WHEN WILL AYUMU MAKE HIS MOVE?

3

SOICHIRO YAMAMOTO
EDITORIAL ASSISTANCE:
MADOKA KITAO / NEKOMADO

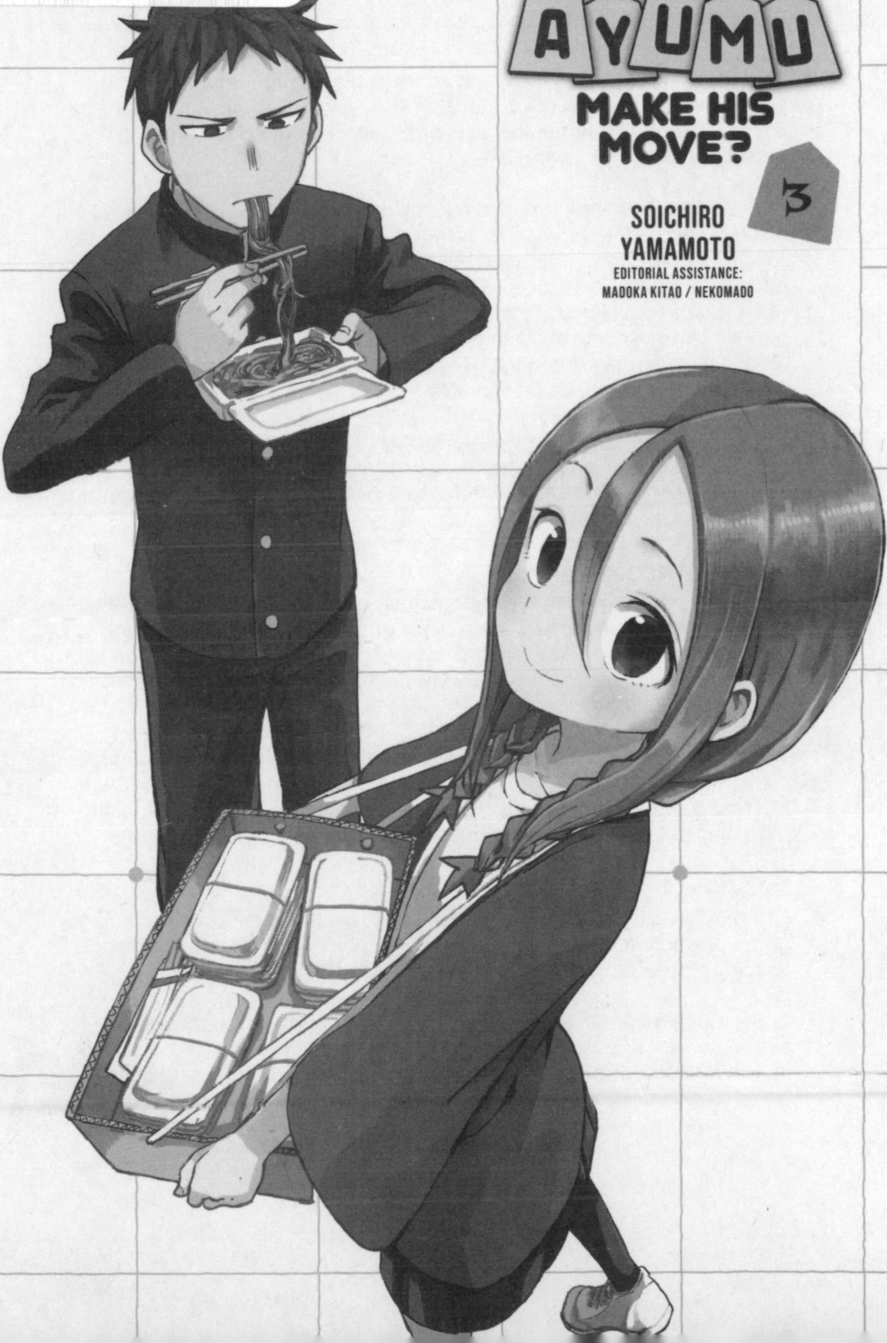

ABOUT SHOGI

This manga is a nearly-rom-com set in a high school shogi club. This game isn't well known outside Japan, but if you're familiar with chess, it's easy to grasp! Check out this explainer before reading, or jump right in and come back if you want to learn more!

Shogi is a two-player board game in the same family as chess. It's ancestor arrived in Japan over a thousand years ago and evolved into roughly its current form around the sixteenth century. Two players face off across a board with nine ranks (rows) and nine files (columns). Each player has a small army of pieces that start on their side of the board, and players can move one of these pieces per turn. The goal, like in chess, is to "checkmate" the other player's king piece by putting it into a situation where it cannot avoid being captured.

The two players are called *sente* and *gote* ("moves first" and "moves next"). These are sometimes called "black" and "white" in English; however, all pieces in shogi are the same color. They are differentiated by orientation, with the pointed end facing the opposing player.

PIECES AND MOVES

There are many different types of pieces, each with its own set of legal moves. Some of these will be familiar to chess players: For example, pawns move one square forward, while bishops move any number of squares diagonally. See the following pages for a detailed list of pieces and their moves.

When a piece legally moves into a square already occupied by an enemy piece, the enemy piece is "captured"—meaning that it is removed from the board and held "in hand" by the capturing player. (Pieces cannot move into squares occupied by friendly pieces.)

DROPPING

One big difference between shogi and chess is that, instead of moving a piece, players can use their turn to place a piece they have in hand back on the board under their control. This is called "dropping" a piece.

A piece can be dropped almost anywhere on the board, although there are some restrictions. A player can never have two unpromoted pawns on the same file, and a piece cannot be dropped onto a square from which it has no legal move.

PROMOTION

If a piece reaches the three ranks at the far end of the board (the "enemy camp"), it can be "promoted." The piece is flipped over to reveal its other side, and gains a new set of moves. For example, a promoted pawn becomes a *tokin*, which moves like a gold general. (Note that kings and gold generals cannot be promoted.)

Promotion is not compulsory unless the piece would have no legal move otherwise. If a piece is left unpromoted, it can be promoted at the end of any subsequent move that begins within the enemy camp.

CHECK AND CHECKMATE

Moving a piece into a position that would let the enemy king be captured on the next move is called an *ote* ("king move"). This corresponds to "check" in chess. The "checked" player must protect their king, either by moving it, capturing the checking piece, or placing (or dropping) another piece in between the two. If the checked player has no way to save the king, they lose the game. This corresponds to "checkmate" in chess. As in chess, it is also against the rules for a player to make a move that puts their own king in check.

CASTLES

A key concept in shogi strategy is the castle (in Japanese, *kakoi*, "enclosure"). A castle is a formation of pieces that protects your king. Over the centuries, shogi players have come up with many types of castles, and also ways to undermine and attack them.

Note that building a castle involves arranging pieces using standard legal moves. This makes it different from the special move of "castling" in chess, although the objective (protect the king) is similar.

SHOGI PIECES

歩 FUHYO

English name: Pawn (P)
Move: One square directly forward
Comments: Unlike in chess, pawns do not capture diagonally

TOKIN

English name: Tokin (+P)
Move: Replaced by gold general rules
Comments: Most English-speaking players use the Japanese name for this piece instead of "promoted pawn"

香 KYOSHA

English name: Lance (L)
Move: Any number of squares directly forward

仝 NARIKYO

English name: Promoted lance (+L)
Move: Replaced by gold general rules

桂 KEIMA

English name: Knight (N)
Move: L-shaped "jump" two squares forward and one square to left or right
Comments: Knights can "jump" over pieces that are in their way. Unlike in chess, they cannot jump in any direction.

圭 NARIKEI

English name: Promoted knight (+N)
Move: Replaced by gold general rules

銀 GINSHO

English name: Promoted knight (S)
Move: One square in any direction except left, right, or directly back

全 NARIGIN

English name: Promoted silver (+S)
Move: Replaced by gold general rules

金 KINSHO

English name: Gold general (or just "Gold") (G)
Move: One square in any direction except diagonally backward (left or right)
Comments: Gold generals cannot be promoted.

角 KAKUGYO

English name: Bishop (B)
Move: Any number of squares diagonally

馬 RYUMA

English name: Promoted bishop (or "Dragon horse") (+B)
Move: Any number of squares diagonally OR one square in any direction

飛 HISHA

English name: Rook (R)
Move: Any number of squares forward, back, left, or right

龍 RYUO

English name: Promoted rook (or "Dragon king") (+R)
Move: Any number of squares forward, back, left, or right, OR one square in any direction

王 OSHO

English name: King (K)
Move: One square in any direction
Comments: Kings cannot be promoted. This tile is used by the higher-ranking player, while the lower-ranking player traditionally uses the *gyokusho* tile (below) for their king.

玉 GYOKUSHO

English name: King (or "Jewel") (K)
Move: One square in any direction
Comments: This tile is used as the king of the lower-ranking player, but the rules are the same as for the *osho* tile.

Contents

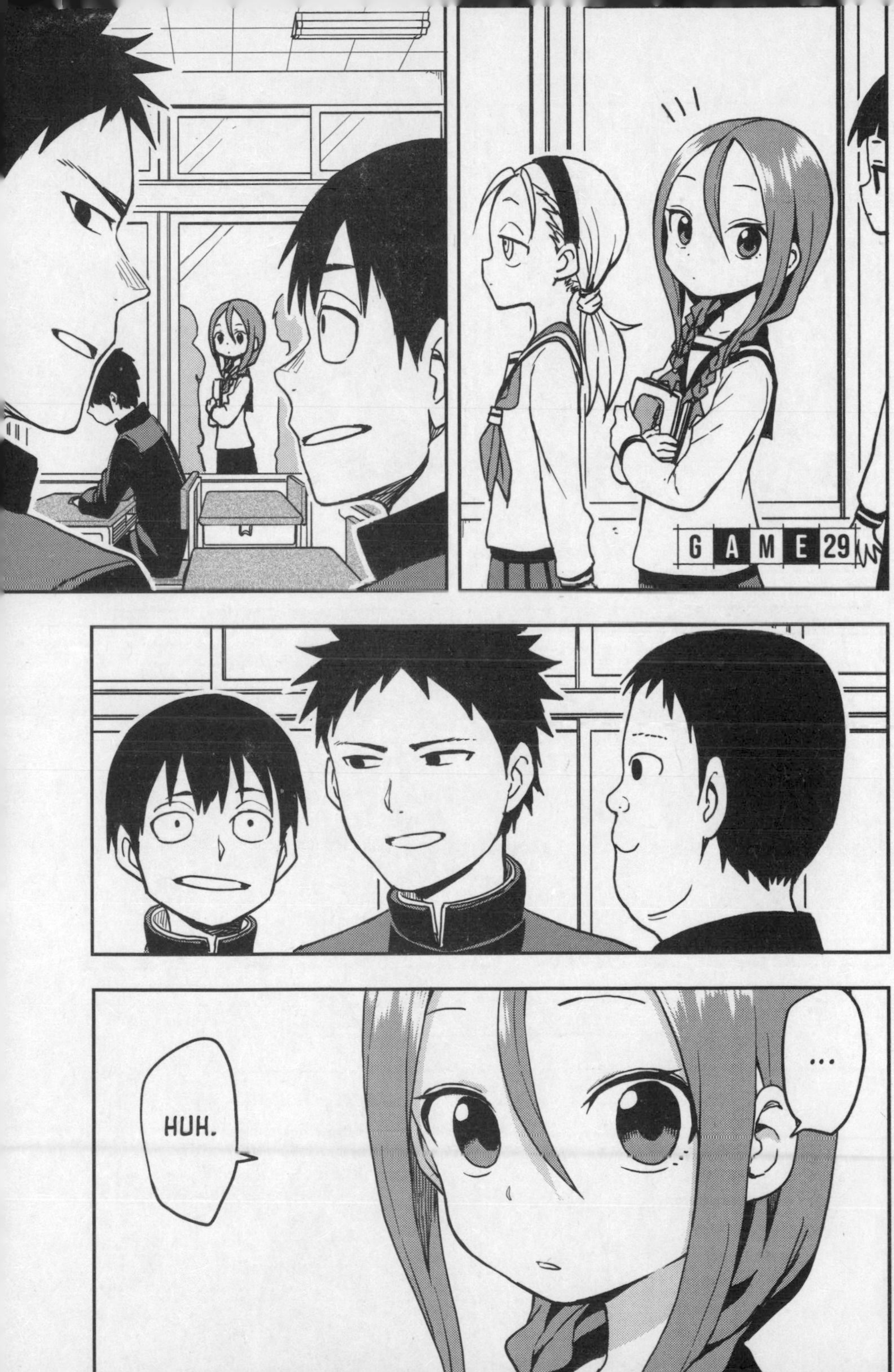
GAME 29
...
HUH.

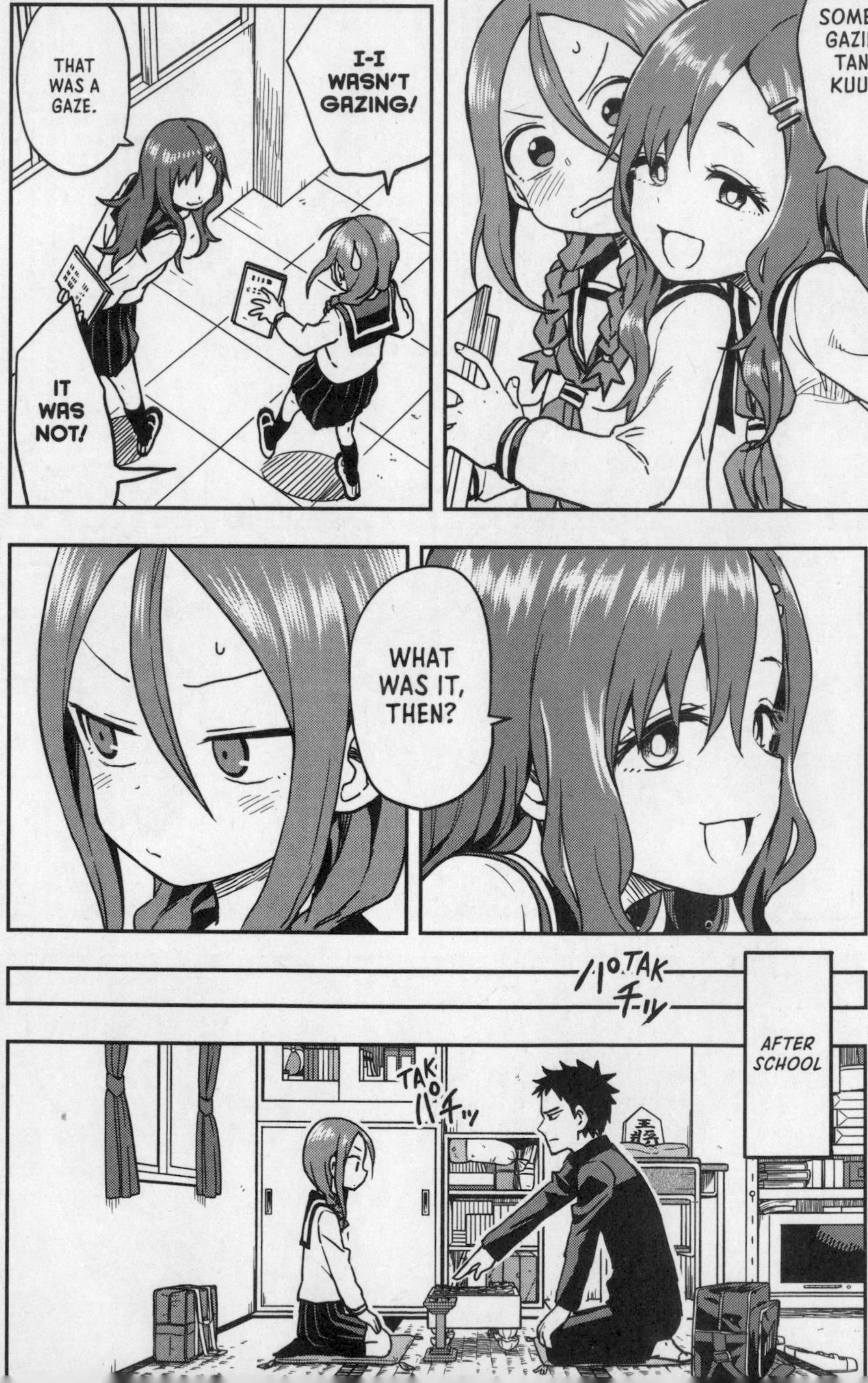
SOMEONE'S GAZING AT TANAKA-KUUUN...
I-I WASN'T GAZING!
THAT WAS A GAZE.
IT WAS NOT!
WHAT WAS IT, THEN?
TAK
AFTER SCHOOL
TAK

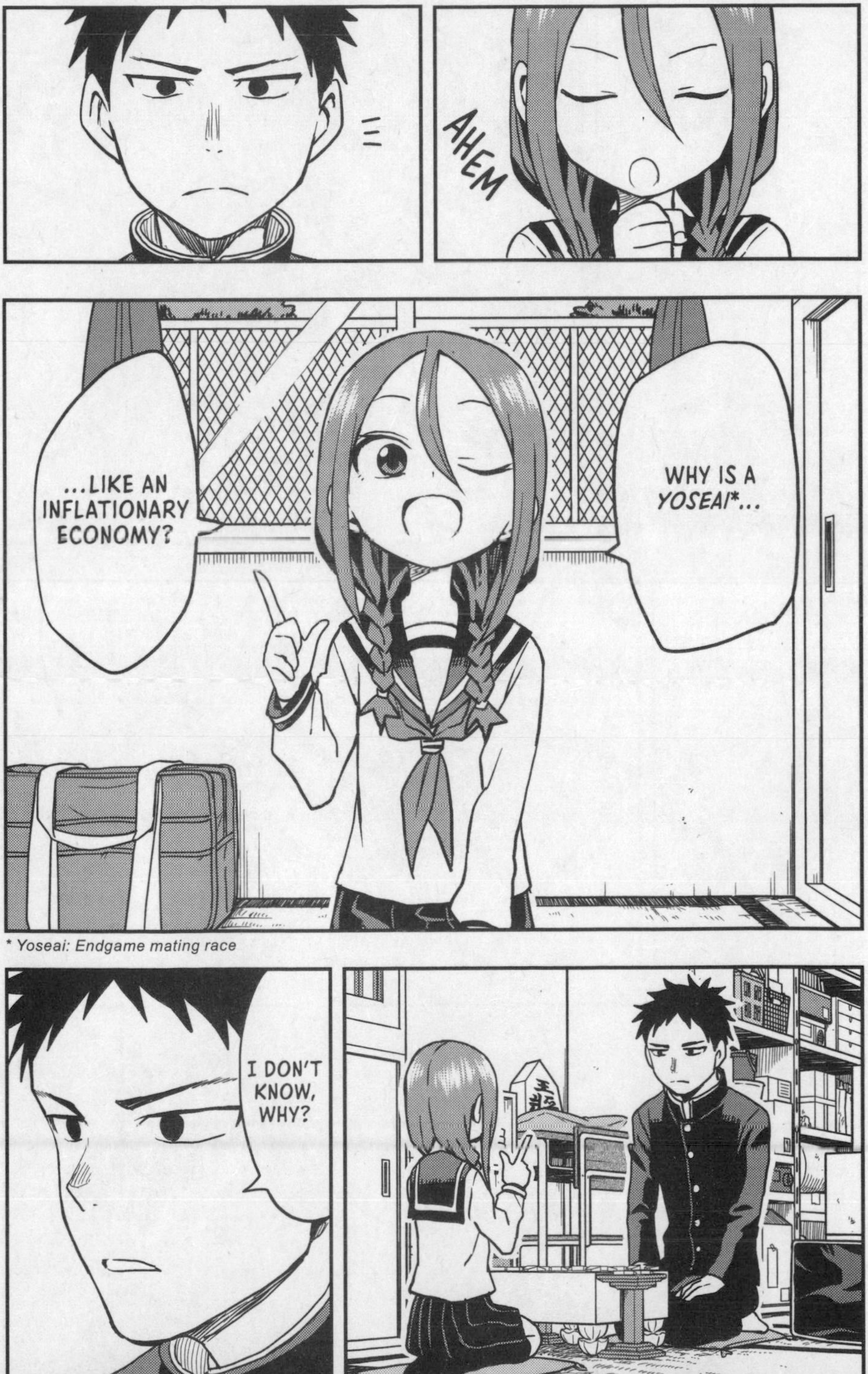
AHEM
WHY IS A *YOSEAI**...
...LIKE AN INFLATIONARY ECONOMY?
I DON'T KNOW, WHY?
* *Yoseai: Endgame mating race*

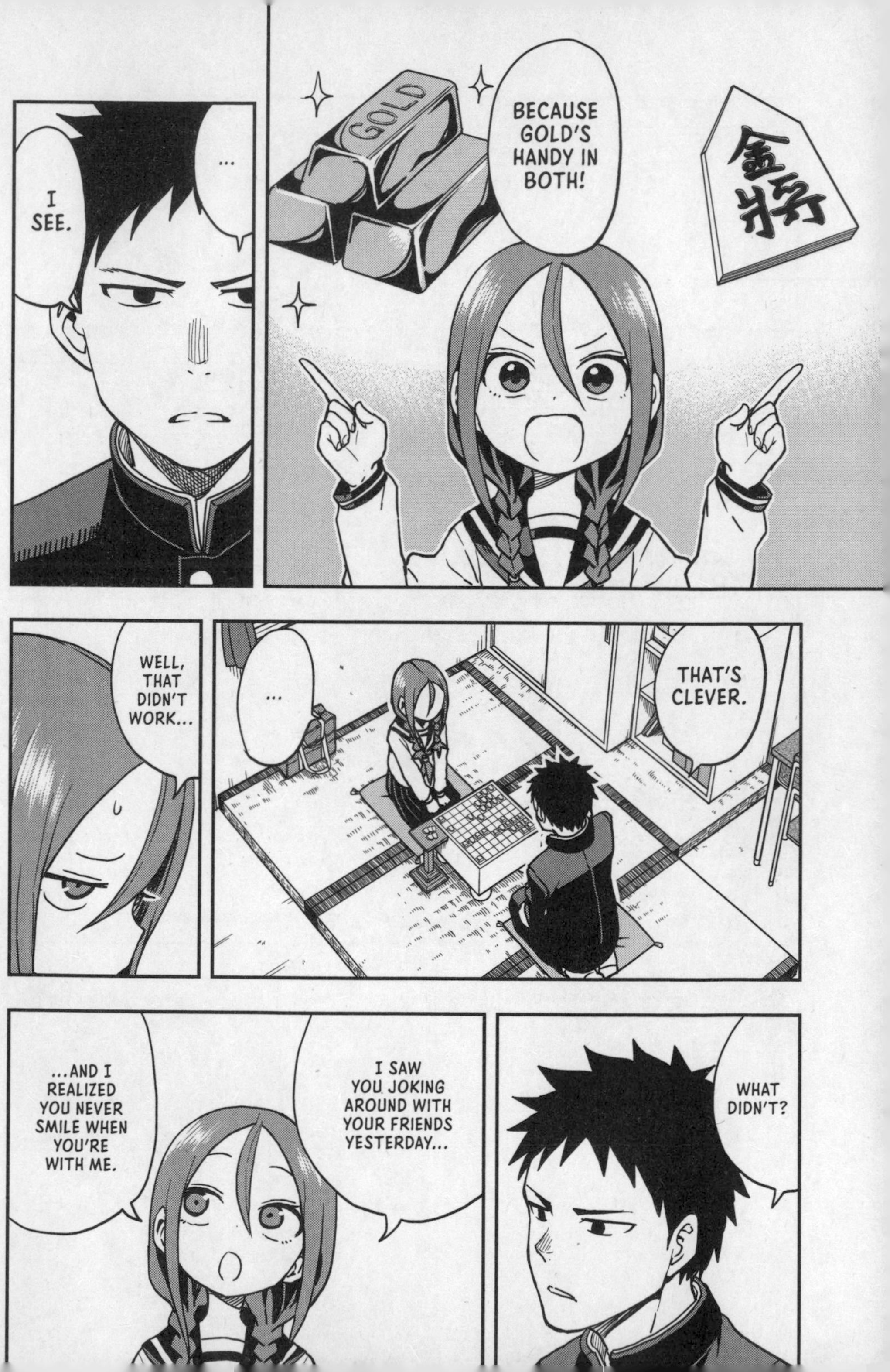

GOLD
BECAUSE GOLD'S HANDY IN BOTH!
金将
...
I SEE.
THAT'S CLEVER.
...
WELL, THAT DIDN'T WORK...
WHAT DIDN'T?
I SAW YOU JOKING AROUND WITH YOUR FRIENDS YESTERDAY...
...AND I REALIZED YOU NEVER SMILE WHEN YOU'RE WITH ME.

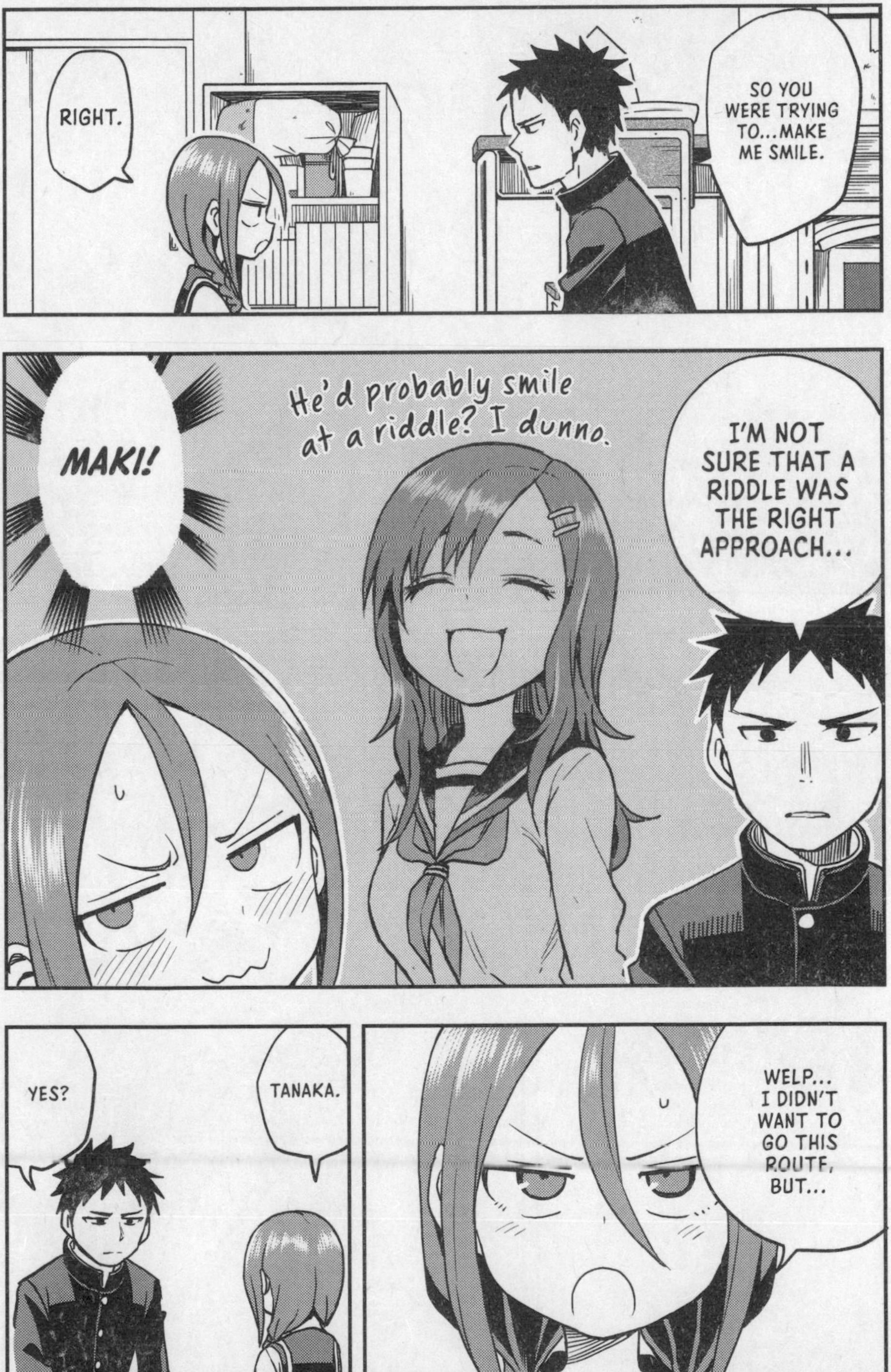
SO YOU WERE TRYING TO...MAKE ME SMILE.
RIGHT.
I'M NOT SURE THAT A RIDDLE WAS THE RIGHT APPROACH...
He'd probably smile at a riddle? I dunno.
MAKI!
WELP... I DIDN'T WANT TO GO THIS ROUTE, BUT...
TANAKA.
YES?

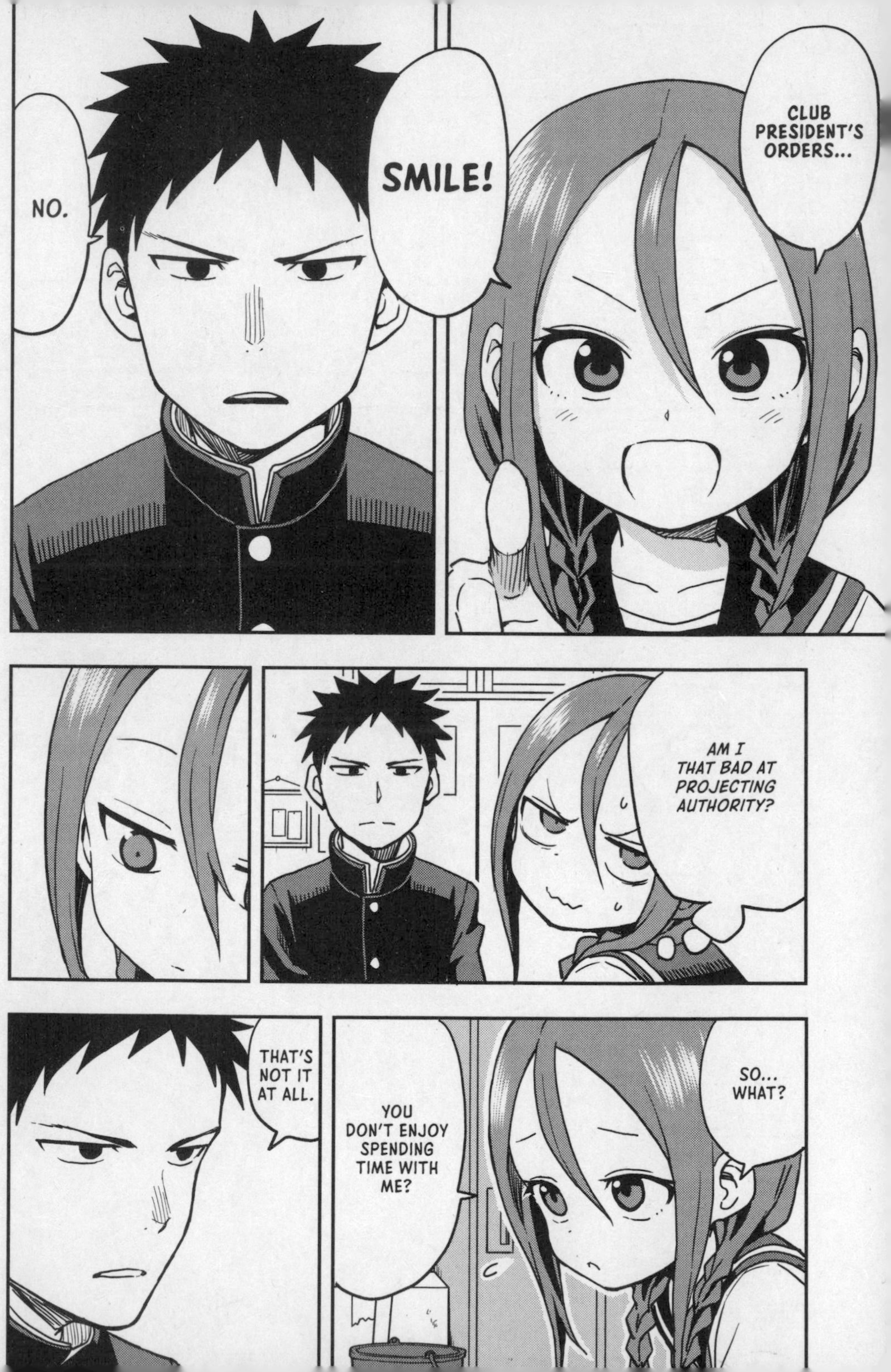
CLUB PRESIDENT'S ORDERS...
SMILE!
NO.
AM I THAT BAD AT PROJECTING AUTHORITY?
SO... WHAT?
YOU DON'T ENJOY SPENDING TIME WITH ME?
THAT'S NOT IT AT ALL.

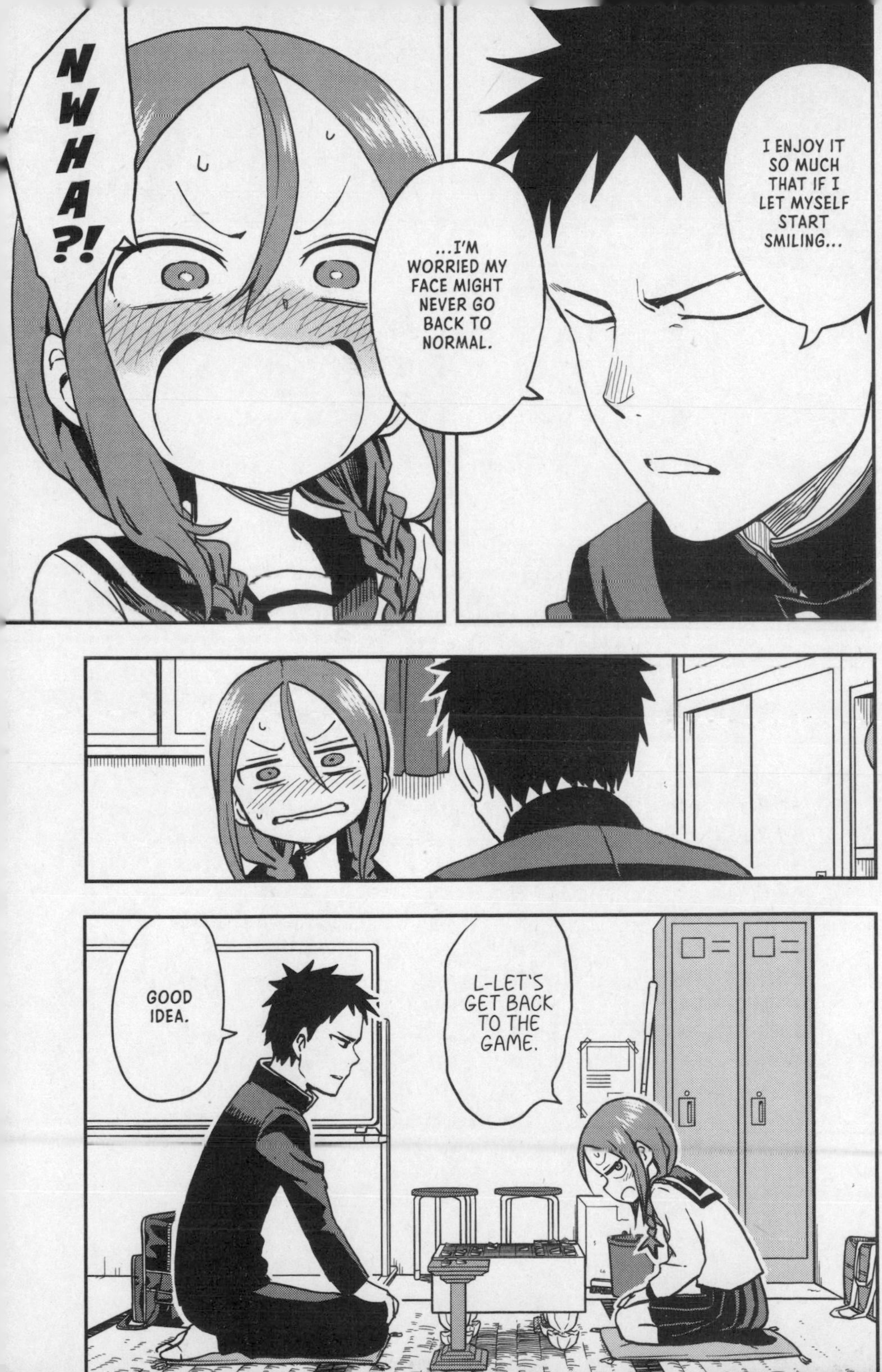
I ENJOY IT SO MUCH THAT IF I LET MYSELF START SMILING...
...I'M WORRIED MY FACE MIGHT NEVER GO BACK TO NORMAL.
NWHA?!
L-LET'S GET BACK TO THE GAME.
GOOD IDEA.

▲ BLACK (SENTE): AYUMU TANAKA △ WHITE (GOTE): URUSHI YAOTOME

(DIAGRAM SHOWS BOARD AFTER MOVE 74, △ +G×2I)

BECAUSE GOLD'S HANDY IN BOTH!

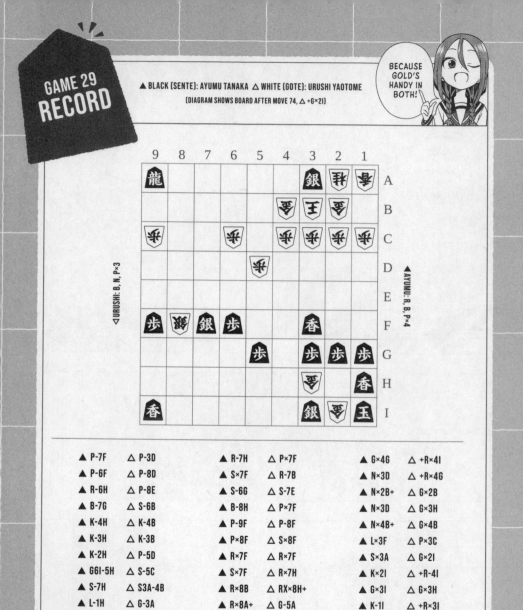

◁URUSHI: B, N, P×3

▲AYUMU: R, B, P×4

	▲	△		▲	△		▲	△
	P-7F	P-3D		R-7H	P×7F		G×4G	+R×4I
	P-6F	P-8D		S×7F	R-7B		N×3D	+R×4G
	R-6H	P-8E		S-6G	S-7E		N×2B+	G×2B
	B-7G	S-6B		B-8H	P×7F		N×3D	G×3H
	K-4H	K-4B		P-9F	P-8F		N×4B+	G×4B
	K-3H	K-3B		P×8F	S×8F		L×3F	P×3C
	K-2H	P-5D		R-7F	R×7F		S×3A	G×2I
	G6I-5H	S-5C		S×7F	R×7H		K×2I	+R-4I
	S-7H	S3A-4B		R-8B	RX×8H+		G×3I	G×3H
	L-1H	G-3A		R-8A+	G-5A		K-1I	+R×3I
	K-1I	P-7D		+R×9A	+R×8I		S×3I	G×2I
	S-6G	S-6D		G5H-4H	N×3E		(WHITE WINS AT MOVE 74)	
	S-2H	P-7E		N×4F	N×4G+			

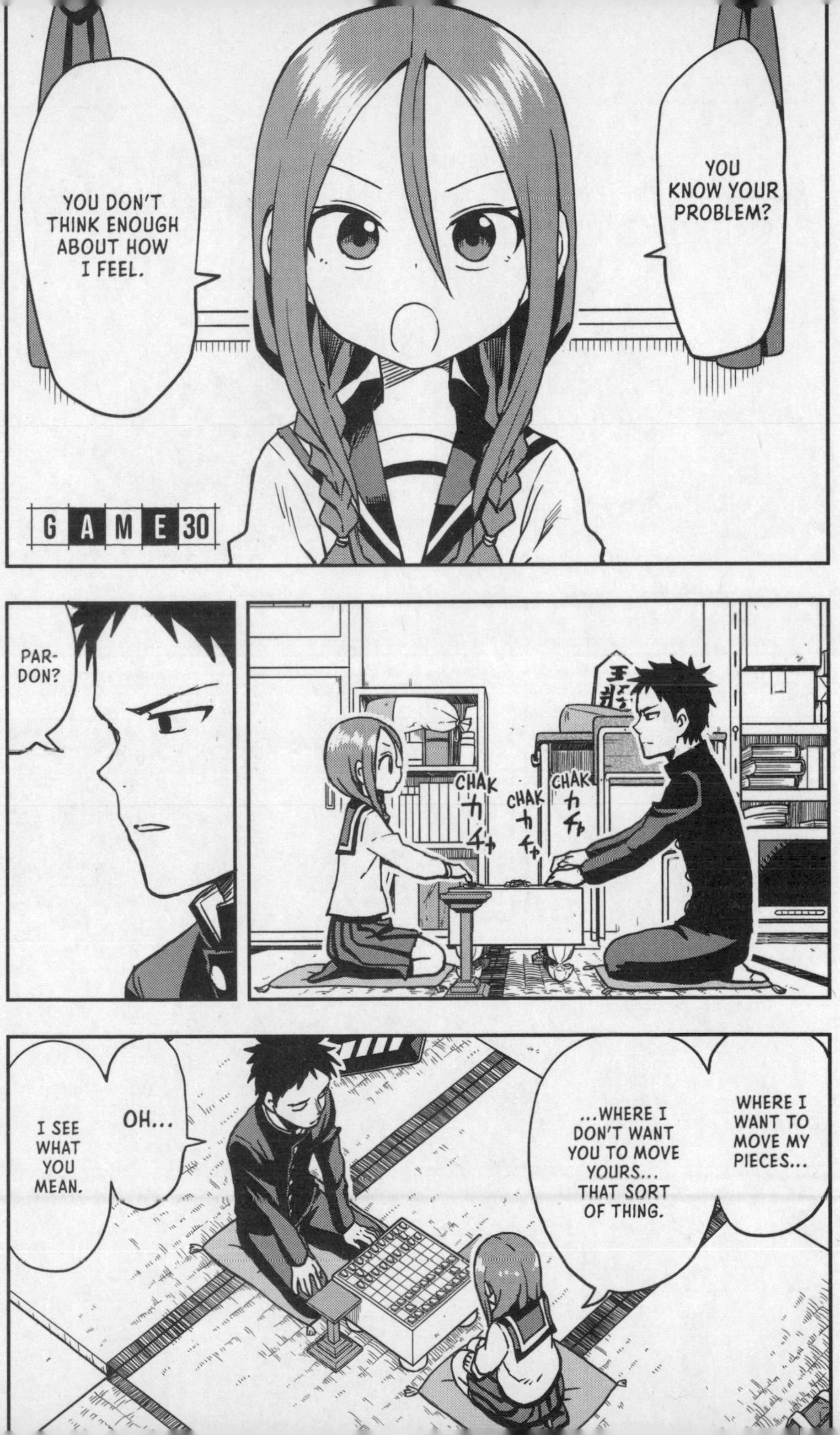
YOU KNOW YOUR PROBLEM?
YOU DON'T THINK ENOUGH ABOUT HOW I FEEL.
GAME 30
CHAK カチャ
CHAK カチャ
CHAK カチャ
PAR-DON?
WHERE I WANT TO MOVE MY PIECES...
...WHERE I DON'T WANT YOU TO MOVE YOURS... THAT SORT OF THING.
OH...
I SEE WHAT YOU MEAN.

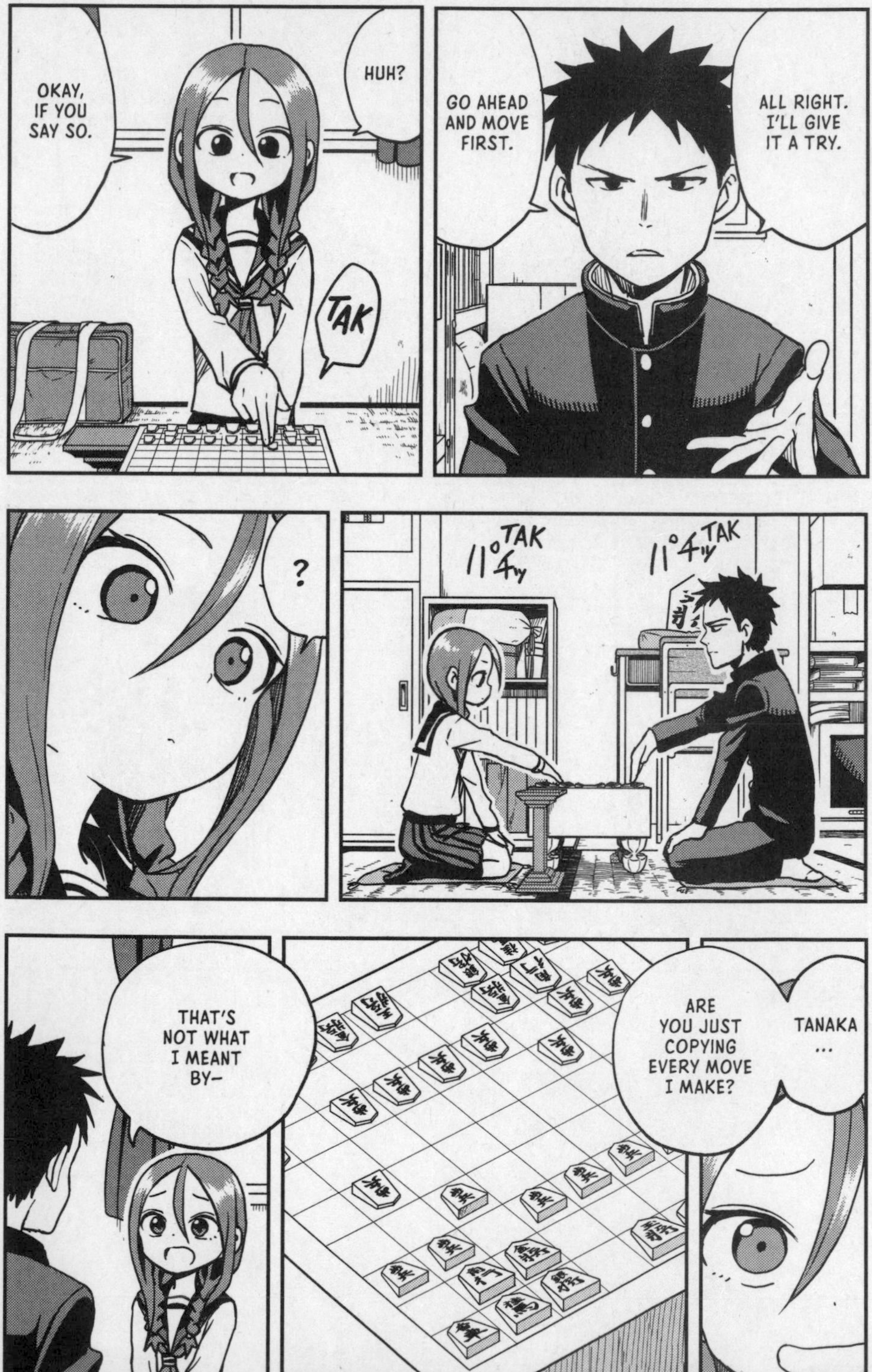
ALL RIGHT. I'LL GIVE IT A TRY.
GO AHEAD AND MOVE FIRST.
HUH?
OKAY, IF YOU SAY SO.
TAK
パチッ TAK
パチッ TAK
?
...
TANAKA ...
ARE YOU JUST COPYING EVERY MOVE I MAKE?
...
THAT'S NOT WHAT I MEANT BY–

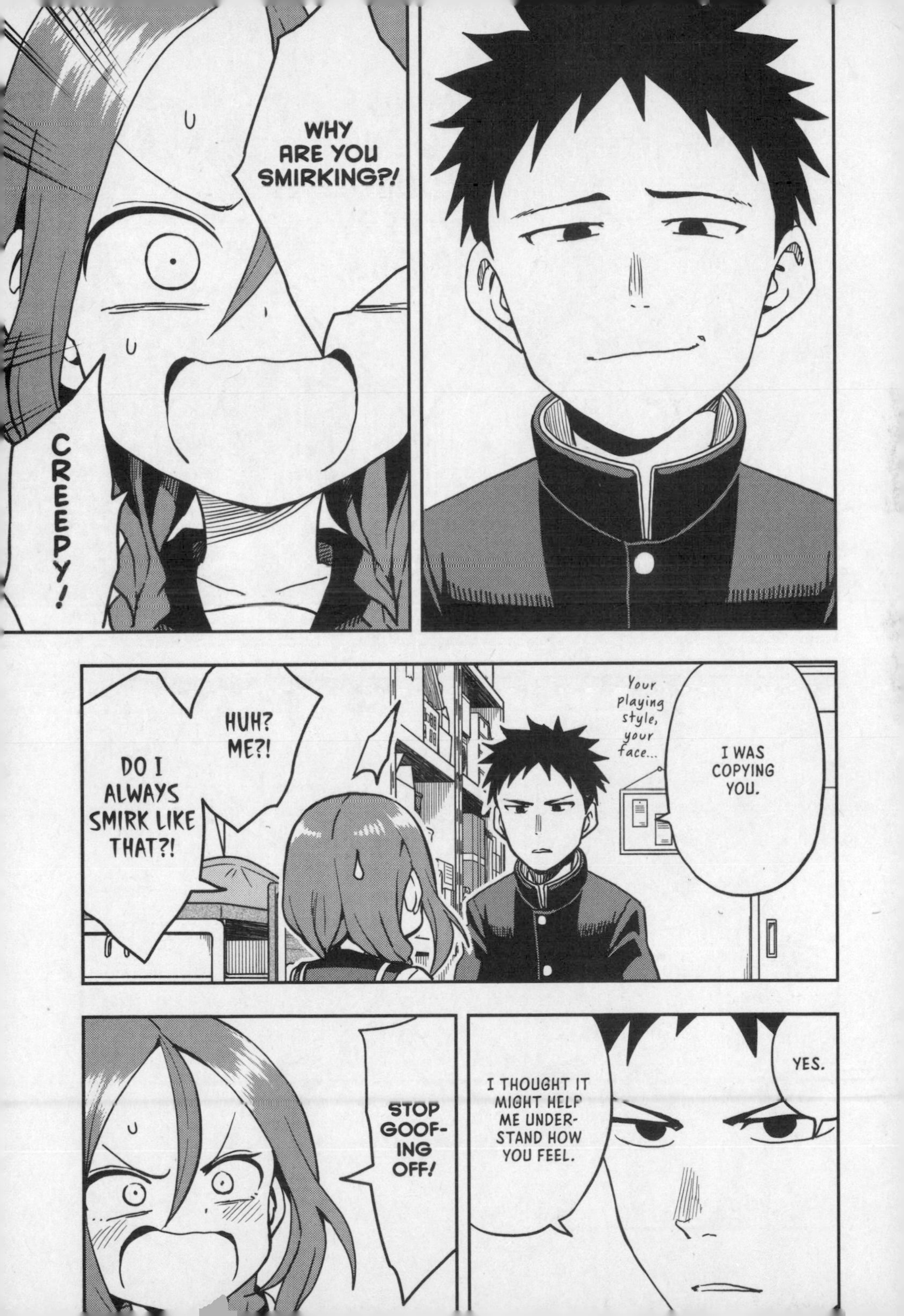
WHY ARE YOU SMIRKING?!
CREEPY!
I WAS COPYING YOU.
Your playing style, your face...
HUH? ME?!
DO I ALWAYS SMIRK LIKE THAT?!
YES.
I THOUGHT IT MIGHT HELP ME UNDER-STAND HOW YOU FEEL.
STOP GOOF-ING OFF!

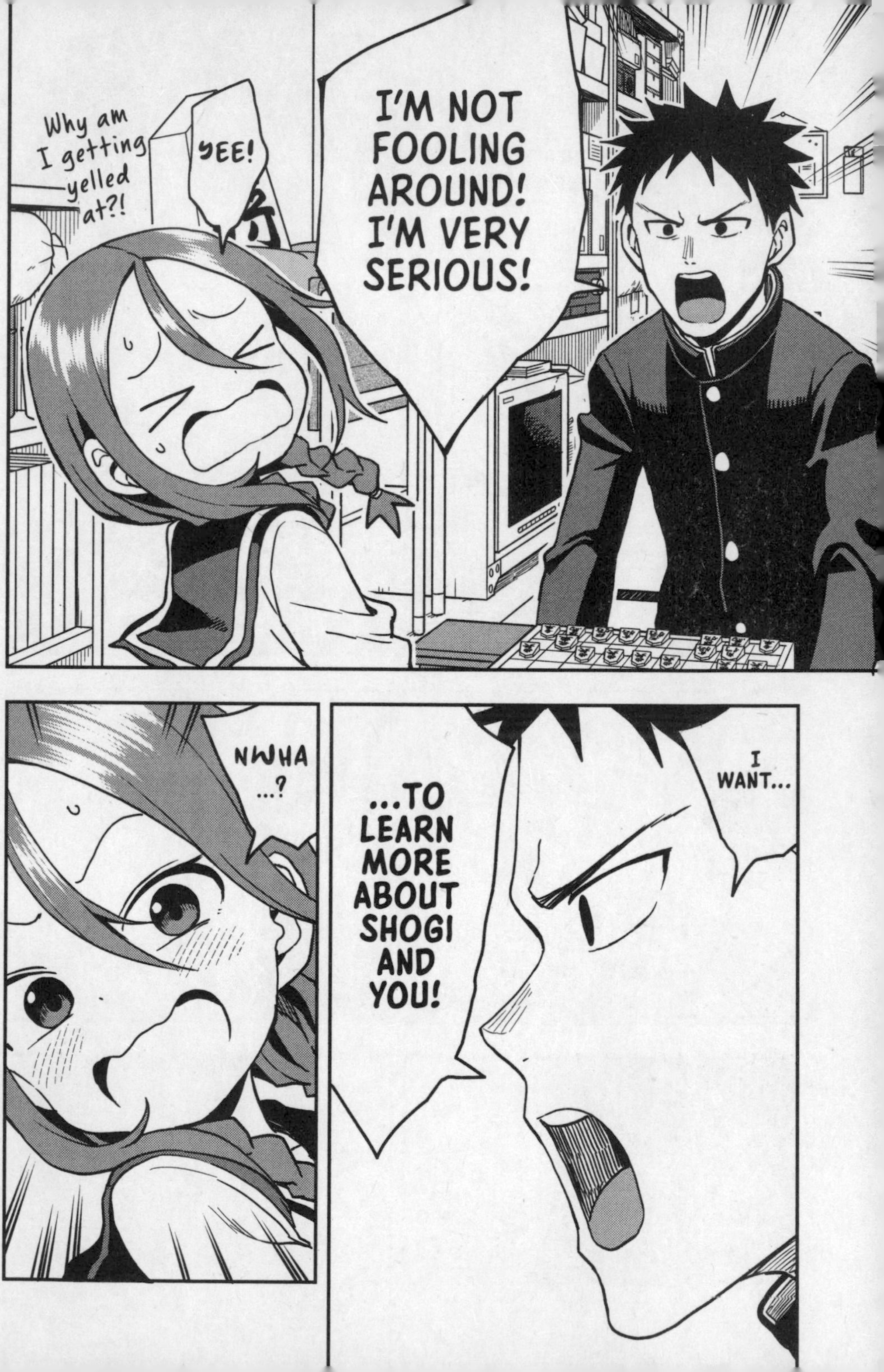
I'M NOT FOOLING AROUND! I'M VERY SERIOUS!
YEE!
Why am I getting yelled at?!
I WANT...
...TO LEARN MORE ABOUT SHOGI AND YOU!
NWHA ...?

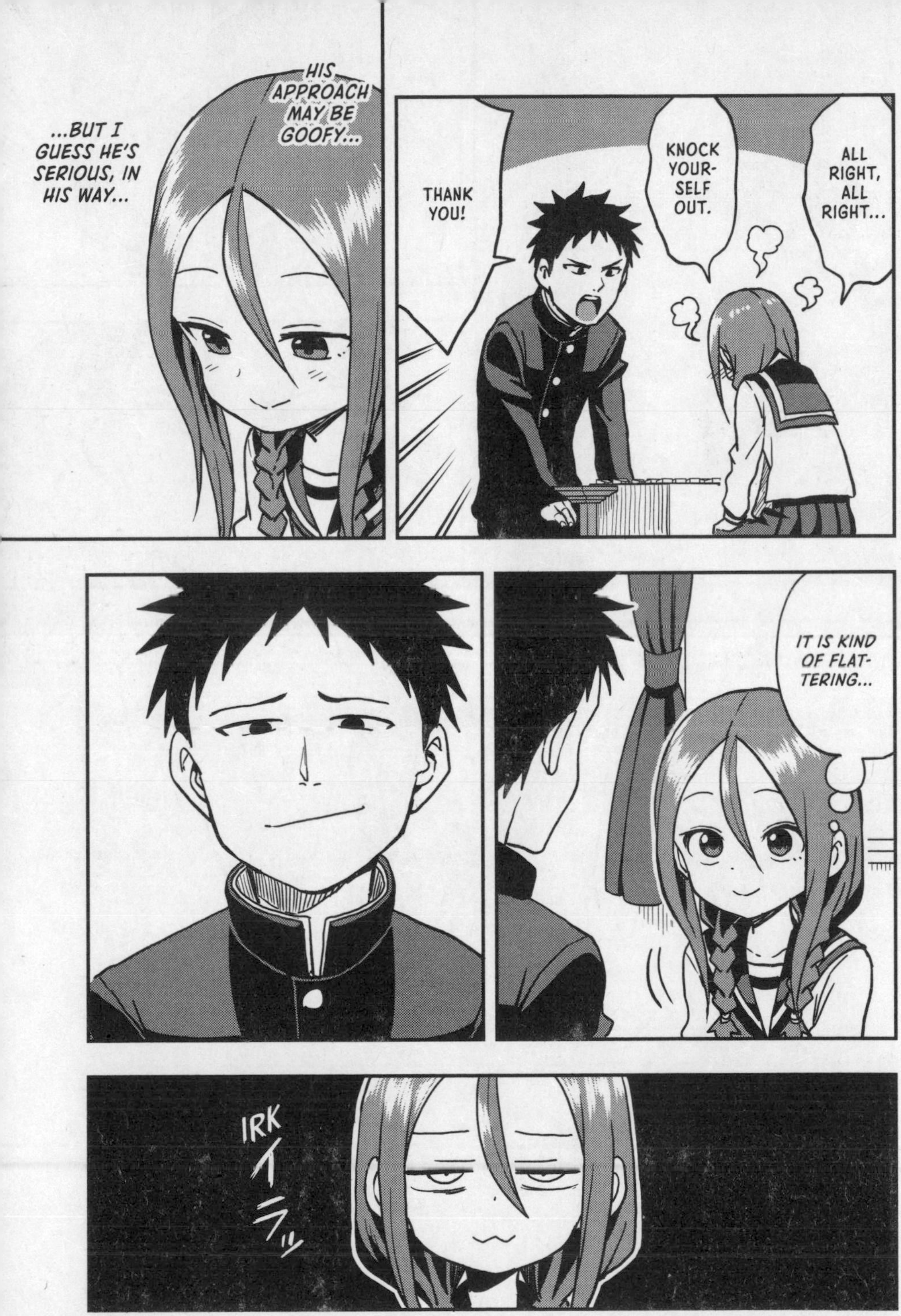
ALL RIGHT, ALL RIGHT...
KNOCK YOUR-SELF OUT.
THANK YOU!
HIS APPROACH MAY BE GOOFY...
...BUT I GUESS HE'S SERIOUS, IN HIS WAY...
IT IS KIND OF FLAT-TERING...
IRK
イラッ

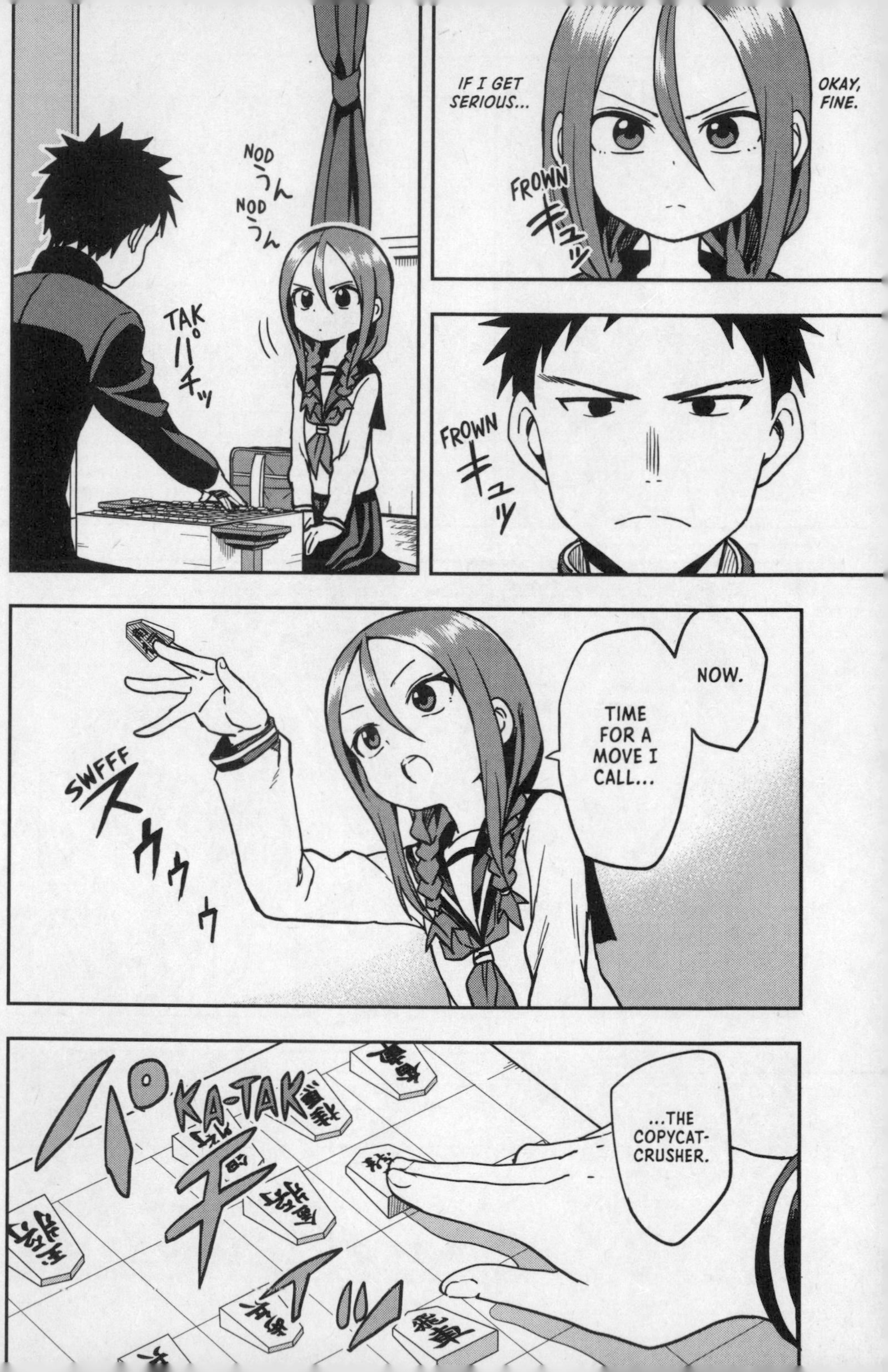
OKAY, FINE.
IF I GET SERIOUS...
FROWN
キュッ
FROWN
キュッ
NOD
うん
NOD
うん
TAK
パチッ
NOW.
TIME FOR A MOVE I CALL...
SWFFF
スウウウ
...THE COPYCAT-CRUSHER.
KA-TAK

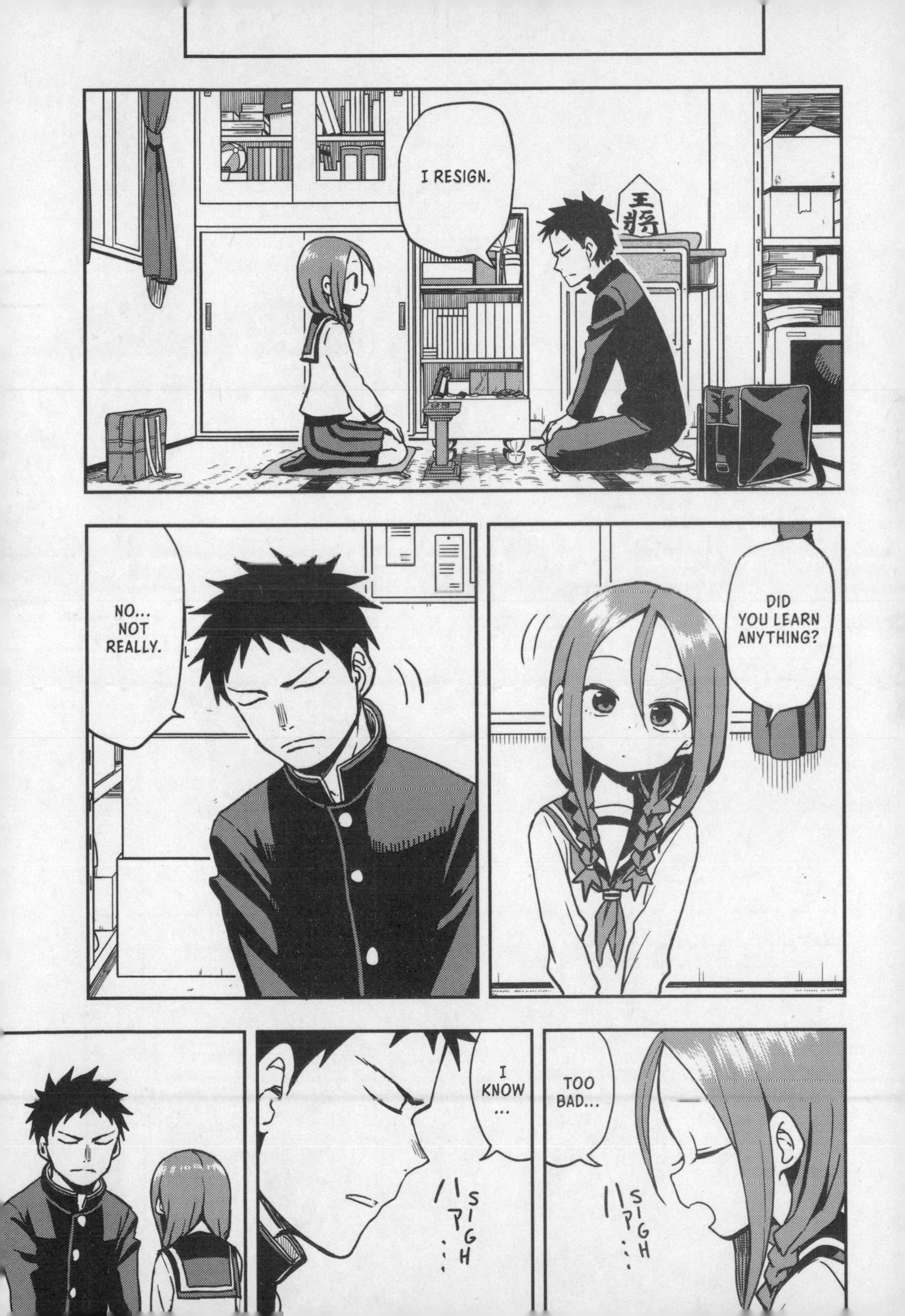
王将
I RESIGN.
DID YOU LEARN ANYTHING?
NO... NOT REALLY.
TOO BAD...
ハァ... SIGH
I KNOW...
ハァ... SIGH

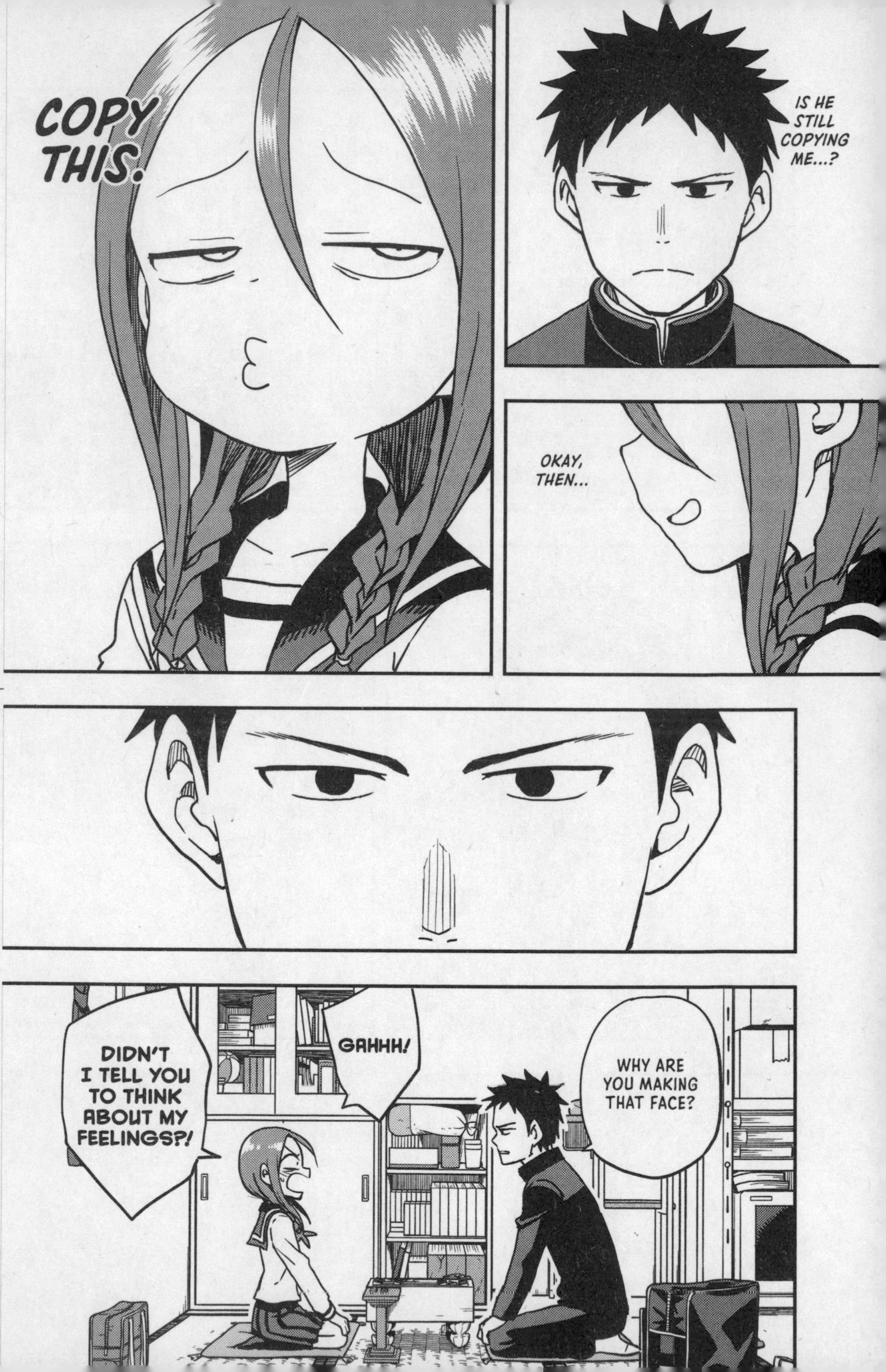
IS HE STILL COPYING ME...?
OKAY, THEN...
COPY THIS.
WHY ARE YOU MAKING THAT FACE?
GAHHH!
DIDN'T I TELL YOU TO THINK ABOUT MY FEELINGS?!

GAME 30 RECORD

...THE COPYCAT-CRUSHER.

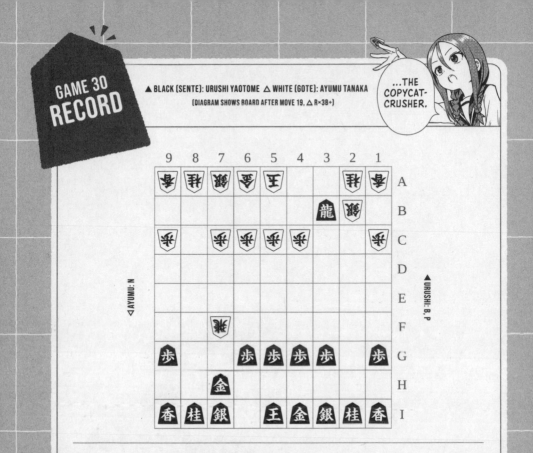

▲ BLACK (SENTE): URUSHI YAOTOME △ WHITE (GOTE): AYUMU TANAKA

(DIAGRAM SHOWS BOARD AFTER MOVE 19, △ R×3B+)

◁AYUMU: N

9
8
7
6
5
4
3
2
1
A
B
C
D
E
F
G
H
I

▲URUSHI: B, P

▲ P-7F	△ P-3D
▲ P-2F	△ P-8D
▲ P-2E	△ P-8E
▲ G-7H	△ G-3B
▲ P-2D	△ P×2D
▲ R×2D	△ P-8F
▲ P×8F	△ R×8F
▲ R×3D	△ R×7F
▲ B×2B+	△ S×2B
▲ R×3B+	

(BLACK WINS AT MOVE 19)

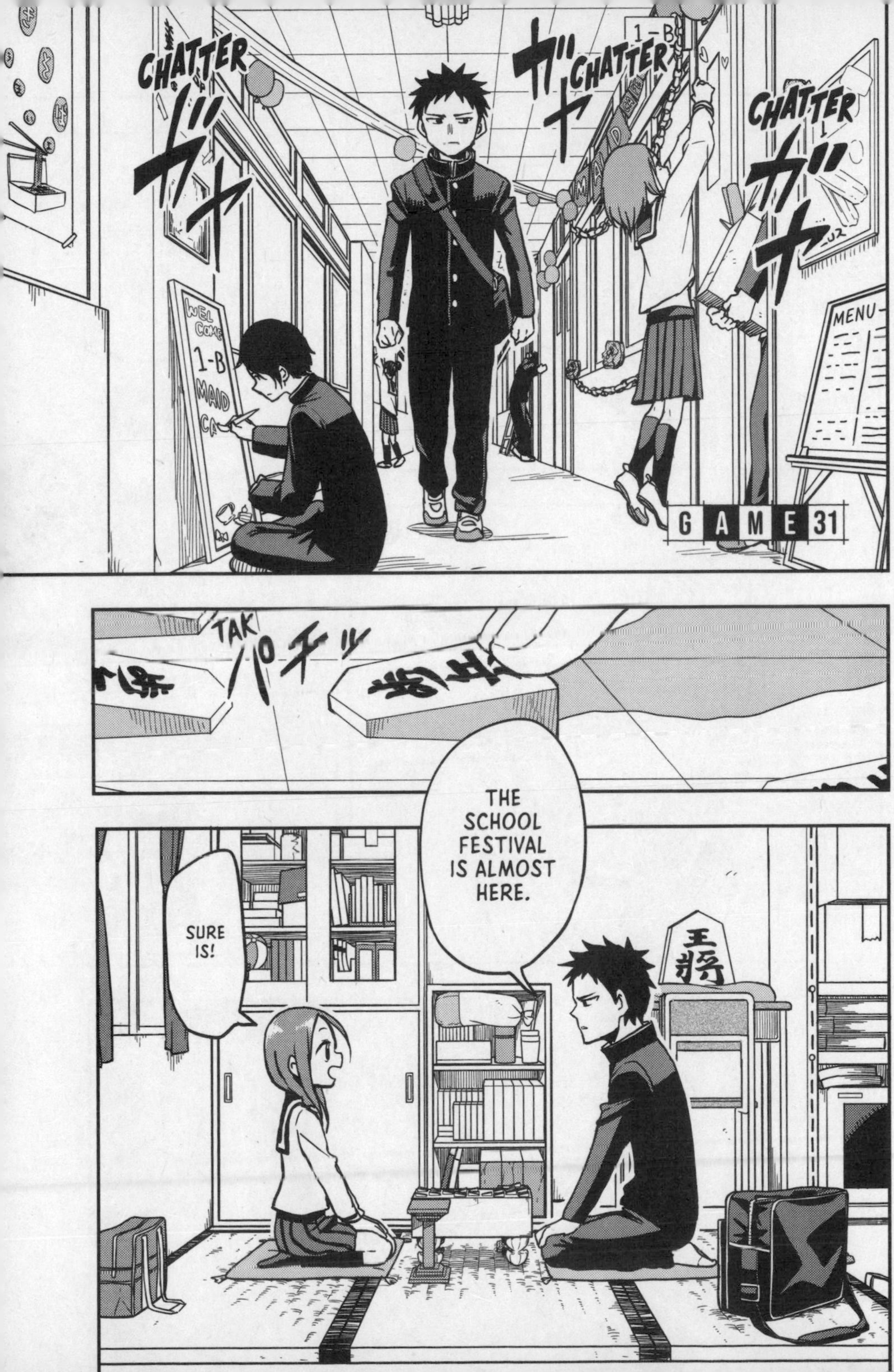
CHATTER
ガヤ
MENU
CHATTER
ガヤ
1-B
CHATTER
ガヤ
WEL COME 1-B MAID CA
GAME 31
パチッ
TAK
THE SCHOOL FESTIVAL IS ALMOST HERE.
王将
SURE IS!

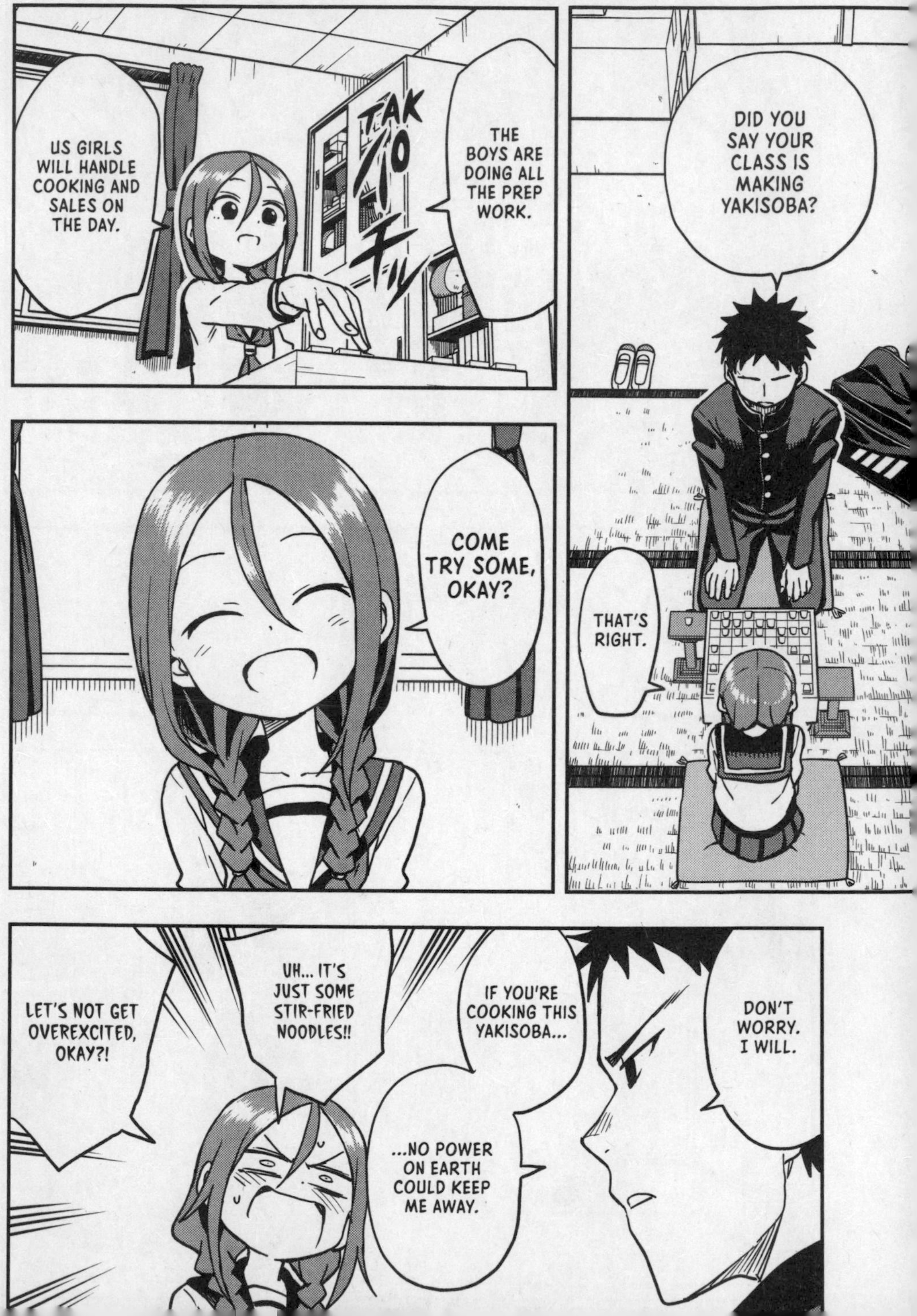
DID YOU SAY YOUR CLASS IS MAKING YAKISOBA?
THAT'S RIGHT.
THE BOYS ARE DOING ALL THE PREP WORK.
TAK
US GIRLS WILL HANDLE COOKING AND SALES ON THE DAY.
COME TRY SOME, OKAY?
DON'T WORRY. I WILL.
IF YOU'RE COOKING THIS YAKISOBA...
...NO POWER ON EARTH COULD KEEP ME AWAY.
UH... IT'S JUST SOME STIR-FRIED NOODLES!!
LET'S NOT GET OVEREXCITED, OKAY?!

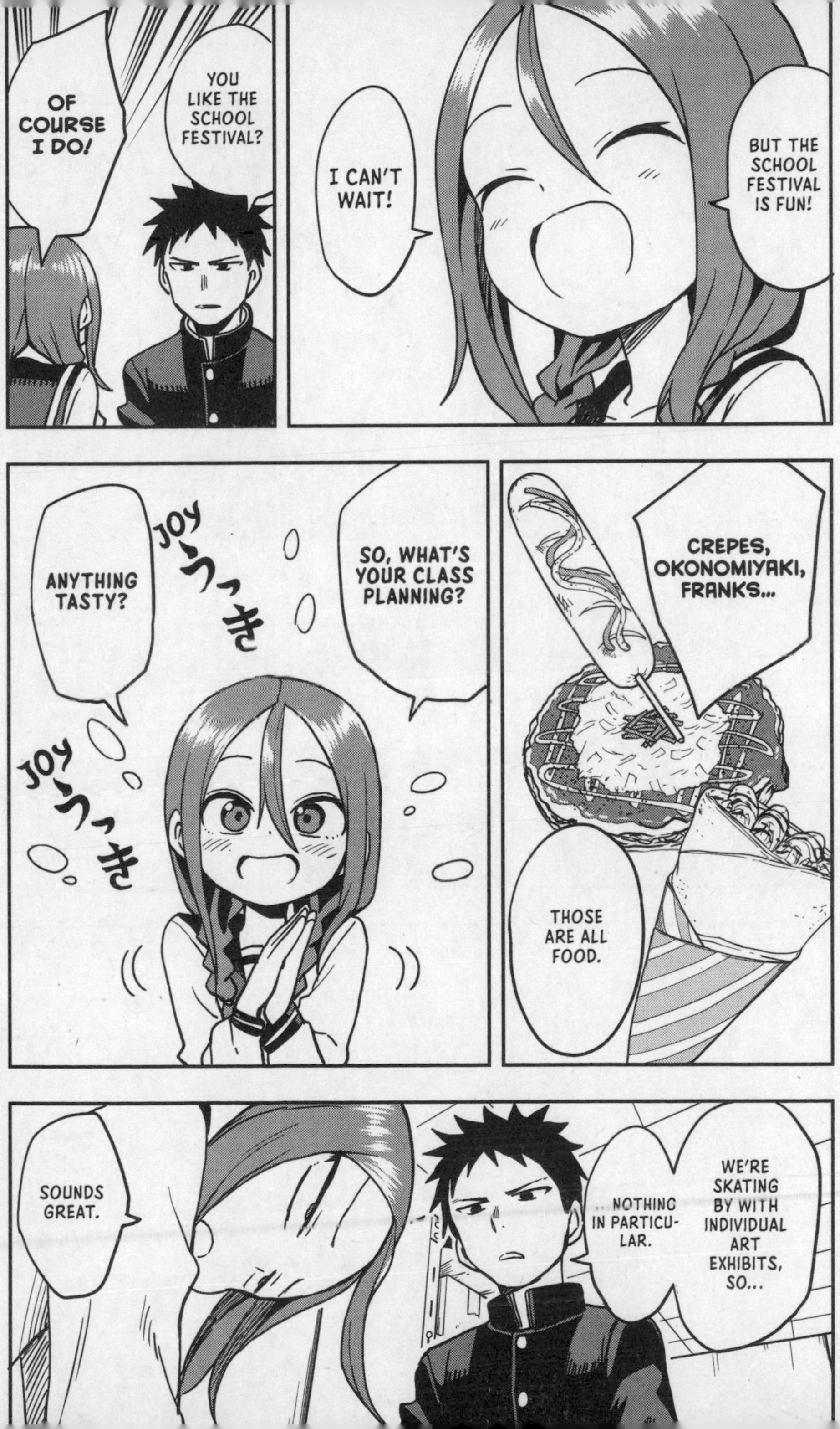
BUT THE SCHOOL FESTIVAL IS FUN!
I CAN'T WAIT!
YOU LIKE THE SCHOOL FESTIVAL?
OF COURSE I DO!
CREPES, OKONOMIYAKI, FRANKS...
THOSE ARE ALL FOOD.
SO, WHAT'S YOUR CLASS PLANNING?
JOY うっき
ANYTHING TASTY?
JOY うっき
WE'RE SKATING BY WITH INDIVIDUAL ART EXHIBITS, SO...
...NOTHING IN PARTICU-LAR.
SOUNDS GREAT.

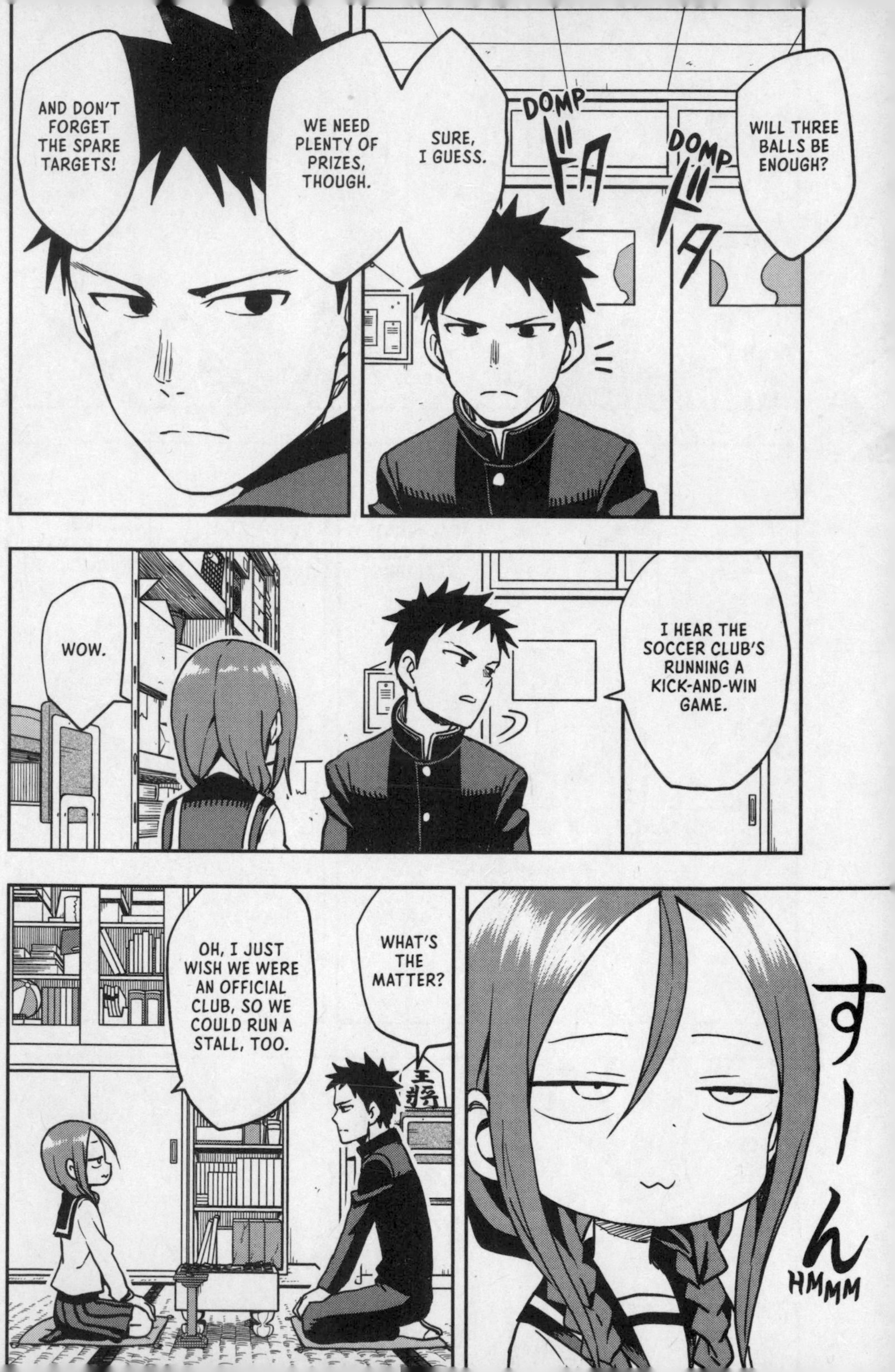
WILL THREE BALLS BE ENOUGH?
DOMP
DOMP
SURE, I GUESS.
WE NEED PLENTY OF PRIZES, THOUGH.
AND DON'T FORGET THE SPARE TARGETS!
I HEAR THE SOCCER CLUB'S RUNNING A KICK-AND-WIN GAME.
WOW.
すーん
HMMM
WHAT'S THE MATTER?
OH, I JUST WISH WE WERE AN OFFICIAL CLUB, SO WE COULD RUN A STALL, TOO.

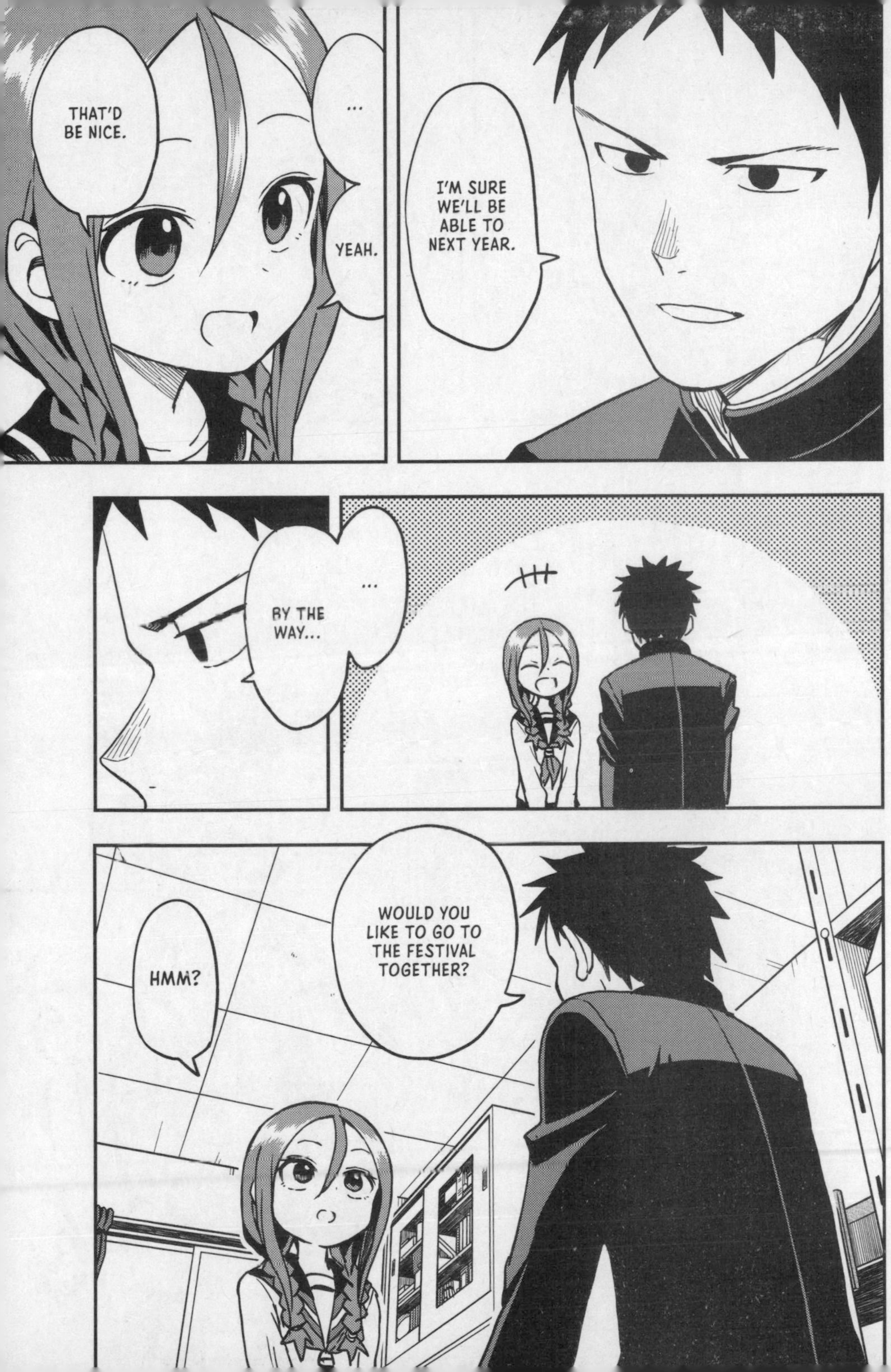
I'M SURE WE'LL BE ABLE TO NEXT YEAR.
...
YEAH.
THAT'D BE NICE.
...
BY THE WAY...
WOULD YOU LIKE TO GO TO THE FESTIVAL TOGETHER?
HMM?

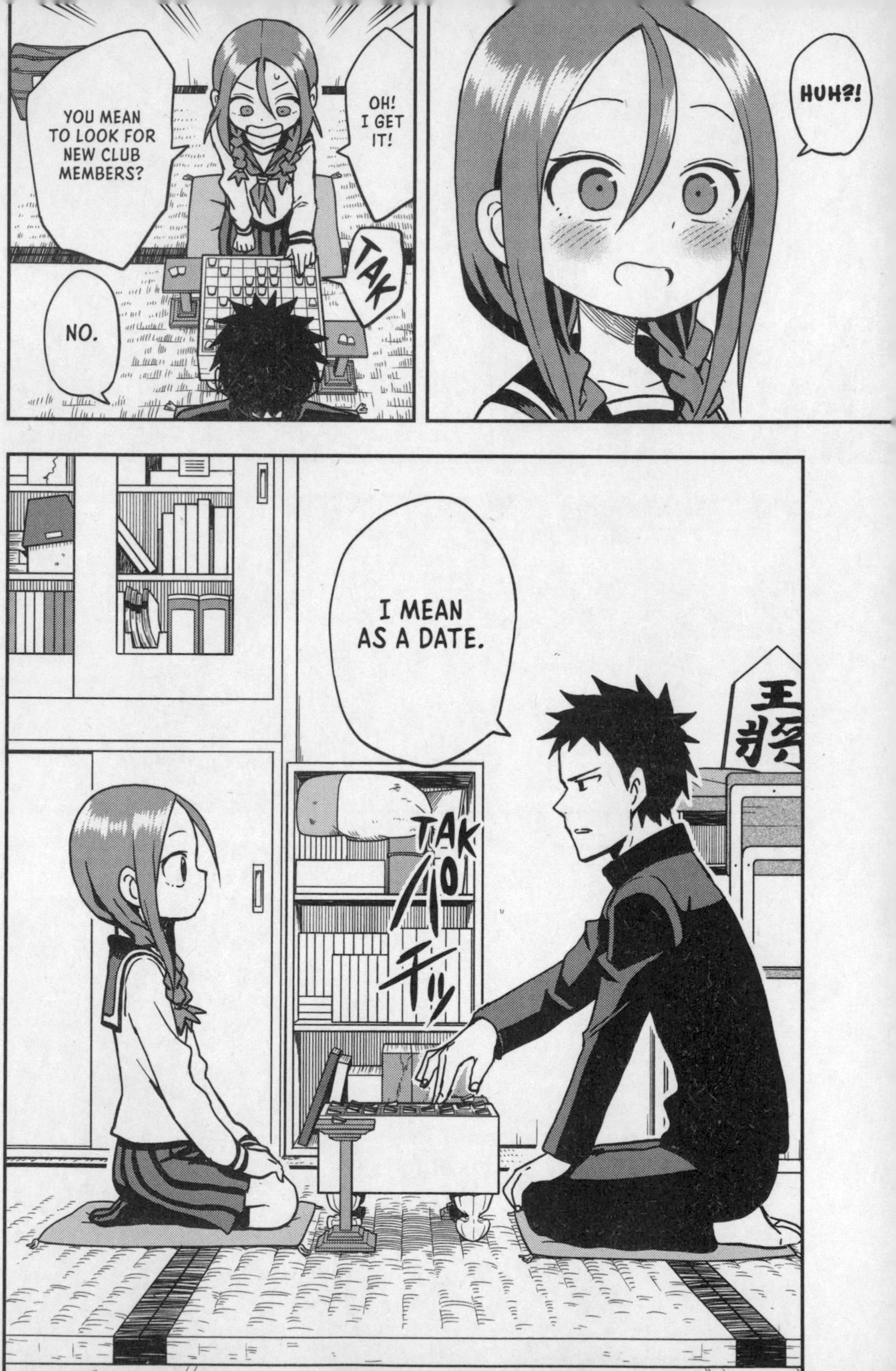
HUH?!
OH! I GET IT!
YOU MEAN TO LOOK FOR NEW CLUB MEMBERS?
TAK
NO.
I MEAN AS A DATE.
王将
TAK
パチッ

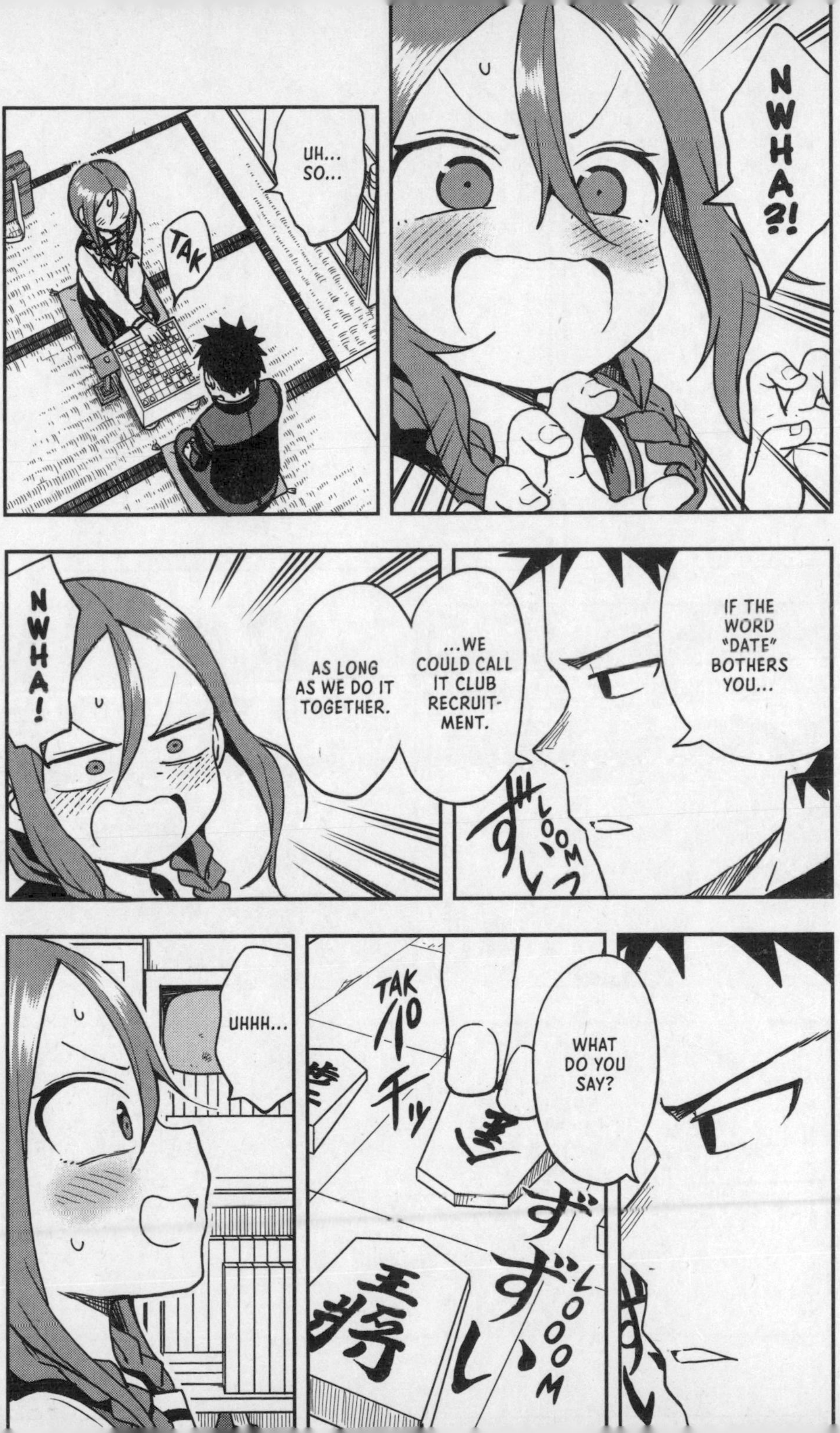
NWHA?!
UH... SO...
TAK
IF THE WORD "DATE" BOTHERS YOU...
...WE COULD CALL IT CLUB RECRUIT-MENT.
AS LONG AS WE DO IT TOGETHER.
LOOM
NWHA!
WHAT DO YOU SAY?
TAK
LOOOOM
UHHH...

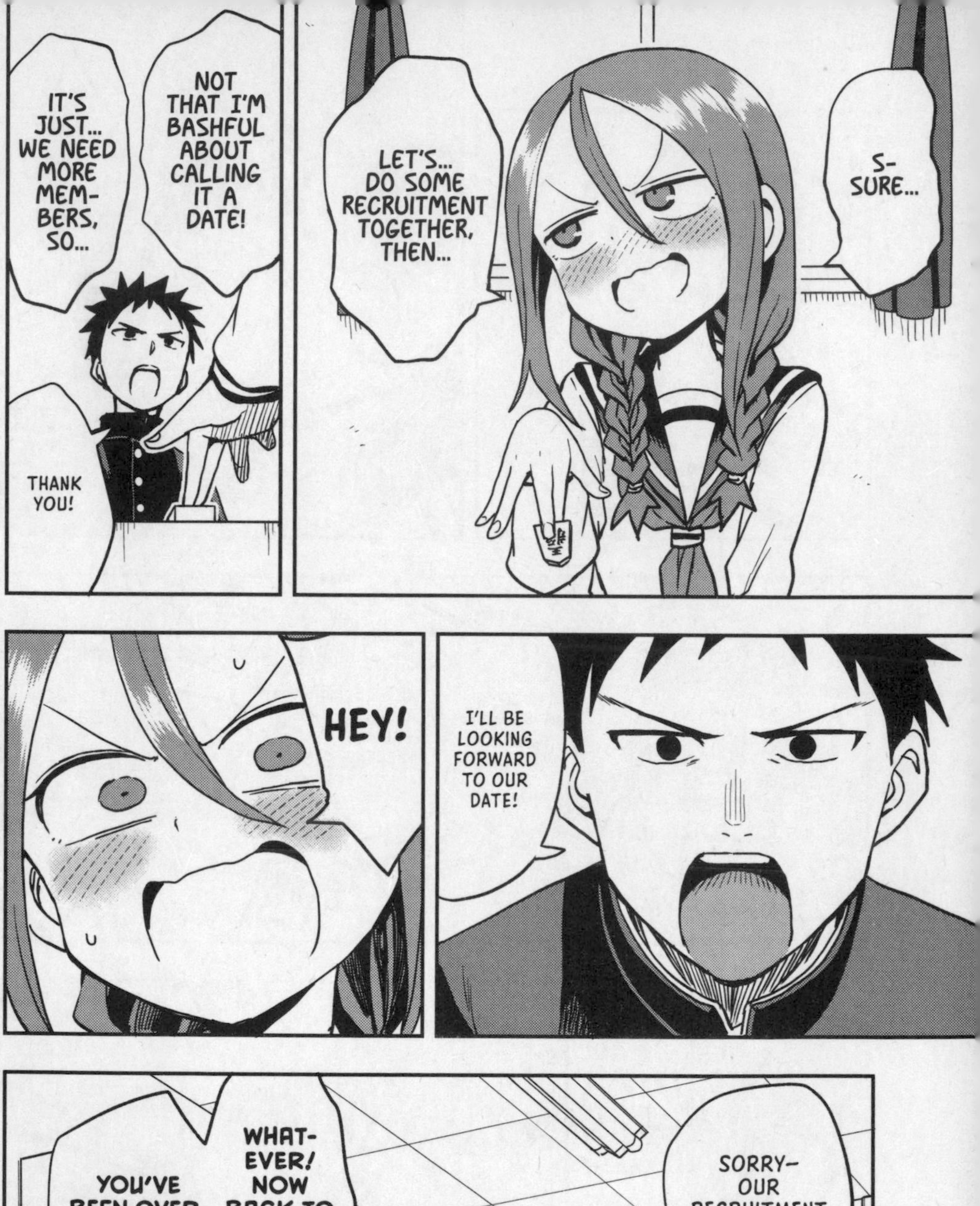
S-SURE...
LET'S... DO SOME RECRUITMENT TOGETHER, THEN...
NOT THAT I'M BASHFUL ABOUT CALLING IT A DATE!
IT'S JUST... WE NEED MORE MEM-BERS, SO...
THANK YOU!
I'LL BE LOOKING FORWARD TO OUR DATE!
HEY!
SORRY— OUR RECRUITMENT DRIVE!
WHAT-EVER! NOW BACK TO SHOGI!
YOU'VE BEEN OVER-EXTENDED FOR HALF THE GAME!

GAME 31 RECORD

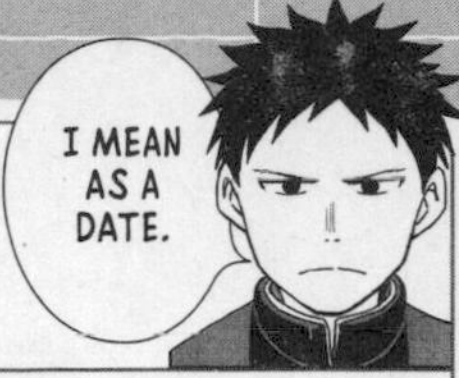
I MEAN AS A DATE.

▲ BLACK (SENTE): AYUMU TANAKA △ WHITE (GOTE): URUSHI YAOTOME

(DIAGRAM SHOWS BOARD AFTER MOVE 42, △K-3B)

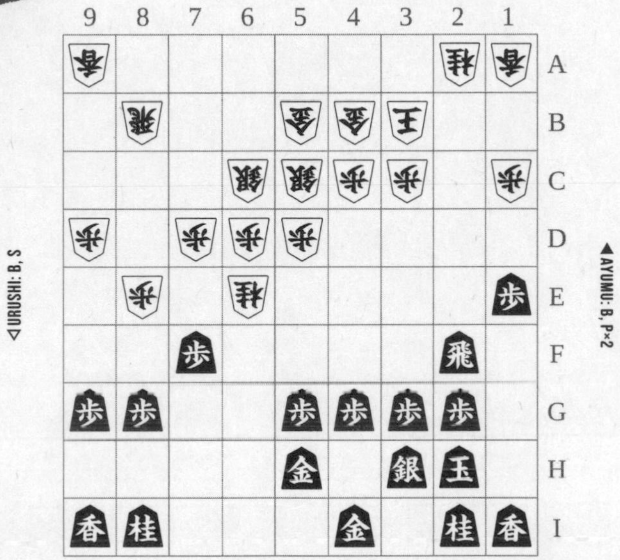
9 8 7 6 5 4 3 2 1
A
B
C
D
E
F
G
H
I
◁URUSHI: B, S
▲AYUMU: B, P×2

▲ P-7F	△ P-3D
▲ P-6F	△ P-8D
▲ R-6H	△ P-8E
▲ B-7G	△ S-6B
▲ S-7H	△ K-4B
▲ K-4H	△ K-3B
▲ K-3H	△ P-5D
▲ S-6G	△ G6A-5B
▲ K-2H	△ S-4B
▲ S-3H	△ S4B-5C
▲ G6I-5H	△ P-6D
▲ P-1F	△ P-7D
▲ S-5F	△ N-7C
▲ S-4E	△ G4A-4B
▲ S×3D	△ S-6C
▲ P-1E	△ P-9D
▲ P-6E	△ N×6E
▲ B×2B+	△ K×2B
▲ R-6F	△ P*3C
▲ S×2C+	△ K×2C
▲ R-2F	△ K-3B
▲ B×2C	△ K-3A
▲ B-5F+	△ P-8F
▲ P×8F	△ R×8F
▲ +B-7H	△ P×2B
▲ P×8G	△ R-8A
▲ N-7G	△ N×7G+
▲ +B×7G	△ B×4D
▲ +B×4D	△ SX4D
▲ N*7I	△ B×8H
▲ P-7E	△ B×7I+
▲ R-8F	△ R×8F
▲ P×8F	△ N×4E
▲ R×8A	△ K-3B
▲ R×9A+	△ N×5G+
▲ G×5G	△ +B×5G
▲ N×2D	△ +B×2D
▲ L×2F	△ N×2E
▲ P×7D	△ R×7I
▲ P-7C+	△ G×4H
▲ B×5G	△ +B×5G
▲ L×2E	△ B×3I
▲ G×3I	△ R×3I+
▲ K-1G	△ +B-3E
▲ B×2F	△ S×2H
▲ K-1F	△ N×2D
▲ L×2D	△ G×2E

(WHITE WINS AT MOVE 94)

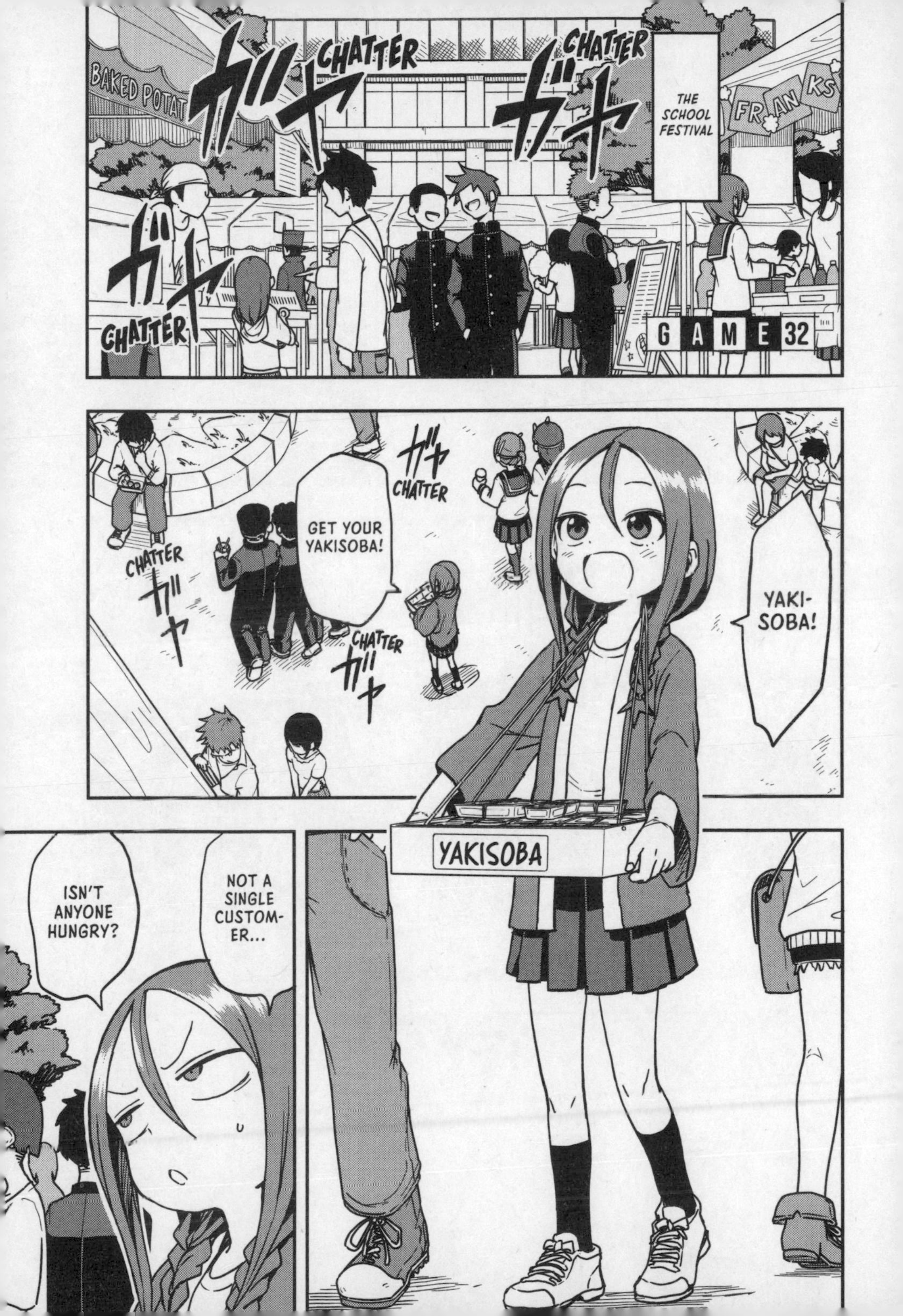
THE SCHOOL FESTIVAL
FRANKS
ガヤ CHATTER
ガヤ CHATTER
BAKED POTAT
ガヤ CHATTER
GAME 32
YAKI-SOBA!
ガヤ CHATTER
GET YOUR YAKISOBA!
CHATTER ガヤ
CHATTER ガヤ
YAKISOBA
NOT A SINGLE CUSTOMER...
ISN'T ANYONE HUNGRY?

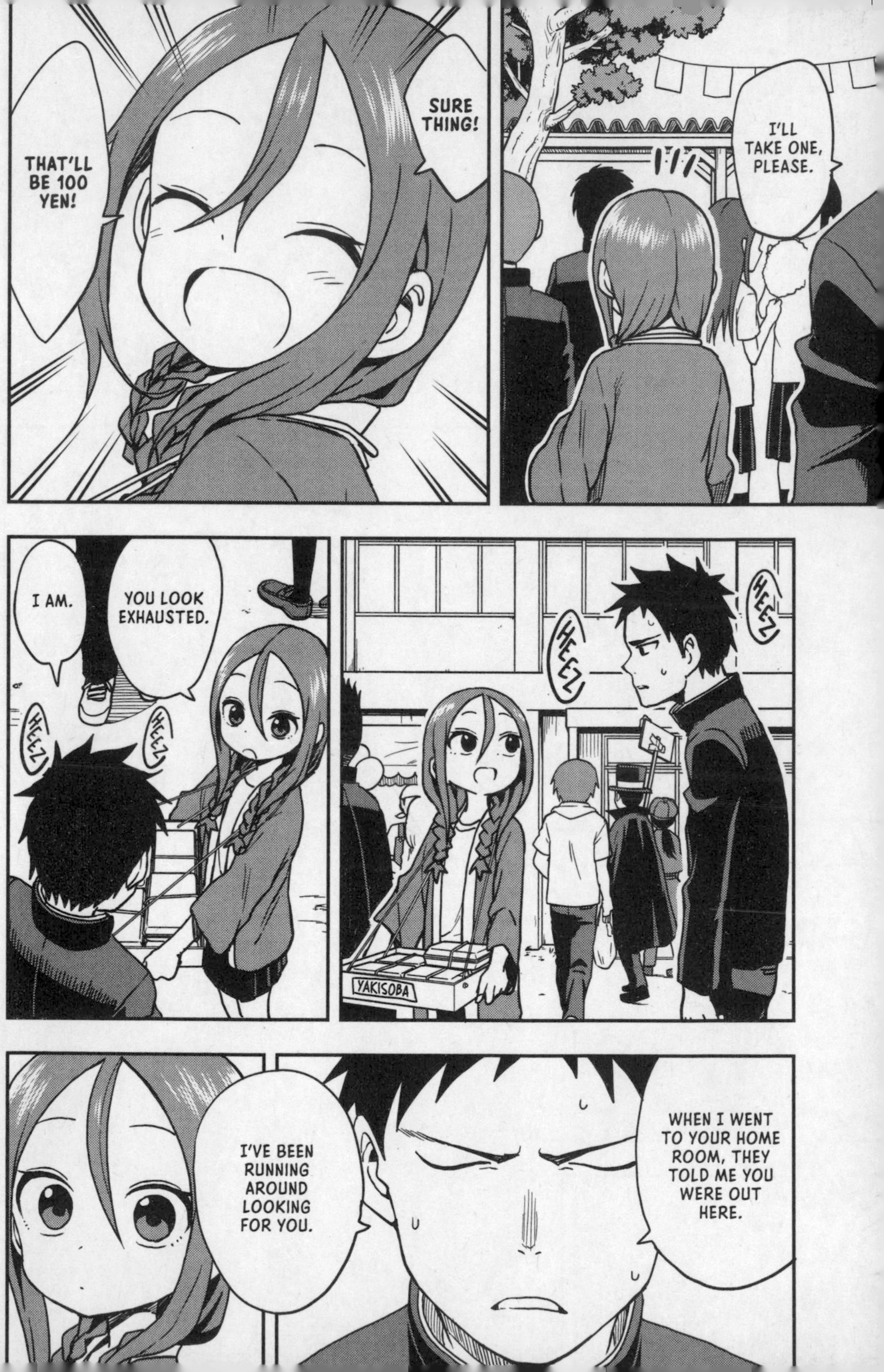
I'LL TAKE ONE, PLEASE.
SURE THING!
THAT'LL BE 100 YEN!
HEEZ
HEEZ
YAKISOBA
YOU LOOK EXHAUSTED.
I AM.
HEEZ
HEEZ
WHEN I WENT TO YOUR HOME ROOM, THEY TOLD ME YOU WERE OUT HERE.
I'VE BEEN RUNNING AROUND LOOKING FOR YOU.

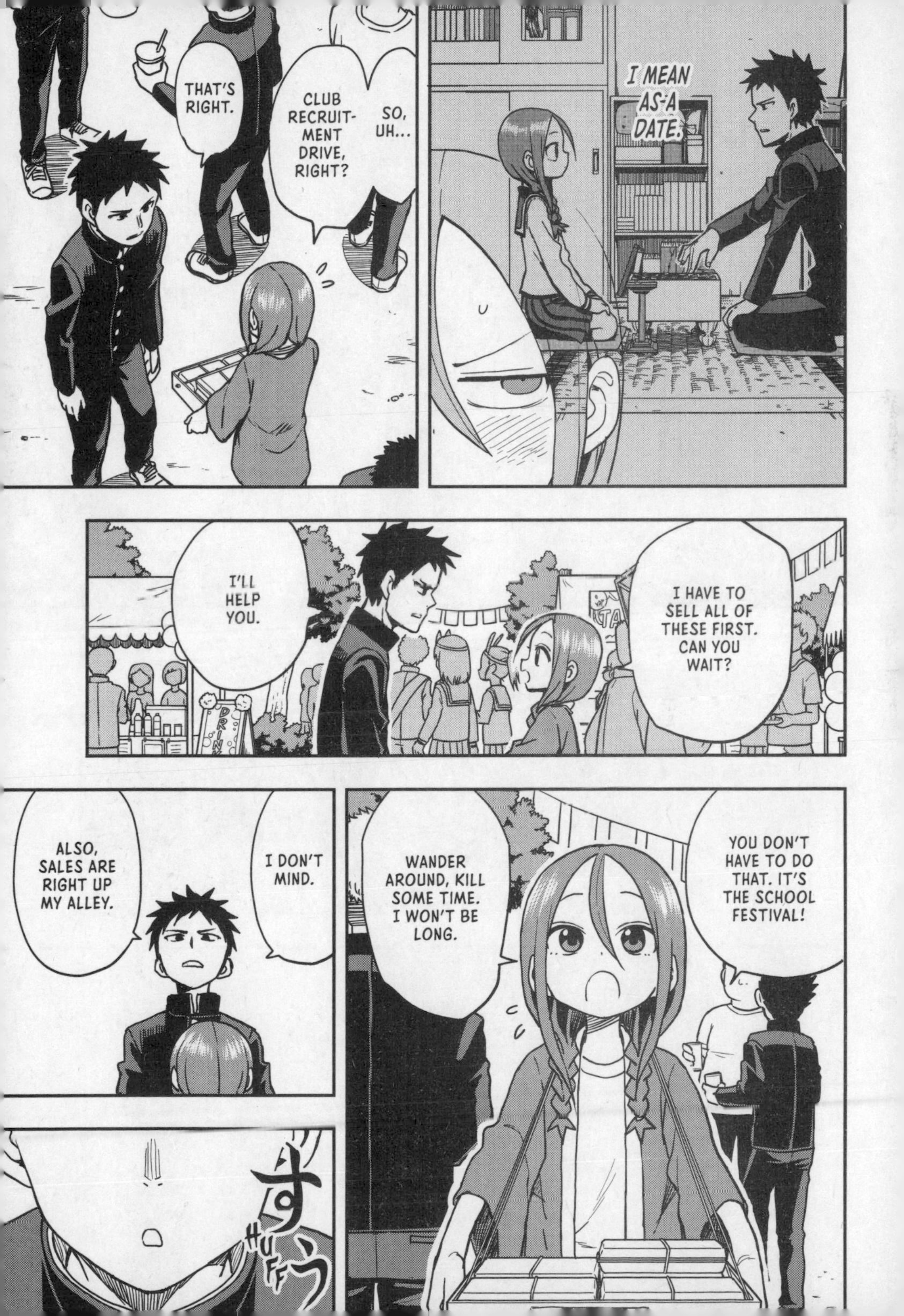
I MEAN AS A DATE.
SO, UH...
CLUB RECRUITMENT DRIVE, RIGHT?
THAT'S RIGHT.
I HAVE TO SELL ALL OF THESE FIRST. CAN YOU WAIT?
I'LL HELP YOU.
YOU DON'T HAVE TO DO THAT. IT'S THE SCHOOL FESTIVAL!
WANDER AROUND, KILL SOME TIME. I WON'T BE LONG.
I DON'T MIND.
ALSO, SALES ARE RIGHT UP MY ALLEY.
すぅ
HUFF

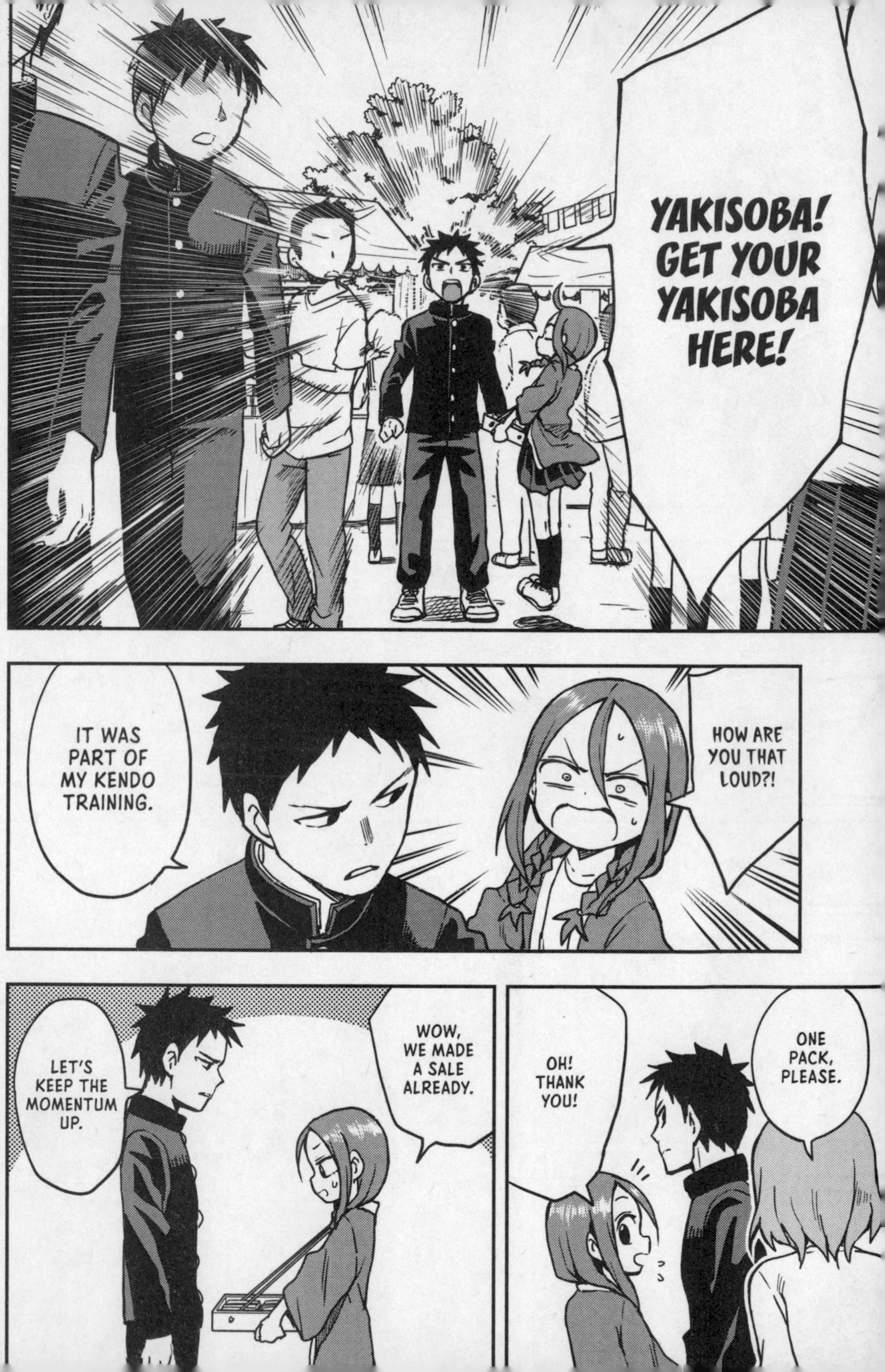
YAKISOBA! GET YOUR YAKISOBA HERE!
HOW ARE YOU THAT LOUD?!
IT WAS PART OF MY KENDO TRAINING.
ONE PACK, PLEASE.
OH! THANK YOU!
WOW, WE MADE A SALE ALREADY.
LET'S KEEP THE MOMENTUM UP.

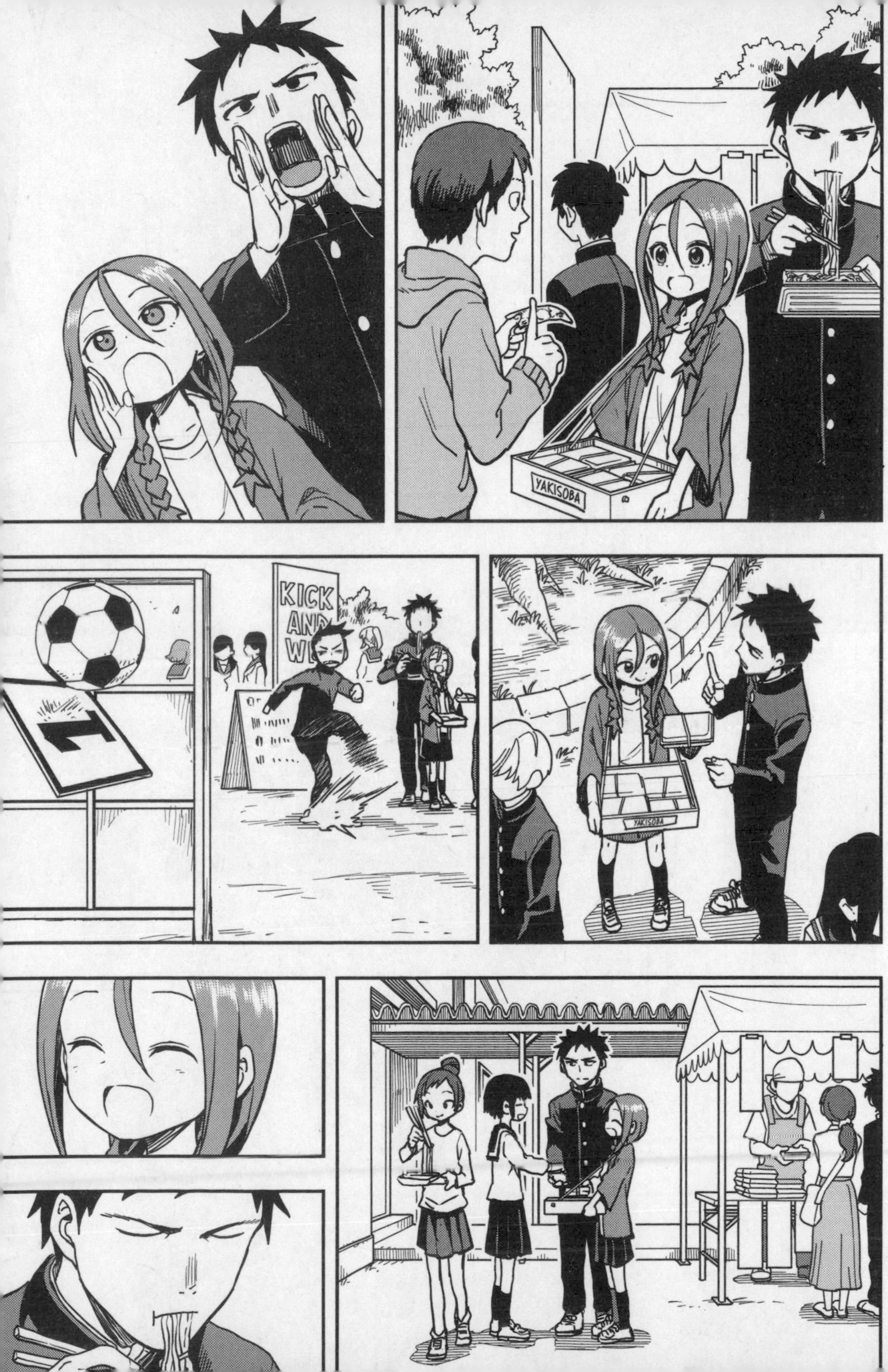
YAKISOBA
YAKISOBA
KICK
AND

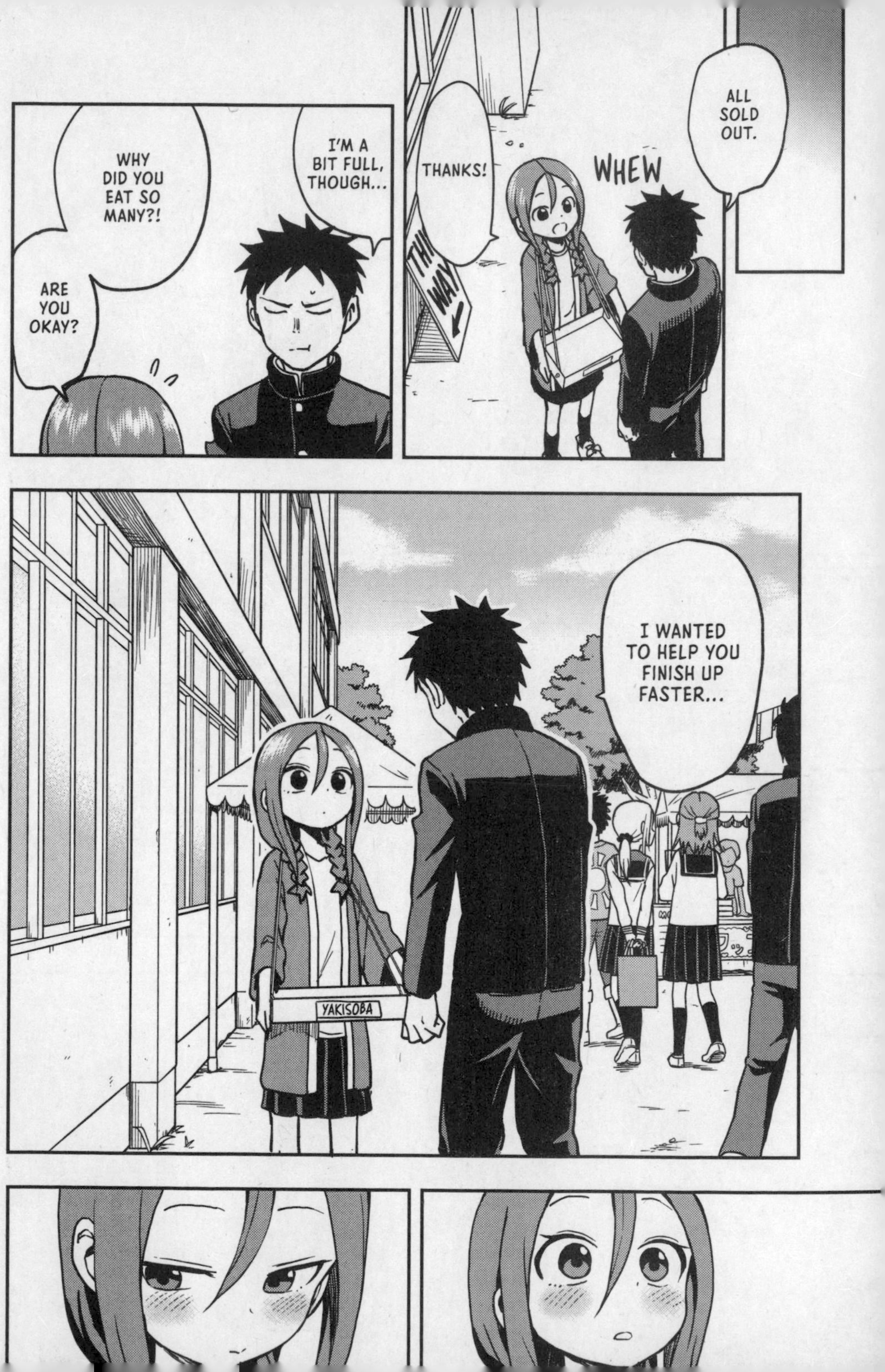
ALL SOLD OUT.
WHEW
THANKS!
I'M A BIT FULL, THOUGH...
WHY DID YOU EAT SO MANY?!
ARE YOU OKAY?
I WANTED TO HELP YOU FINISH UP FASTER...
YAKISOBA

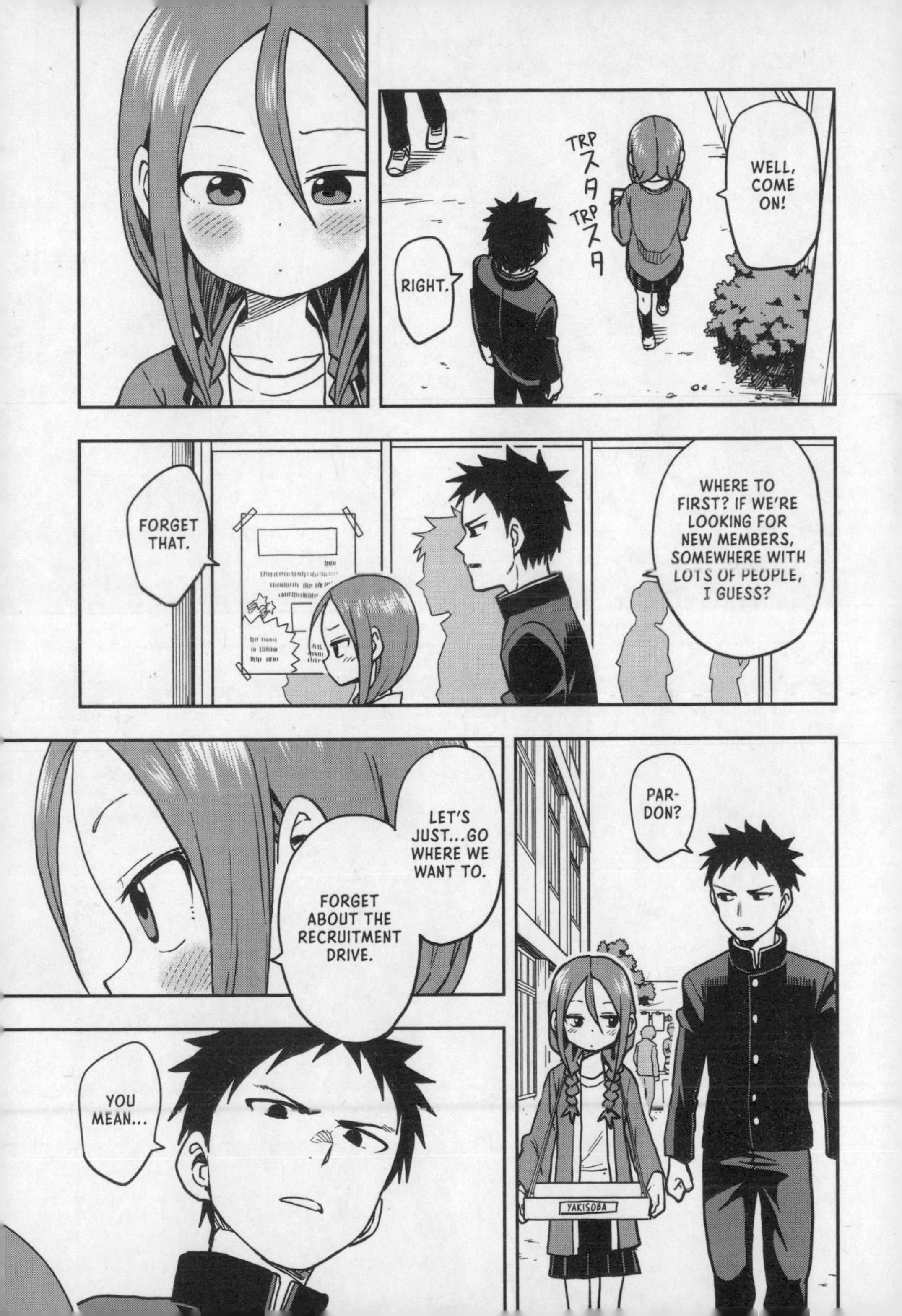
WELL, COME ON!
TRP スタ
TRP スタ
RIGHT.
WHERE TO FIRST? IF WE'RE LOOKING FOR NEW MEMBERS, SOMEWHERE WITH LOTS OF PEOPLE, I GUESS?
FORGET THAT.
PAR-DON?
YAKISOBA
LET'S JUST...GO WHERE WE WANT TO.
FORGET ABOUT THE RECRUITMENT DRIVE.
YOU MEAN...

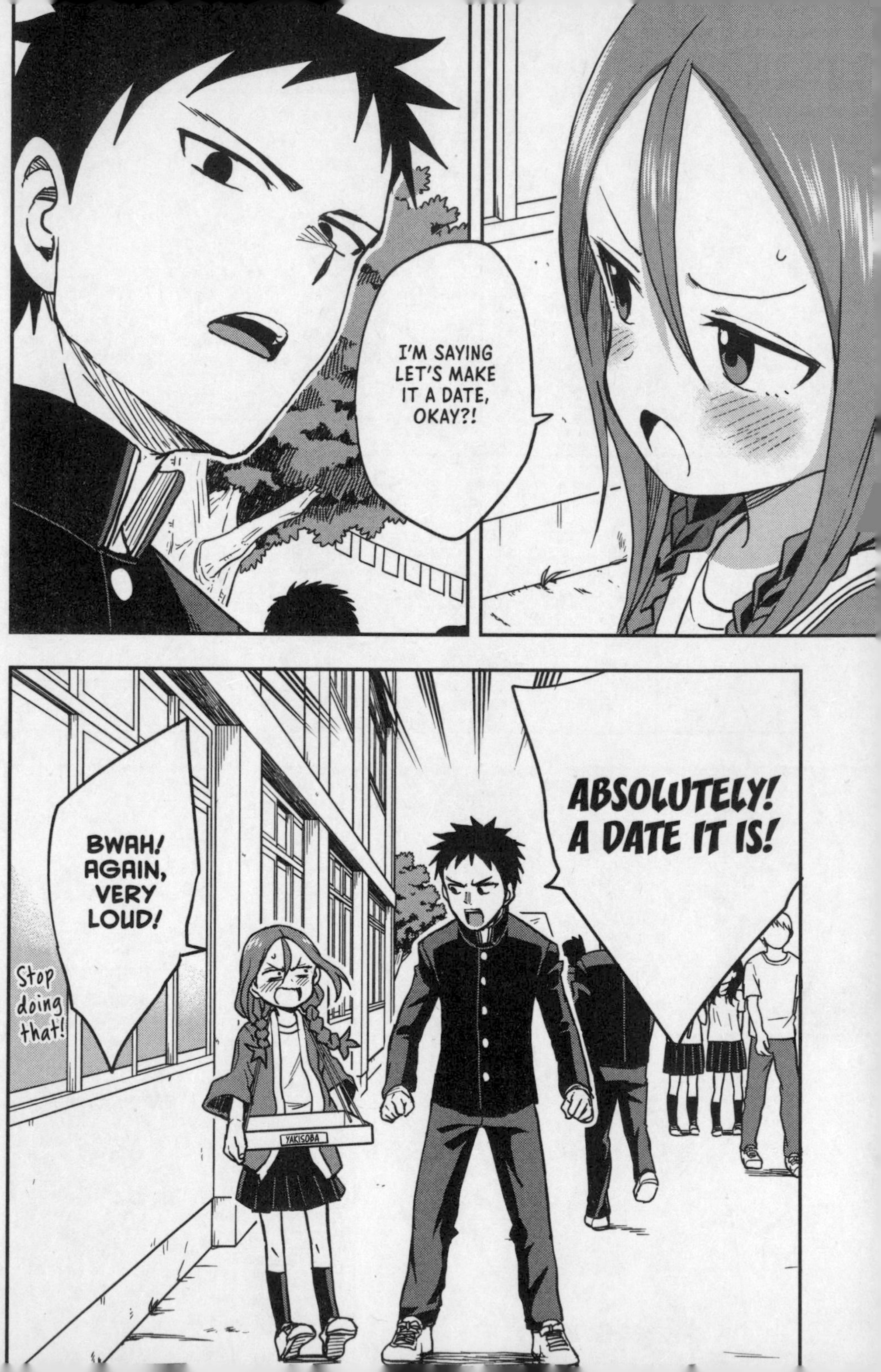
I'M SAYING LET'S MAKE IT A DATE, OKAY?!
ABSOLUTELY! A DATE IT IS!
BWAH! AGAIN, VERY LOUD!
Stop doing that!
YAKISOBA

Leave it to me!

WHEN WILL AYUMU MAKE HIS MOVE?

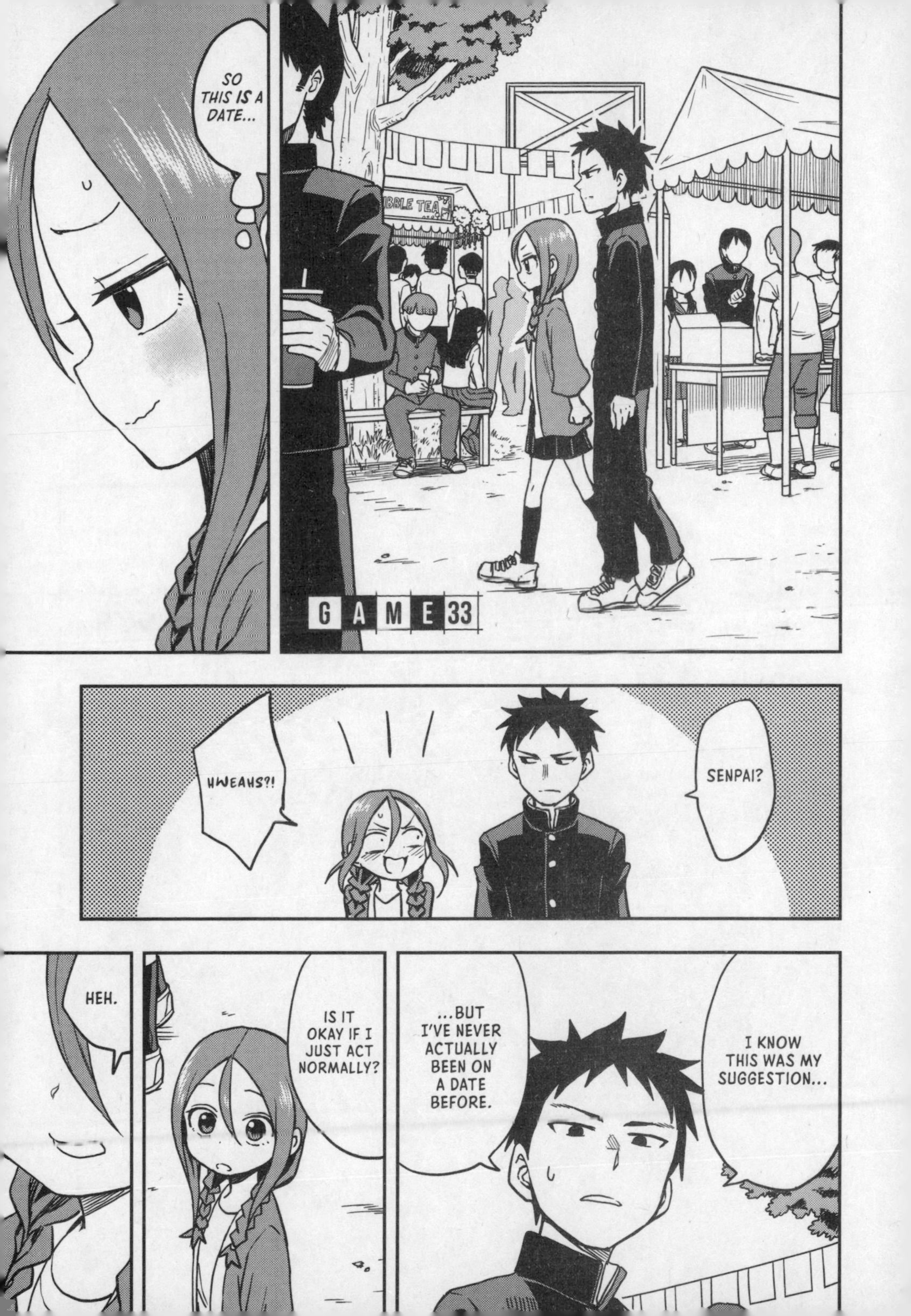
BBLE TEA
GAME 33
SO THIS IS A DATE...
SENPAI?
HWEAHS?!
I KNOW THIS WAS MY SUGGESTION...
...BUT I'VE NEVER ACTUALLY BEEN ON A DATE BEFORE.
IS IT OKAY IF I JUST ACT NORMALLY?
HEH.

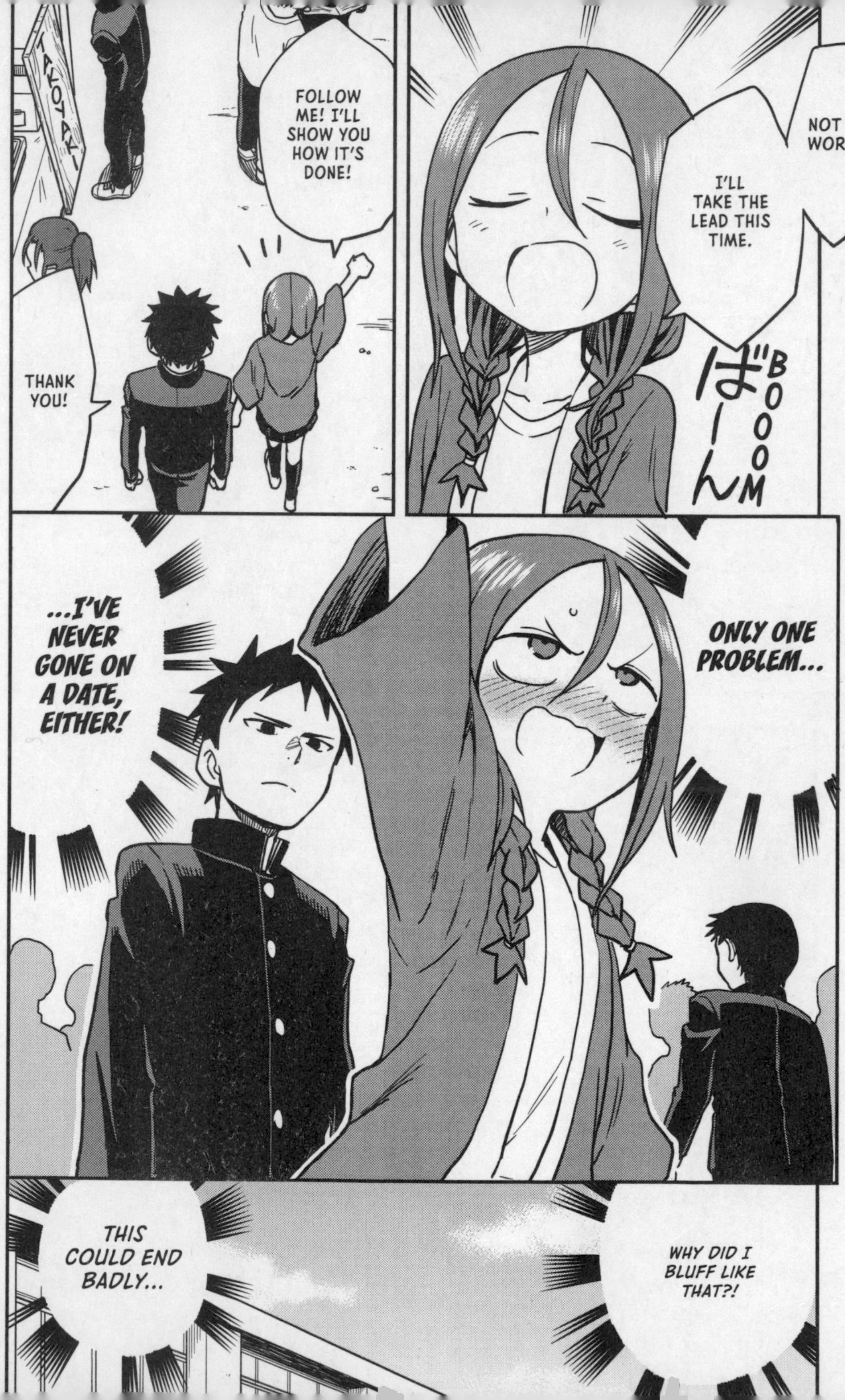
NOT TO WORRY.
I'LL TAKE THE LEAD THIS TIME.
ばーん BOOOOM
FOLLOW ME! I'LL SHOW YOU HOW IT'S DONE!
TAKOYAKI
THANK YOU!
ONLY ONE PROBLEM...
...I'VE NEVER GONE ON A DATE, EITHER!
WHY DID I BLUFF LIKE THAT?!
THIS COULD END BADLY...

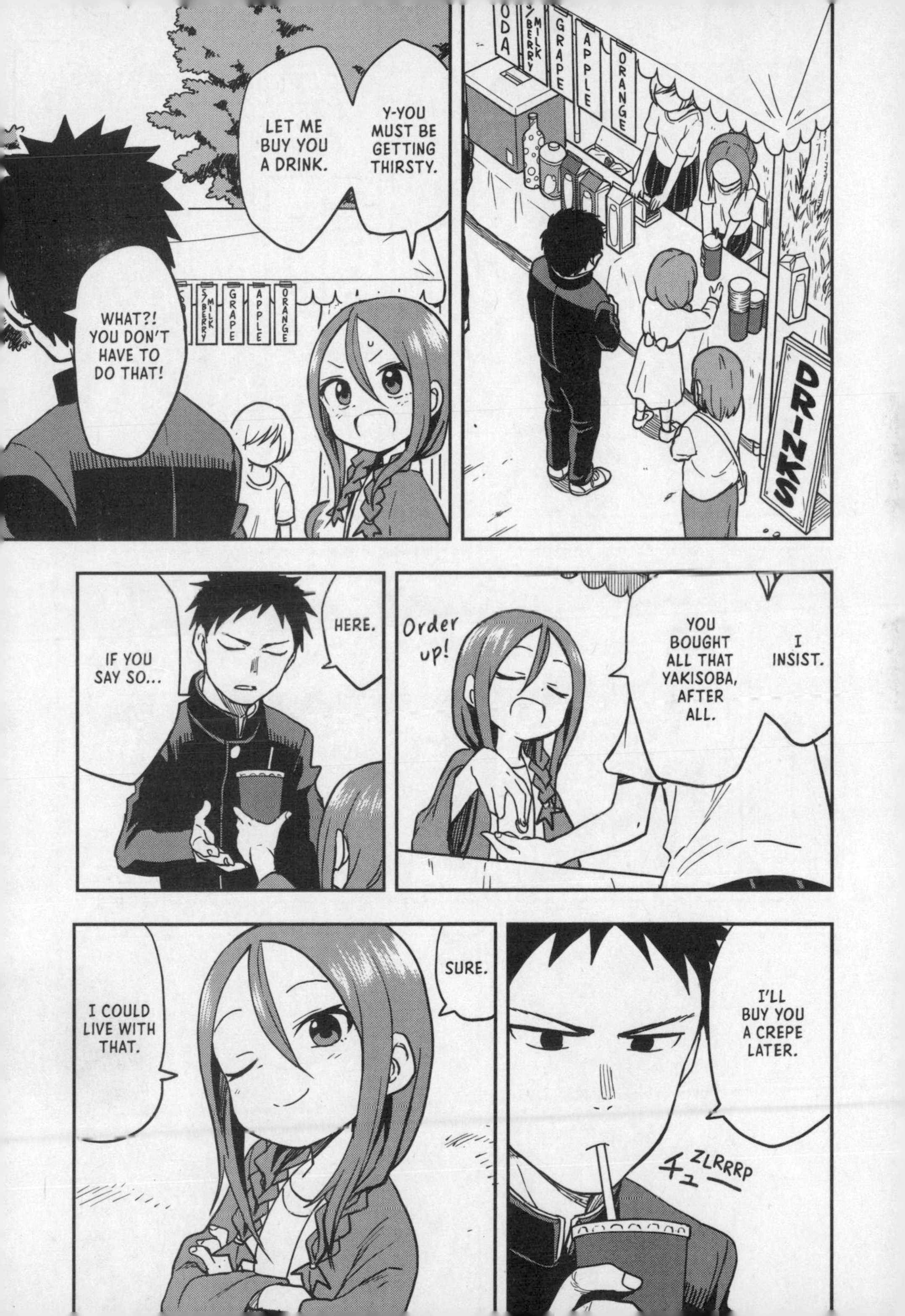
ODA
S/BERRY MILK
GRAPE
APPLE
ORANGE
DRINKS
Y-YOU MUST BE GETTING THIRSTY.
LET ME BUY YOU A DRINK.
S/BERRY MILK
GRAPE
APPLE
ORANGE
WHAT?! YOU DON'T HAVE TO DO THAT!
I INSIST.
YOU BOUGHT ALL THAT YAKISOBA, AFTER ALL.
Order up!
HERE.
IF YOU SAY SO...
I'LL BUY YOU A CREPE LATER.
チュー ZLRRRP
SURE.
I COULD LIVE WITH THAT.

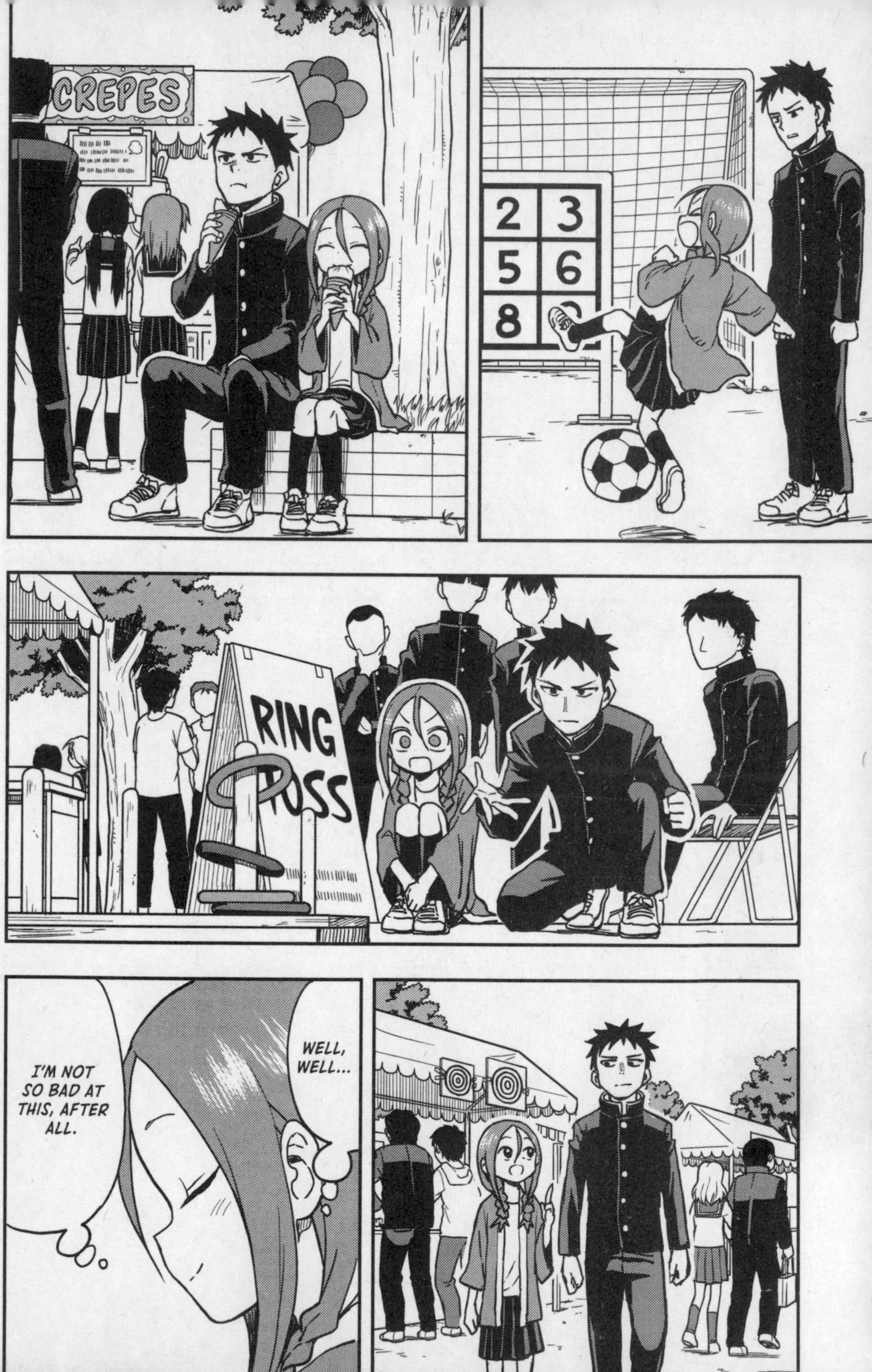
2 3
5 6
8
CREPES
RING
WELL, WELL...
I'M NOT SO BAD AT THIS, AFTER ALL.

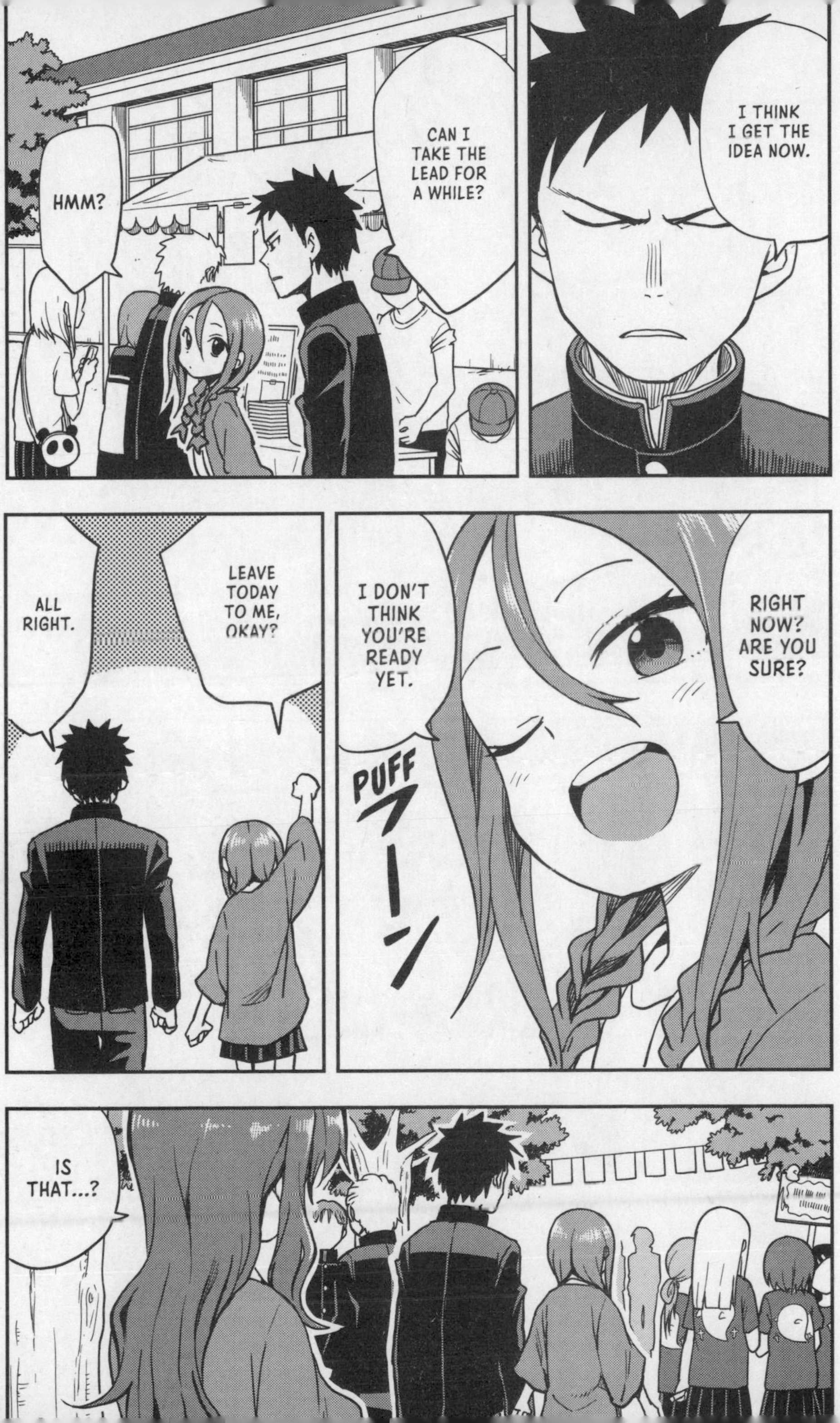
I THINK I GET THE IDEA NOW.
CAN I TAKE THE LEAD FOR A WHILE?
HMM?
RIGHT NOW? ARE YOU SURE?
I DON'T THINK YOU'RE READY YET.
PUFF
フーン
LEAVE TODAY TO ME, OKAY?
ALL RIGHT.
IS THAT...?

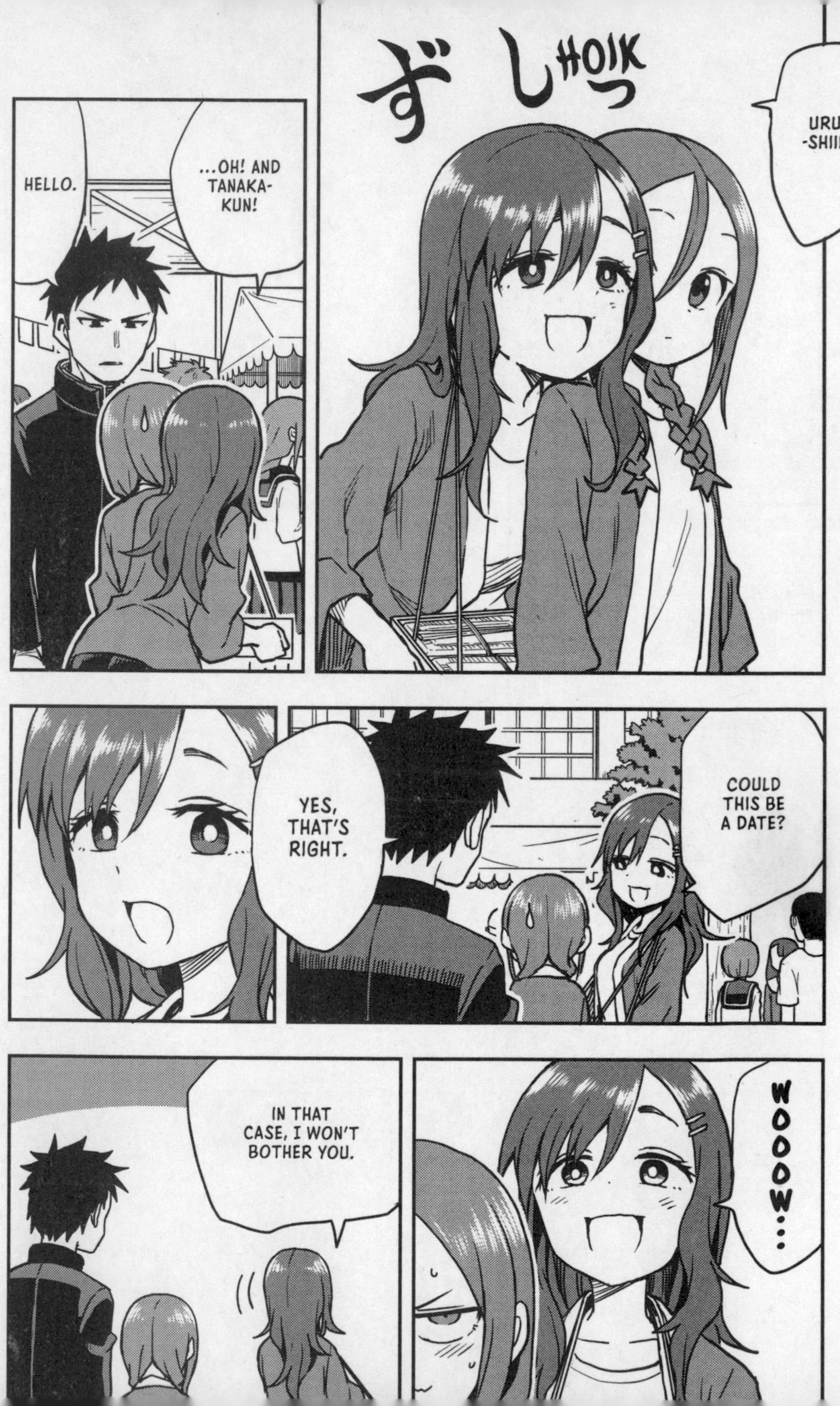
ずしっ HOIK
URU-SHIII.
...OH! AND TANAKA-KUN!
HELLO.
COULD THIS BE A DATE?
YES, THAT'S RIGHT.
WOOOOW...
IN THAT CASE, I WON'T BOTHER YOU.

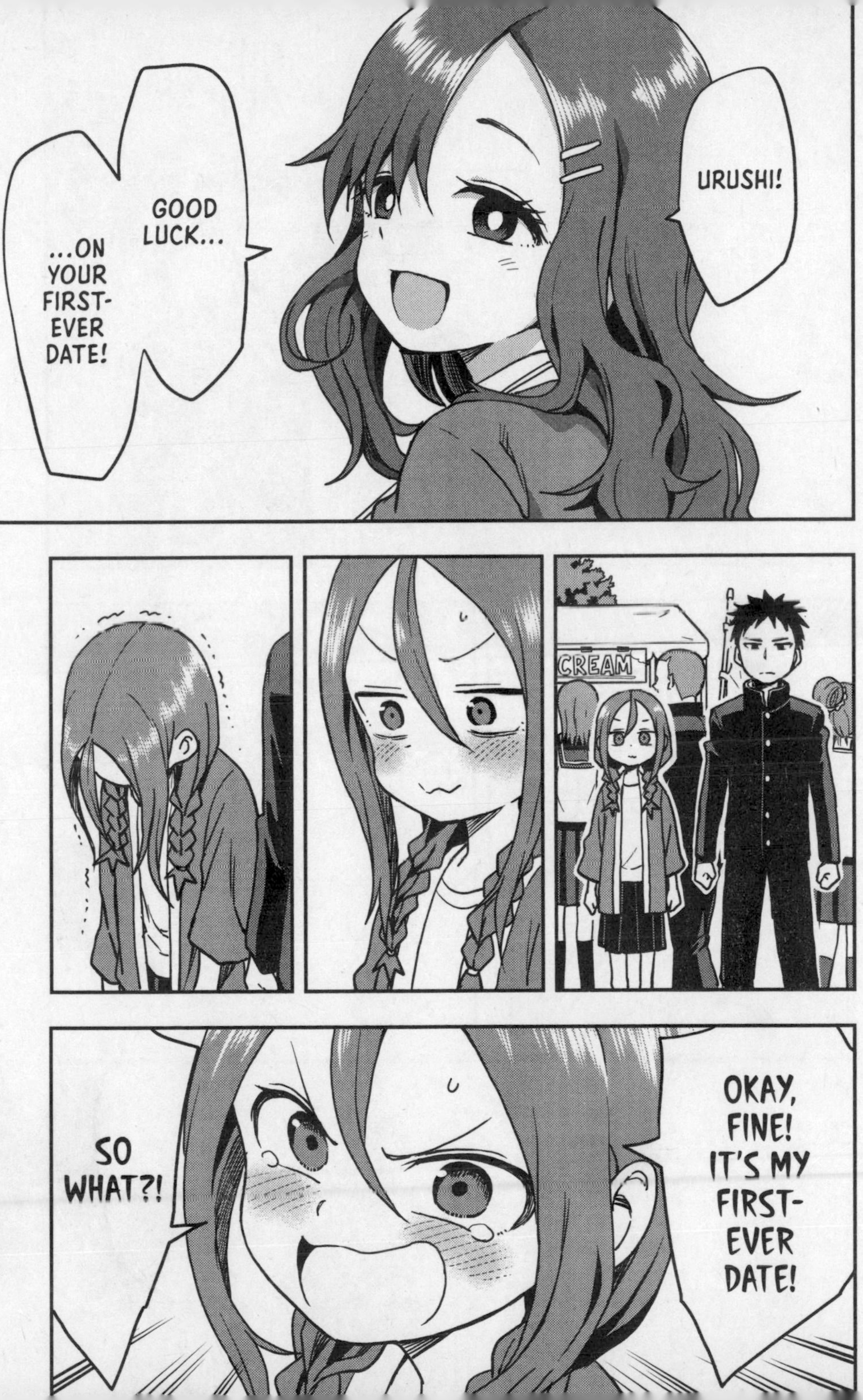
URUSHI!
GOOD LUCK...
...ON YOUR FIRST-EVER DATE!
OKAY, FINE! IT'S MY FIRST-EVER DATE!
SO WHAT?!

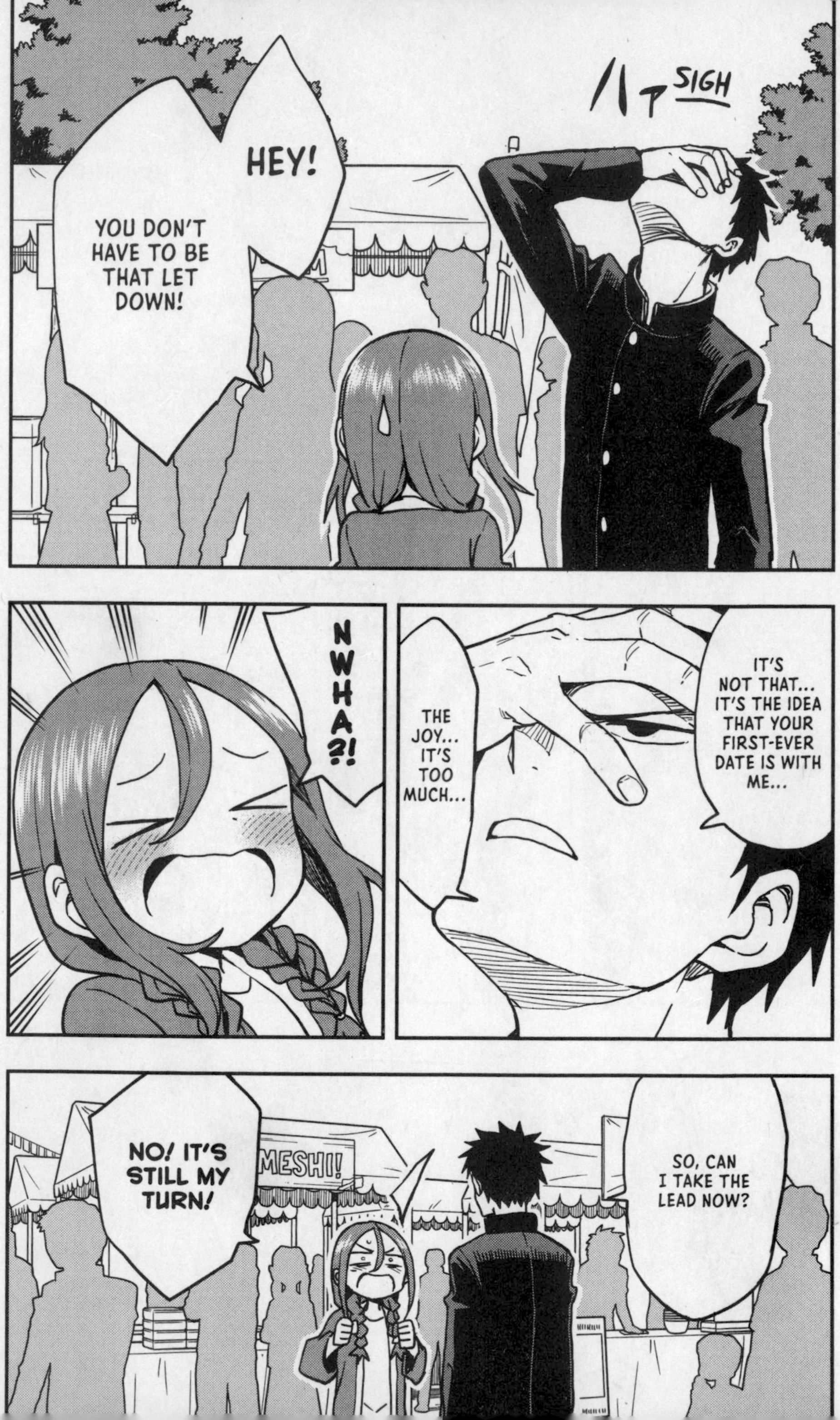
ハア SIGH
HEY! YOU DON'T HAVE TO BE THAT LET DOWN!
IT'S NOT THAT... IT'S THE IDEA THAT YOUR FIRST-EVER DATE IS WITH ME...
THE JOY... IT'S TOO MUCH...
NWHA?!
SO, CAN I TAKE THE LEAD NOW?
MESHI!
NO! IT'S STILL MY TURN!

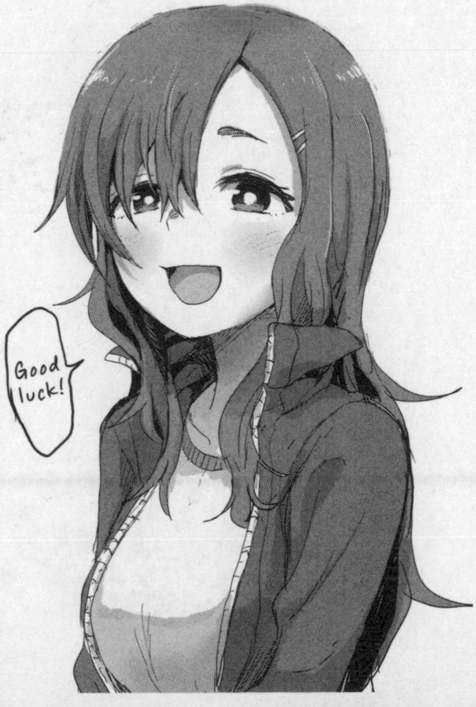
Good luck!

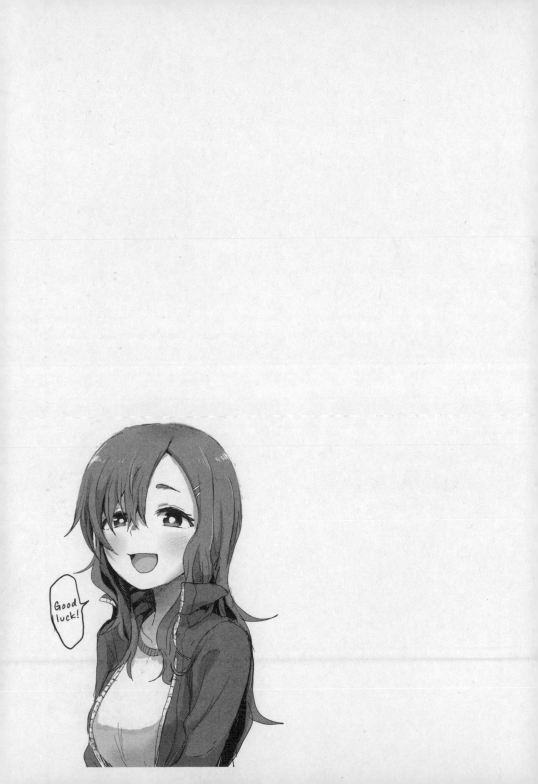

WHEN WILL AYUMU MAKE HIS MOVE?

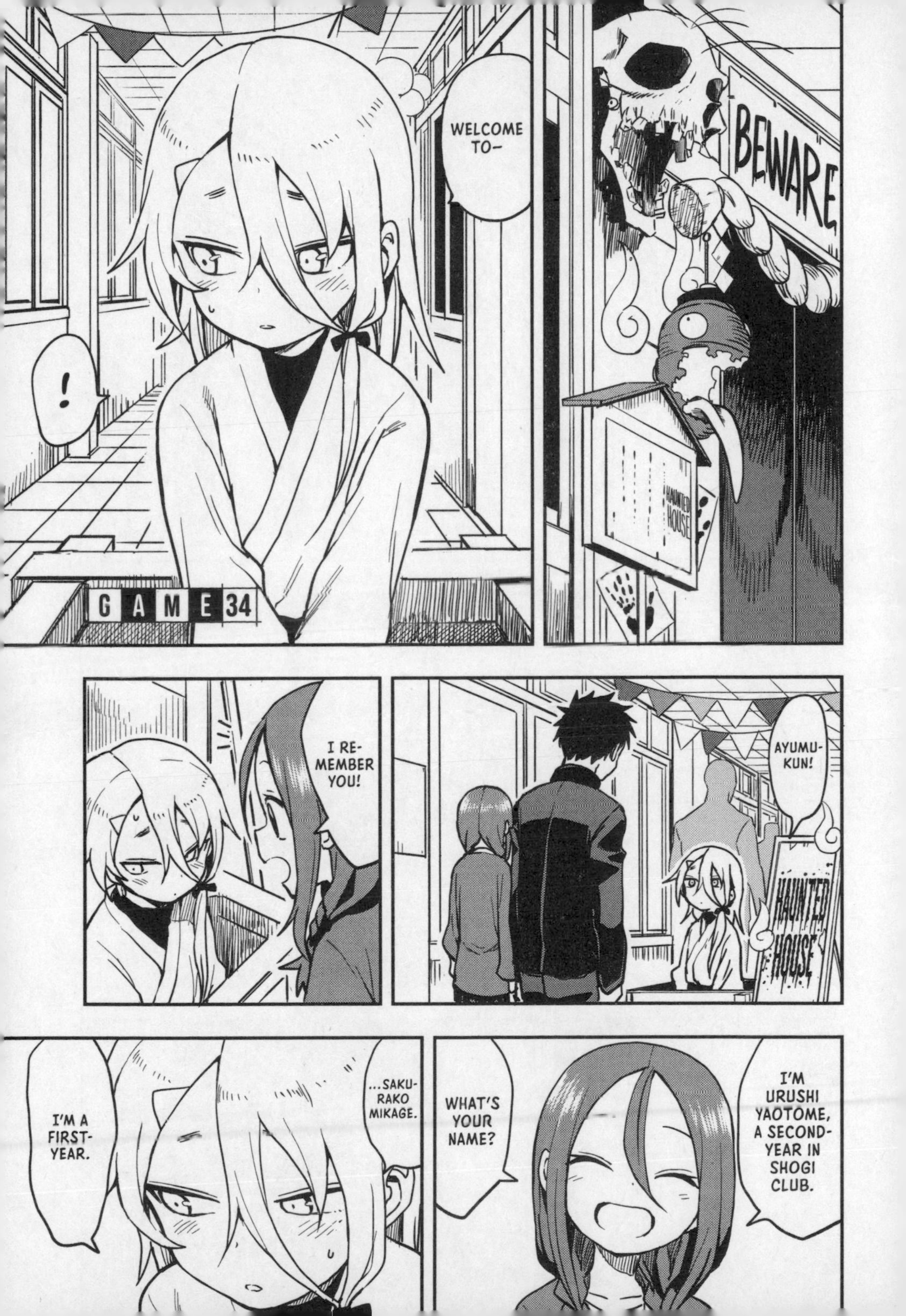
BEWARE
HAUNTED HOUSE
WELCOME TO–
!
GAME 34
AYUMU-KUN!
HAUNTED HOUSE
I RE-MEMBER YOU!
I'M URUSHI YAOTOME, A SECOND-YEAR IN SHOGI CLUB.
WHAT'S YOUR NAME?
...SAKU-RAKO MIKAGE.
I'M A FIRST-YEAR.

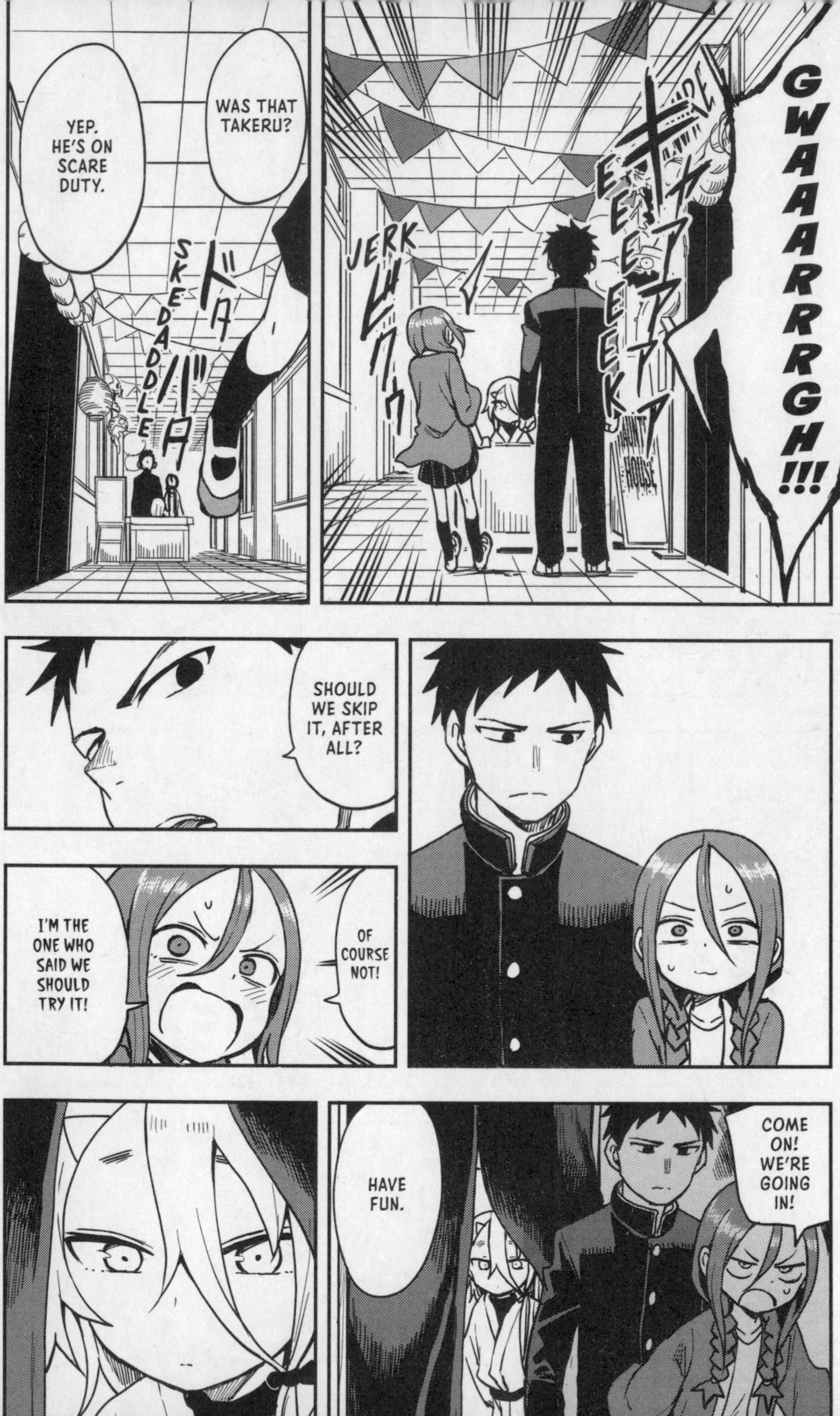
GWAAARRRGH!!!
EEEEEEK
JERK
WAS THAT TAKERU?
YEP. HE'S ON SCARE DUTY.
SKEDADDLE
SHOULD WE SKIP IT, AFTER ALL?
OF COURSE NOT!
I'M THE ONE WHO SAID WE SHOULD TRY IT!
COME ON! WE'RE GOING IN!
HAVE FUN.

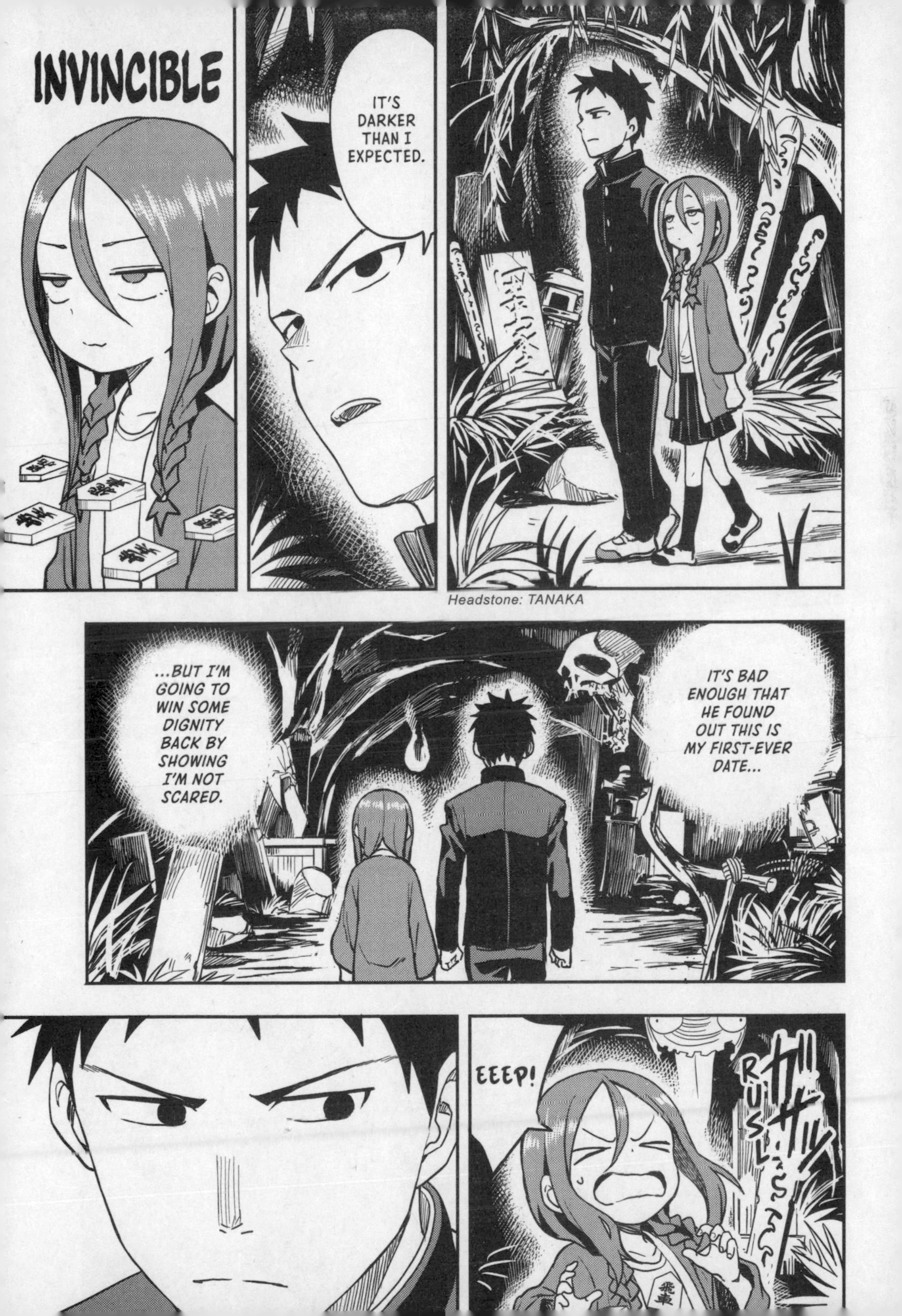
Headstone: TANAKA
IT'S DARKER THAN I EXPECTED.
INVINCIBLE
IT'S BAD ENOUGH THAT HE FOUND OUT THIS IS MY FIRST-EVER DATE...
...BUT I'M GOING TO WIN SOME DIGNITY BACK BY SHOWING I'M NOT SCARED.
RUSTLE
EEEP!

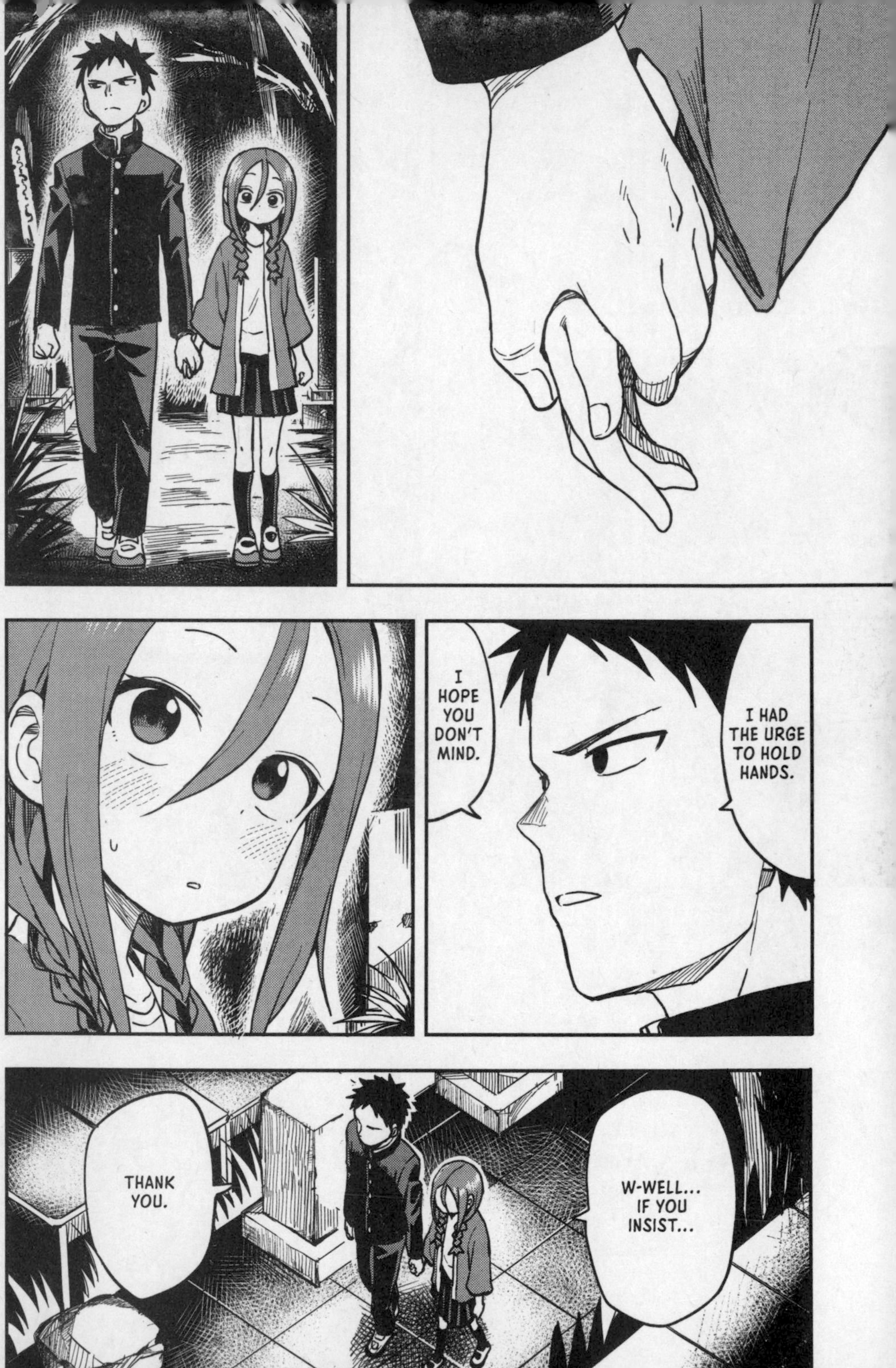
I HAD THE URGE TO HOLD HANDS.
I HOPE YOU DON'T MIND.
W-WELL... IF YOU INSIST...
THANK YOU.

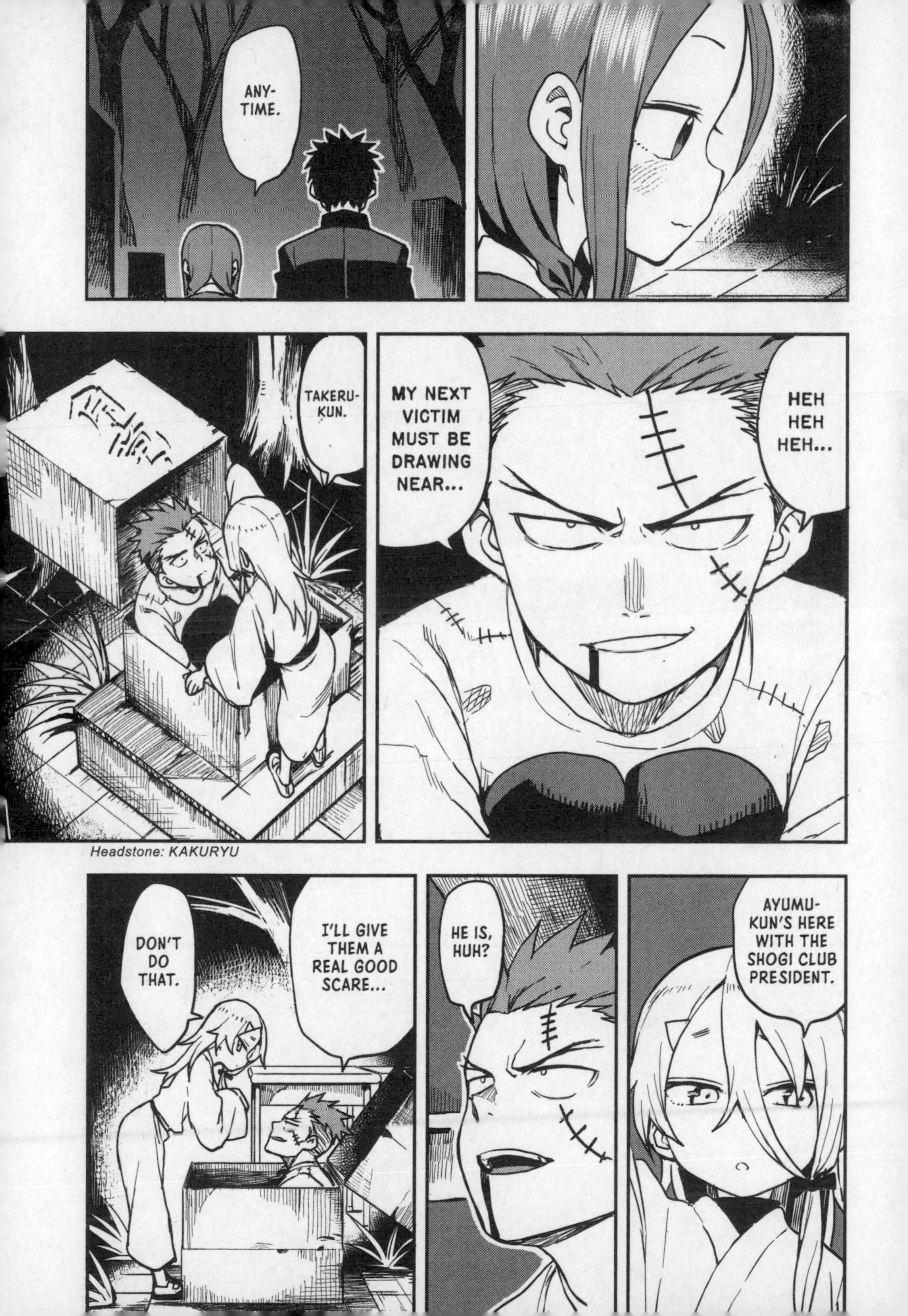
ANY-TIME.
HEH HEH HEH...
MY NEXT VICTIM MUST BE DRAWING NEAR...
TAKERU-KUN.
Headstone: KAKURYU
AYUMU-KUN'S HERE WITH THE SHOGI CLUB PRESIDENT.
HE IS, HUH?
I'LL GIVE THEM A REAL GOOD SCARE...
DON'T DO THAT.

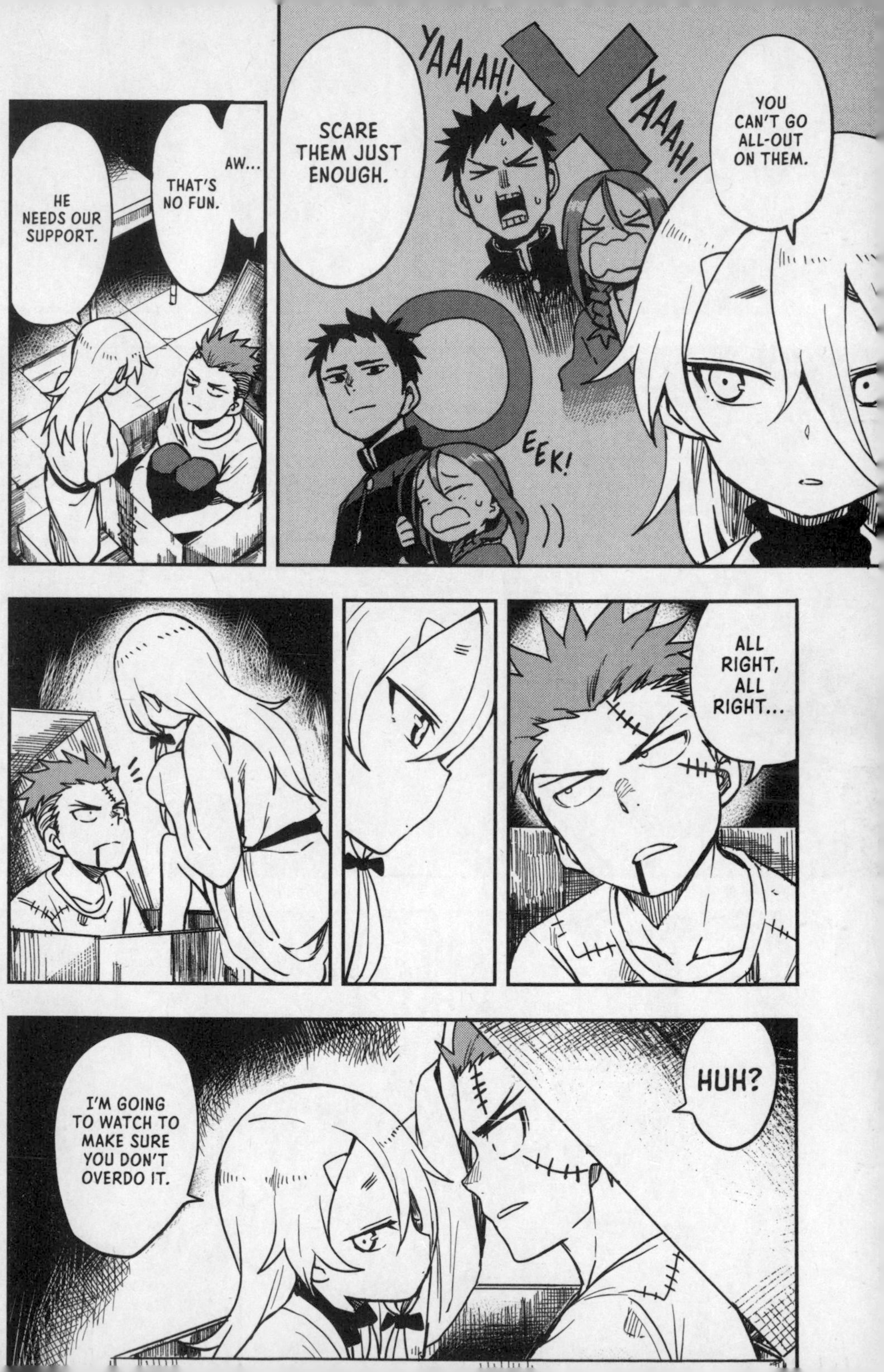
YOU CAN'T GO ALL-OUT ON THEM.
YAAAAH!
YAAAAH!
SCARE THEM JUST ENOUGH.
EEK!
AW... THAT'S NO FUN.
HE NEEDS OUR SUPPORT.
ALL RIGHT, ALL RIGHT...
HUH?
I'M GOING TO WATCH TO MAKE SURE YOU DON'T OVERDO IT.

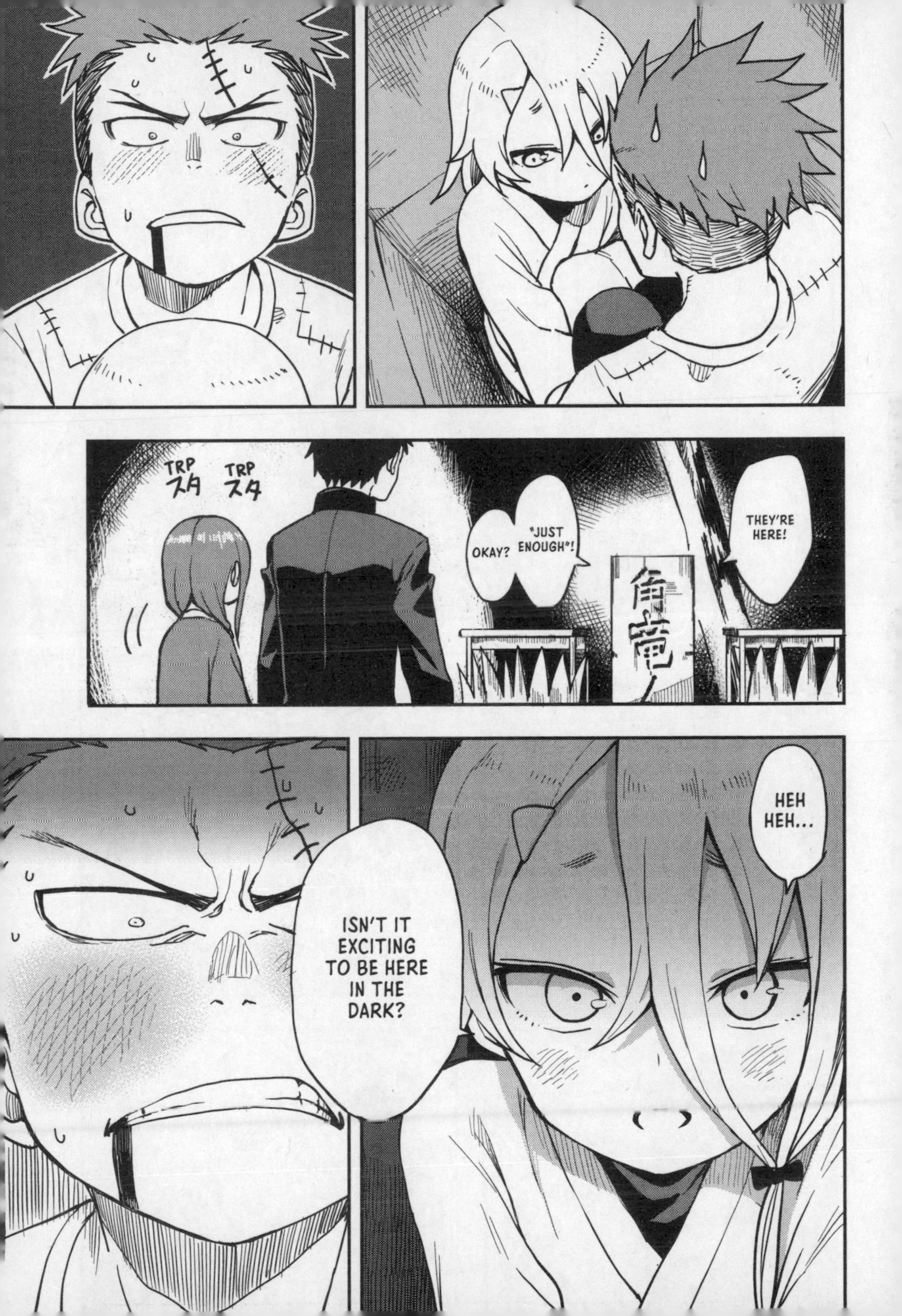
THEY'RE HERE!
"JUST ENOUGH"!
OKAY?
TRP スタ
TRP スタ
HEH HEH...
ISN'T IT EXCITING TO BE HERE IN THE DARK?

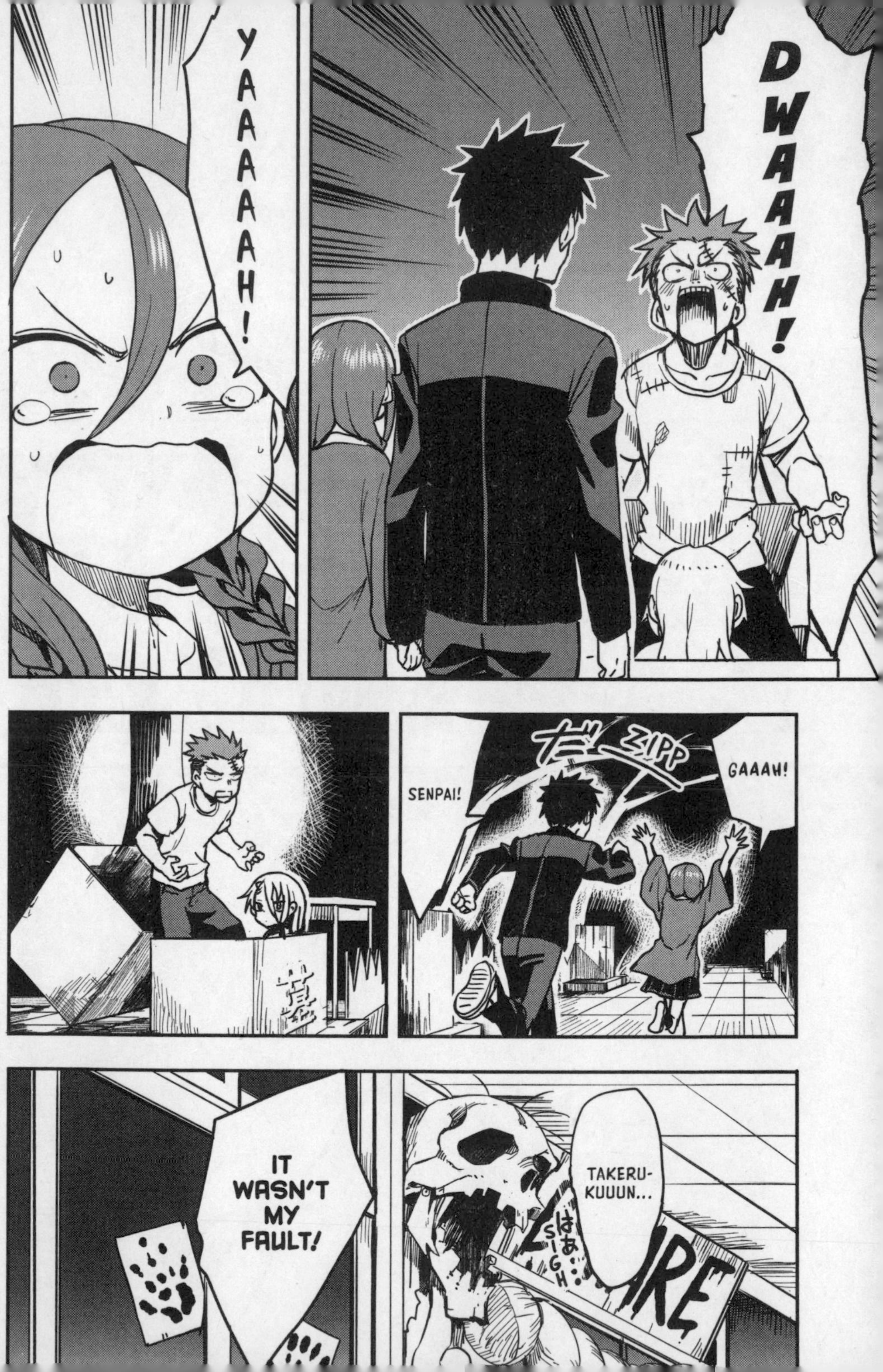
DWAAAAH!
YAAAAAAAH!
GAAAH!
ZIPP
SENPAI!
TAKERU-KUUUN...
はぁ…
SIGH
IT WASN'T MY FAULT!

WHEN WILL
AYUMU
MAKE HIS
MOVE?

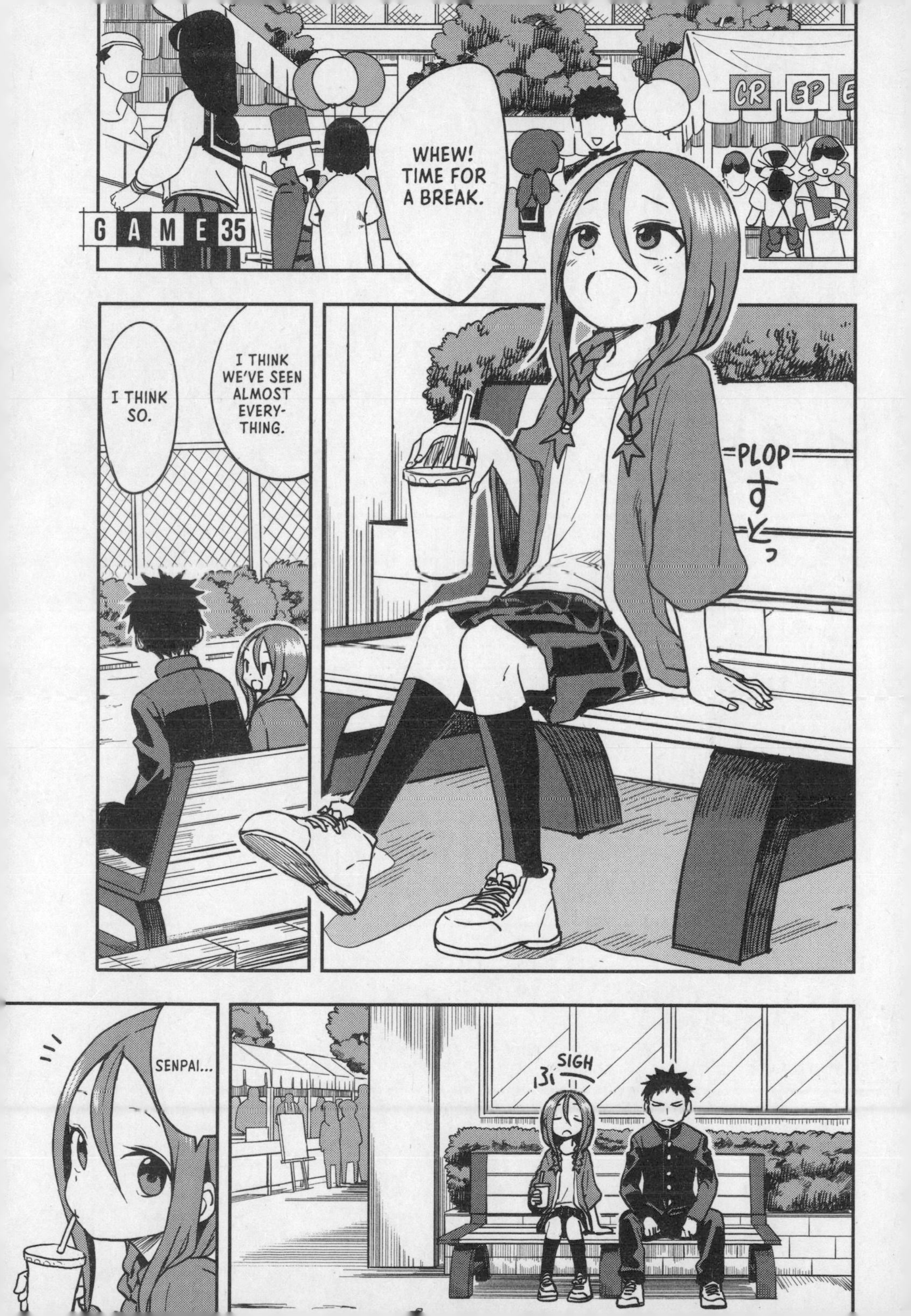
CR EP E
WHEW! TIME FOR A BREAK.
GAME 35
PLOP
すとっ
I THINK WE'VE SEEN ALMOST EVERY-THING.
I THINK SO.
SIGH
ふ
SENPAI...

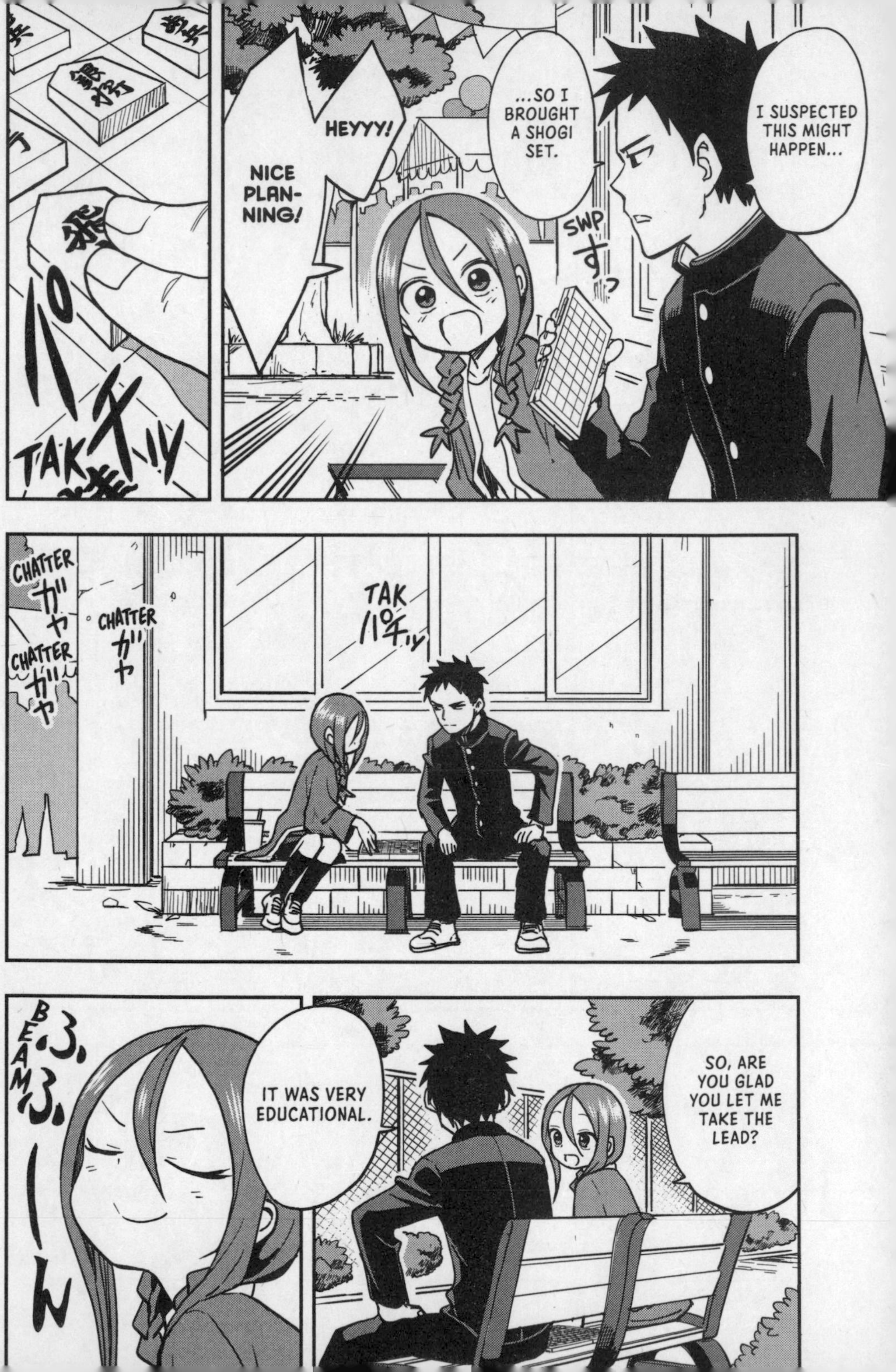
I SUSPECTED THIS MIGHT HAPPEN...
...SO I BROUGHT A SHOGI SET.
SWP
HEYYY!
NICE PLAN-NING!
TAK
TAK
CHATTER
CHATTER
CHATTER
SO, ARE YOU GLAD YOU LET ME TAKE THE LEAD?
IT WAS VERY EDUCATIONAL.
BEAM

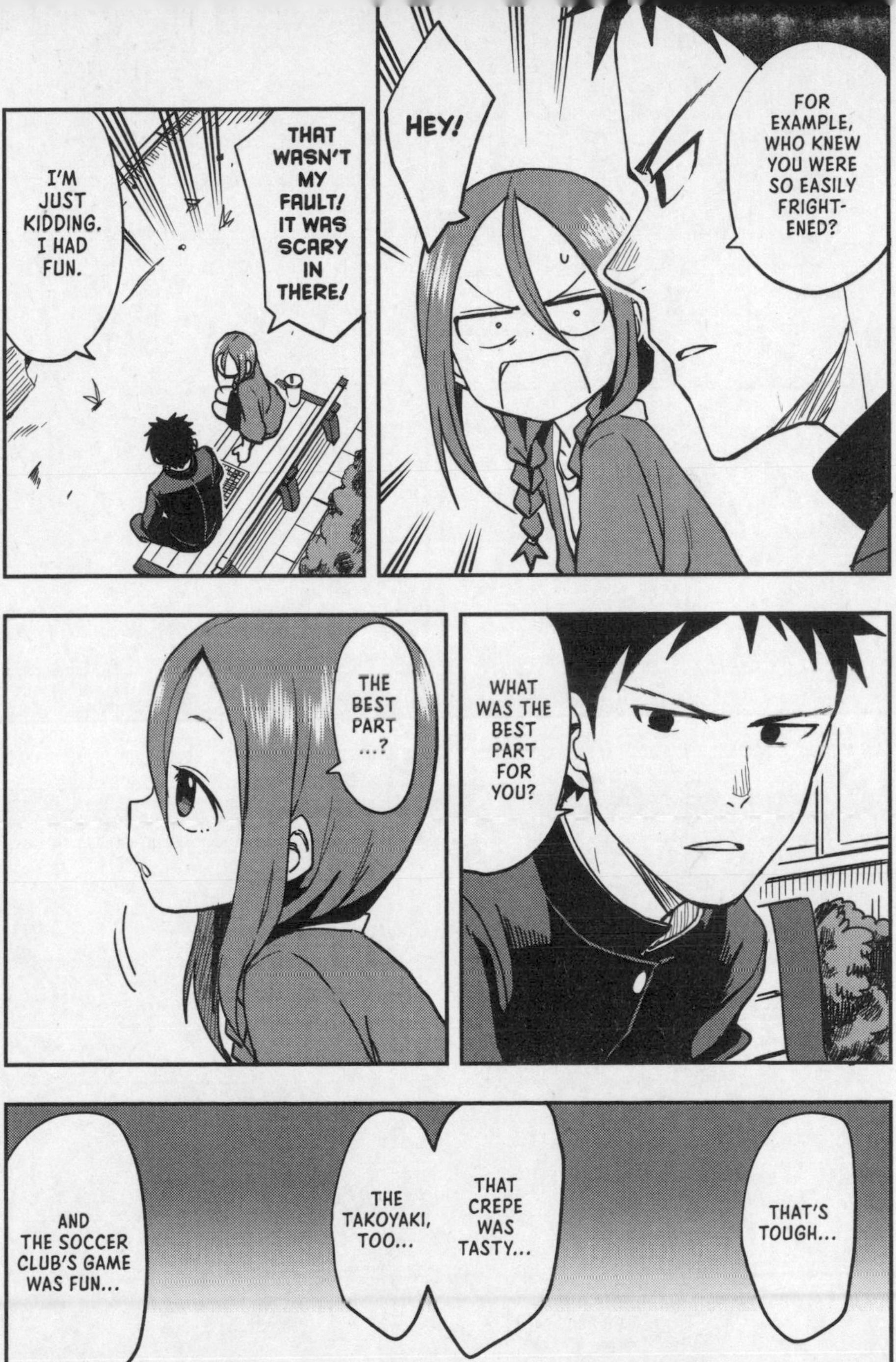
FOR EXAMPLE, WHO KNEW YOU WERE SO EASILY FRIGHT-ENED?
HEY!
THAT WASN'T MY FAULT! IT WAS SCARY IN THERE!
I'M JUST KIDDING. I HAD FUN.
WHAT WAS THE BEST PART FOR YOU?
THE BEST PART ...?
THAT'S TOUGH...
THAT CREPE WAS TASTY...
THE TAKOYAKI, TOO...
AND THE SOCCER CLUB'S GAME WAS FUN...

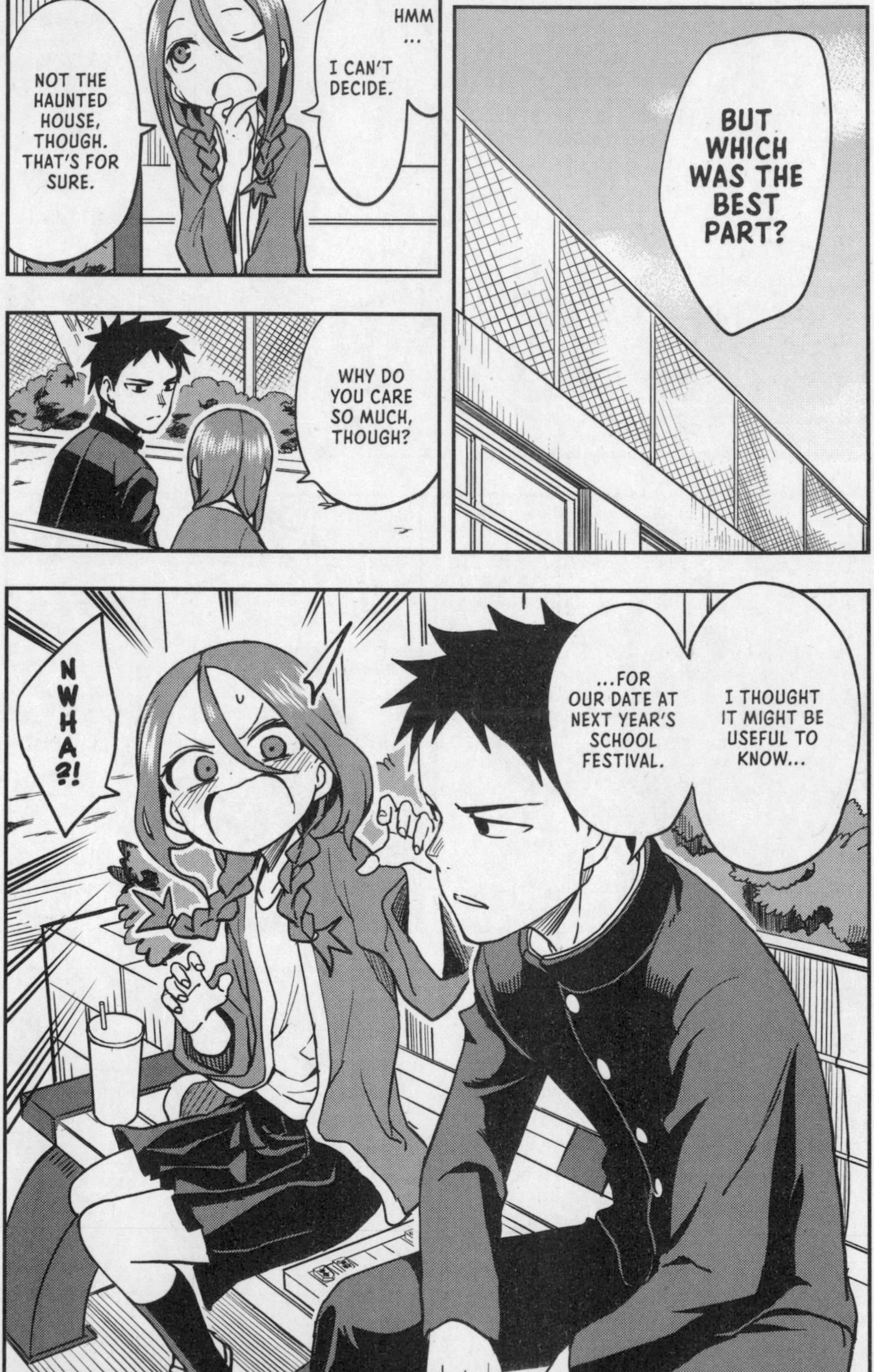
BUT WHICH WAS THE BEST PART?
HMM ... I CAN'T DECIDE.
NOT THE HAUNTED HOUSE, THOUGH. THAT'S FOR SURE.
WHY DO YOU CARE SO MUCH, THOUGH?
I THOUGHT IT MIGHT BE USEFUL TO KNOW...
...FOR OUR DATE AT NEXT YEAR'S SCHOOL FESTIVAL.
NWHA?!

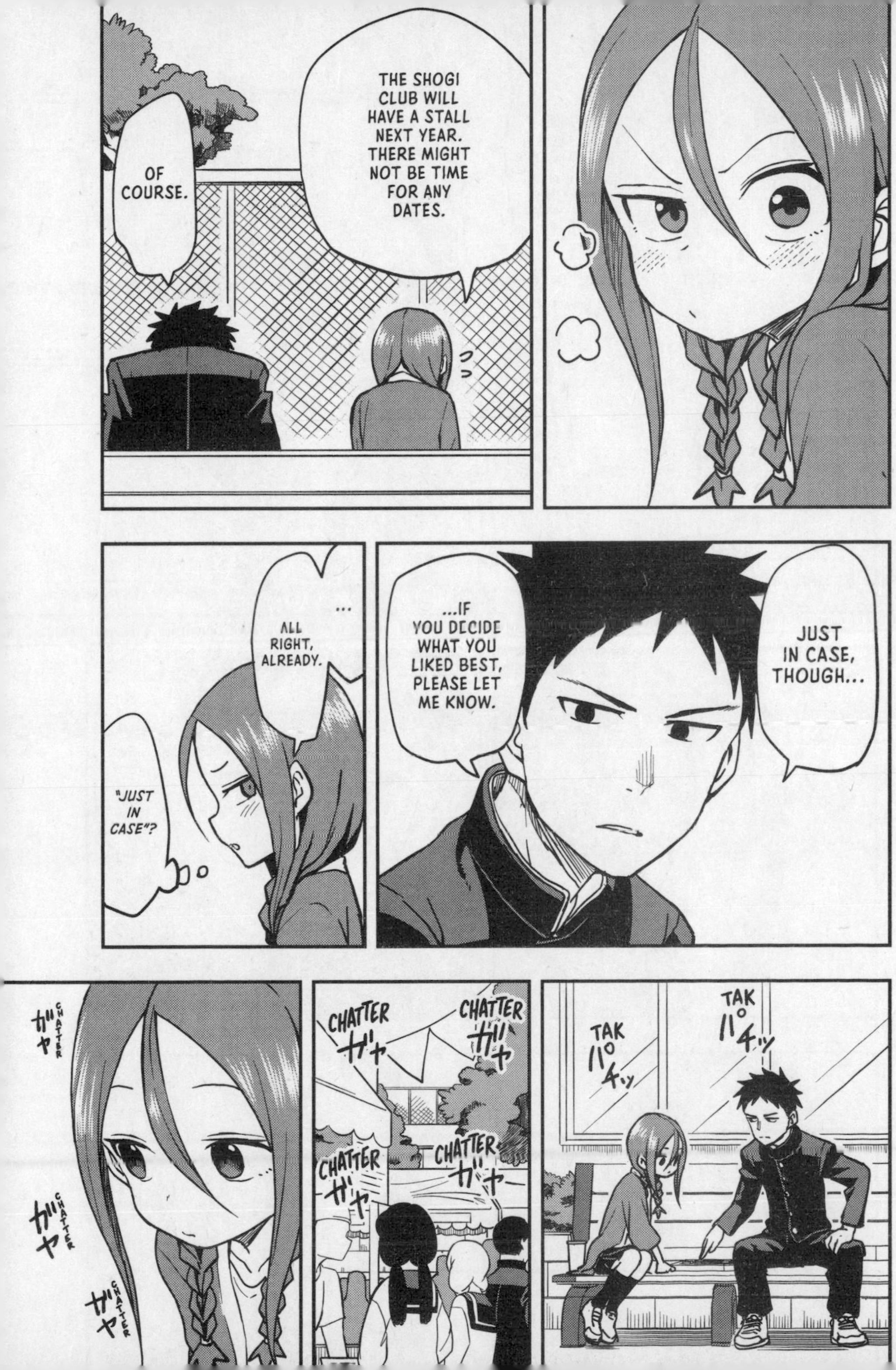
THE SHOGI CLUB WILL HAVE A STALL NEXT YEAR. THERE MIGHT NOT BE TIME FOR ANY DATES.
OF COURSE.
JUST IN CASE, THOUGH...
...IF YOU DECIDE WHAT YOU LIKED BEST, PLEASE LET ME KNOW.
... ALL RIGHT, ALREADY.
"JUST IN CASE"?
TAK パチッ
TAK パチッ
CHATTER ガヤ
CHATTER ガヤ
CHATTER ガヤ
CHATTER ガヤ
CHATTER ガヤ
CHATTER ガヤ
CHATTER ガヤ

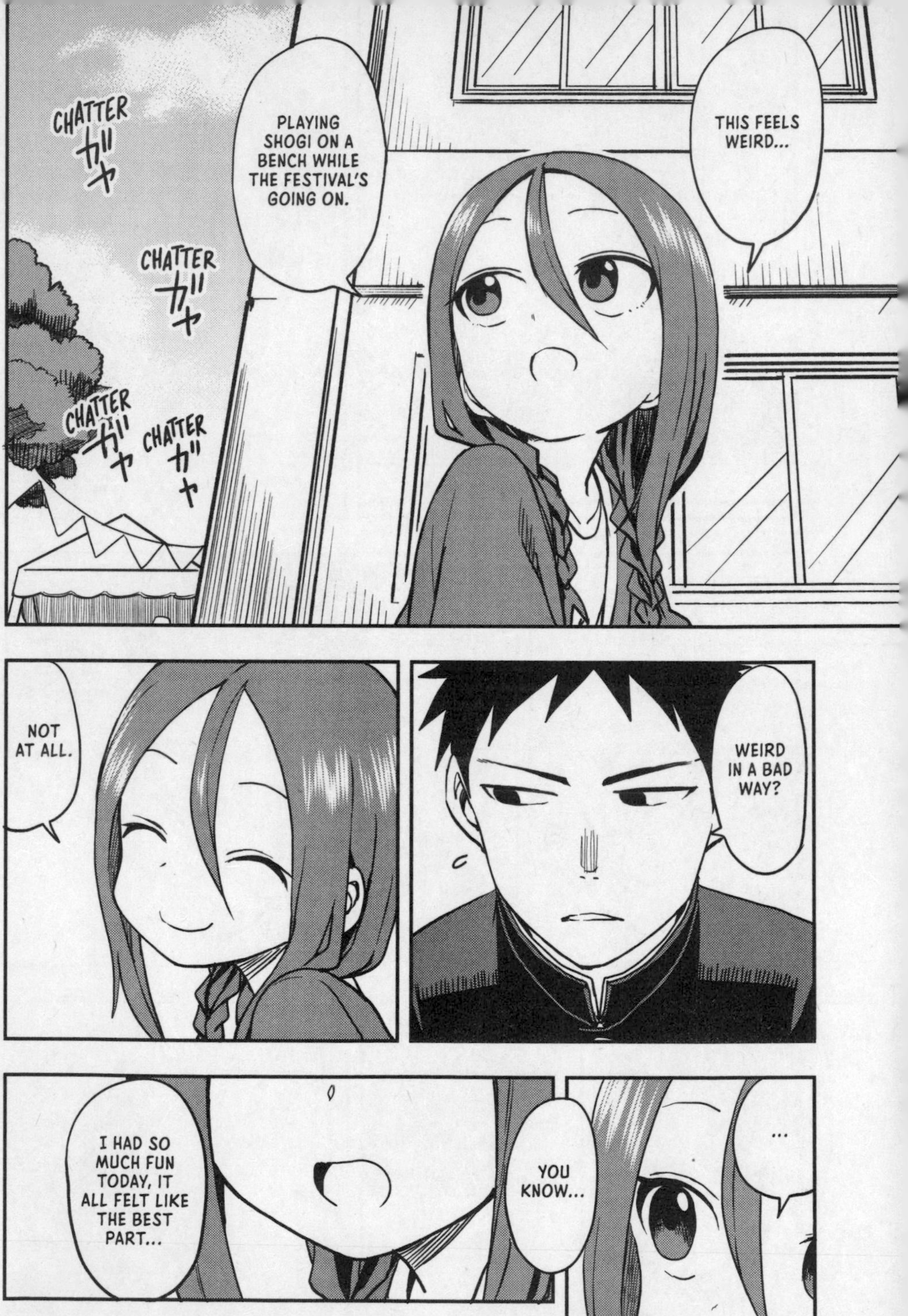
THIS FEELS WEIRD...
PLAYING SHOGI ON A BENCH WHILE THE FESTIVAL'S GOING ON.
CHATTER ガヤ
CHATTER ガヤ
CHATTER ガヤ
CHATTER ガヤ
WEIRD IN A BAD WAY?
NOT AT ALL.
...
YOU KNOW...
I HAD SO MUCH FUN TODAY, IT ALL FELT LIKE THE BEST PART...

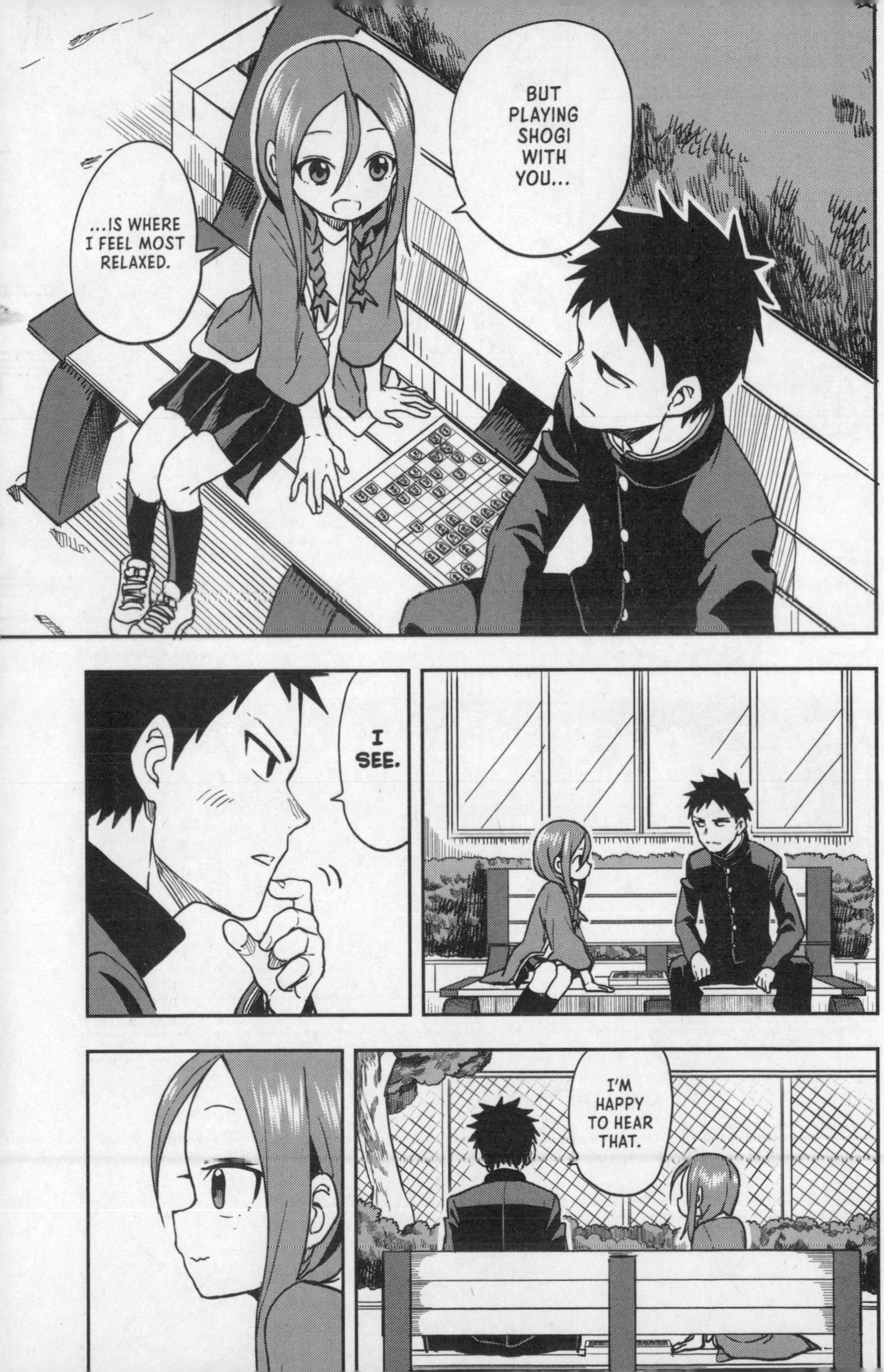
BUT PLAYING SHOGI WITH YOU...
...IS WHERE I FEEL MOST RELAXED.
I SEE.
I'M HAPPY TO HEAR THAT.

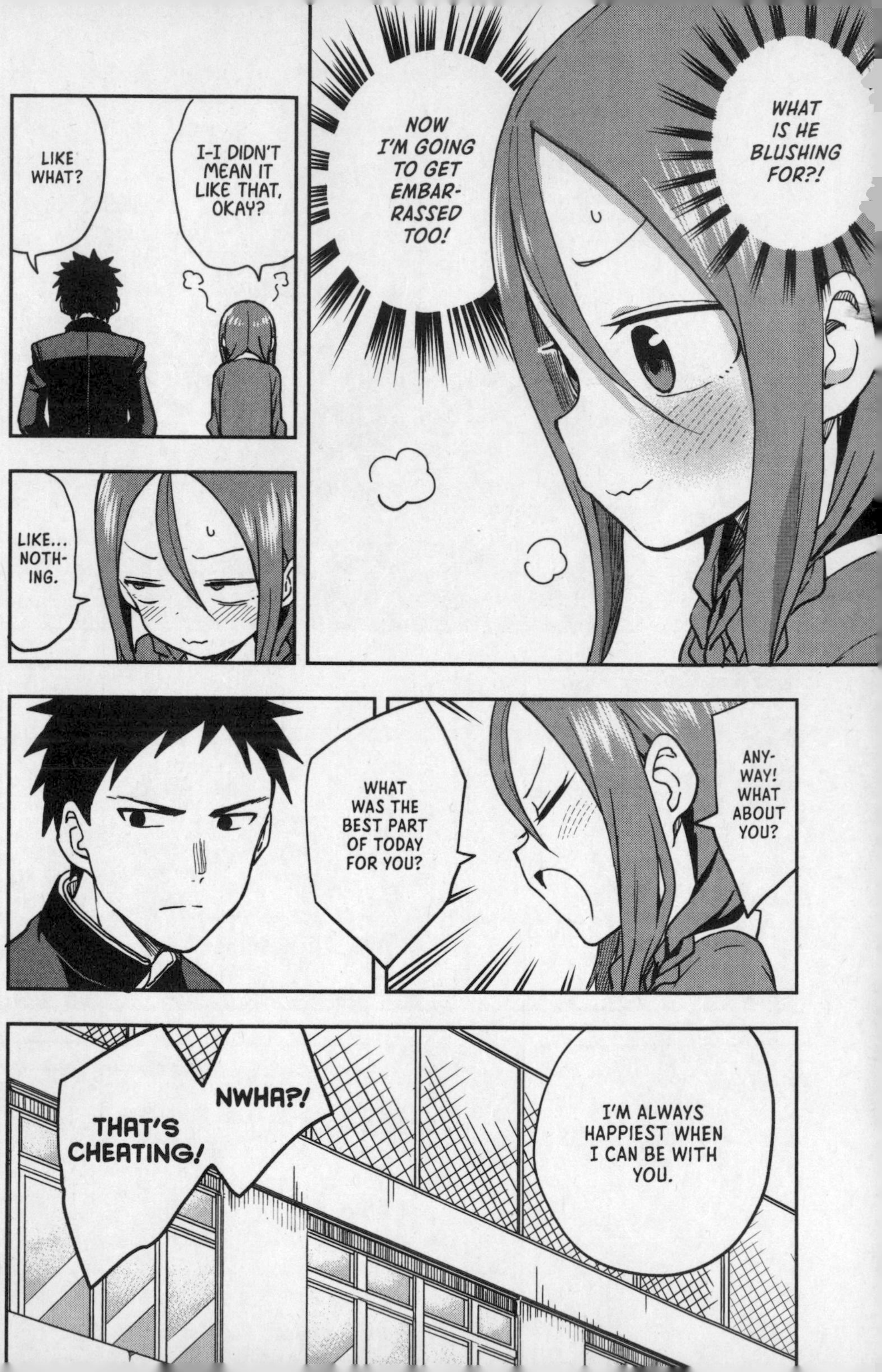
WHAT IS HE BLUSHING FOR?!
NOW I'M GOING TO GET EMBARRASSED TOO!
I-I DIDN'T MEAN IT LIKE THAT, OKAY?
LIKE WHAT?
LIKE... NOTHING.
ANYWAY! WHAT ABOUT YOU?
WHAT WAS THE BEST PART OF TODAY FOR YOU?
I'M ALWAYS HAPPIEST WHEN I CAN BE WITH YOU.
NWHA?!
THAT'S CHEATING!

GAME 35 RECORD

BUT PLAYING SHOGI WITH YOU IS WHERE I FEEL MOST RELAXED.

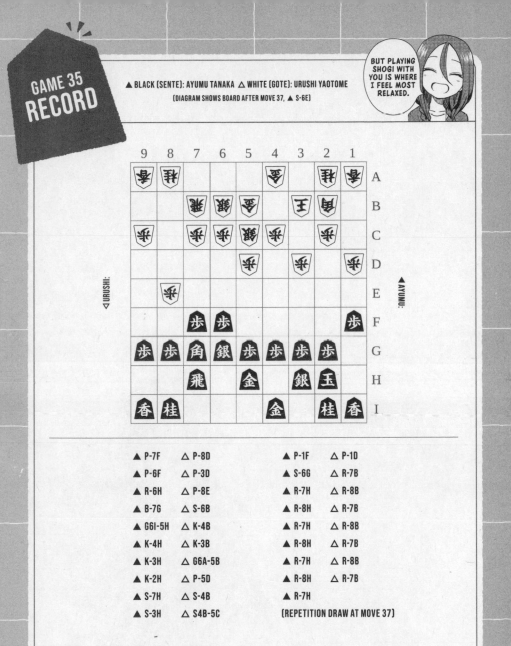

▲ BLACK (SENTE): AYUMU TANAKA △ WHITE (GOTE): URUSHI YAOTOME

(DIAGRAM SHOWS BOARD AFTER MOVE 37, ▲ S-6E)

9 8 7 6 5 4 3 2 1
A
B
C
D
E
F
G
H
I
◁ URUSHI:
▲ AYUMU:

▲ P-7F	△ P-8D	▲ P-1F	△ P-1D
▲ P-6F	△ P-3D	▲ S-6G	△ R-7B
▲ R-6H	△ P-8E	▲ R-7H	△ R-8B
▲ B-7G	△ S-6B	▲ R-8H	△ R-7B
▲ G6I-5H	△ K-4B	▲ R-7H	△ R-8B
▲ K-4H	△ K-3B	▲ R-8H	△ R-7B
▲ K-3H	△ G6A-5B	▲ R-7H	△ R-8B
▲ K-2H	△ P-5D	▲ R-8H	△ R-7B
▲ S-7H	△ S-4B	▲ R-7H	
▲ S-3H	△ S4B-5C	(REPETITION DRAW AT MOVE 37)	

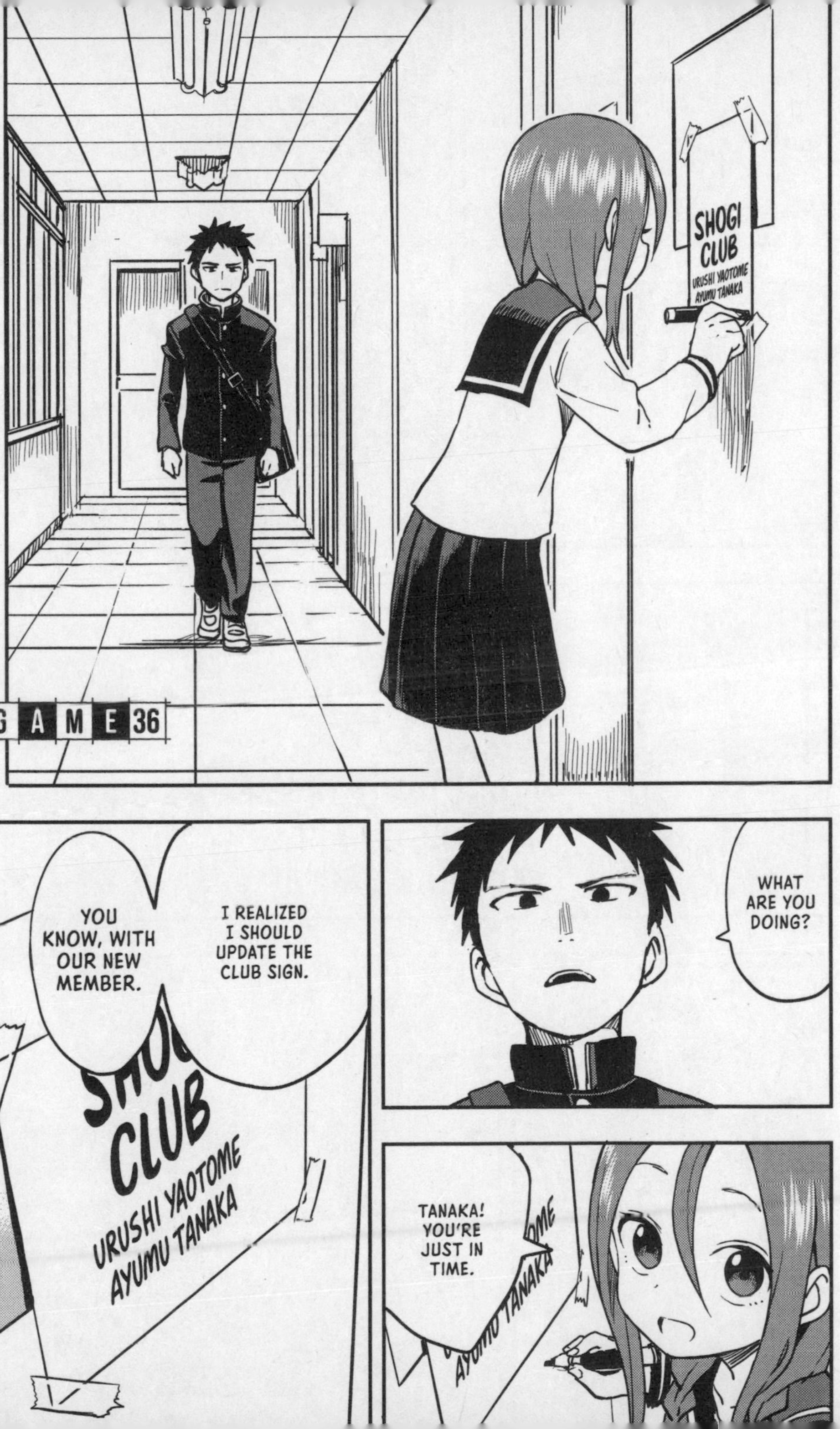
SHOGI CLUB
URUSHI YAOTOME
AYUMU TANAKA
GAME 36
WHAT ARE YOU DOING?
TANAKA! YOU'RE JUST IN TIME.
AYUMU TANAKA
I REALIZED I SHOULD UPDATE THE CLUB SIGN.
YOU KNOW, WITH OUR NEW MEMBER.
CLUB
URUSHI YAOTOME
AYUMU TANAKA

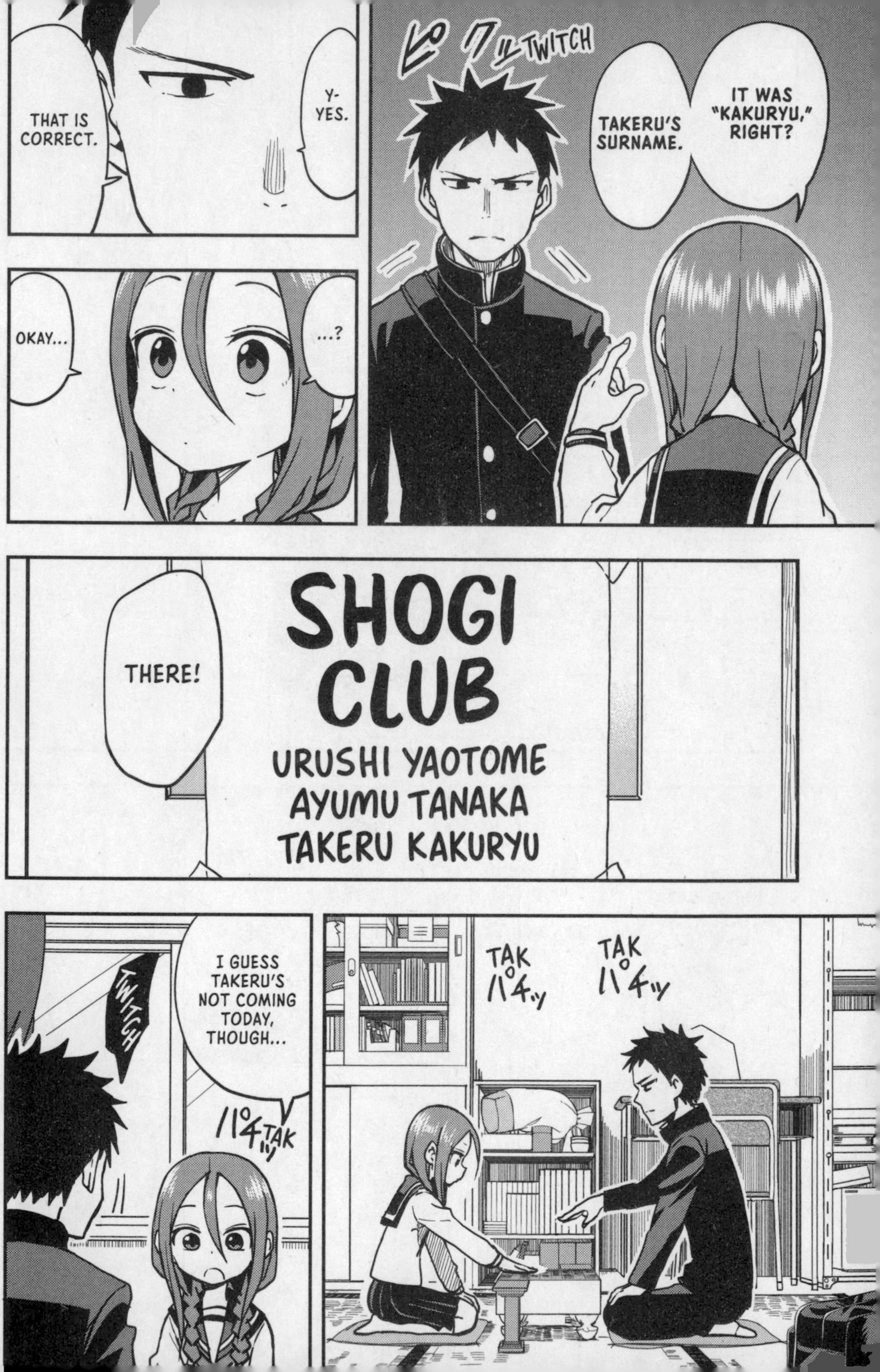
ピクッ TWITCH
IT WAS "KAKURYU," RIGHT?
TAKERU'S SURNAME.
Y-YES.
THAT IS CORRECT.
...?
OKAY...
SHOGI CLUB
URUSHI YAOTOME
AYUMU TANAKA
TAKERU KAKURYU
THERE!
パチッ TAK
パチッ TAK
I GUESS TAKERU'S NOT COMING TODAY, THOUGH...
パチッ TAK
TWITCH

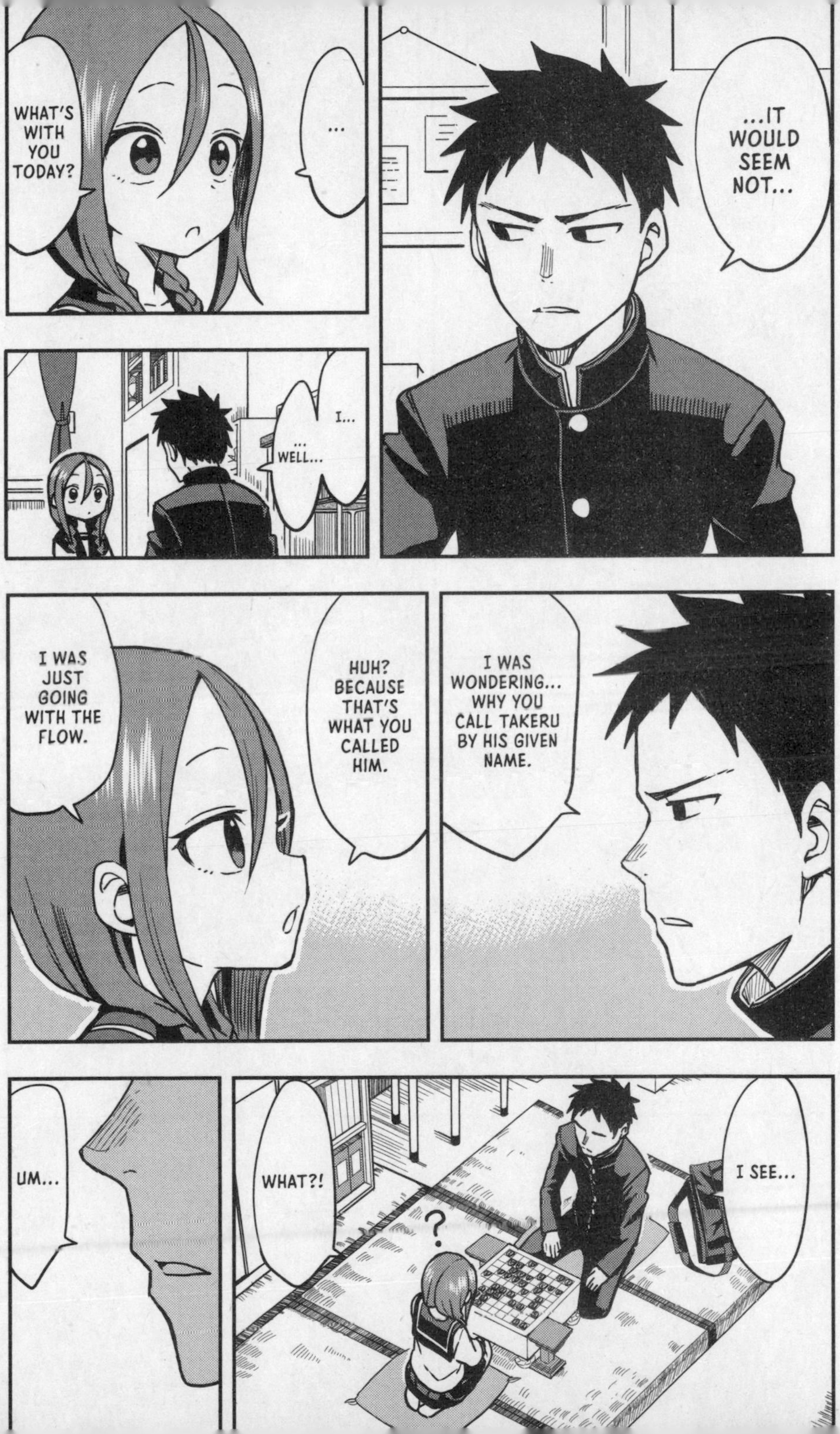
...IT WOULD SEEM NOT...
...
WHAT'S WITH YOU TODAY?
I...
...WELL...
I WAS WONDERING... WHY YOU CALL TAKERU BY HIS GIVEN NAME.
HUH? BECAUSE THAT'S WHAT YOU CALLED HIM.
I WAS JUST GOING WITH THE FLOW.
I SEE...
WHAT?!
?
UM...

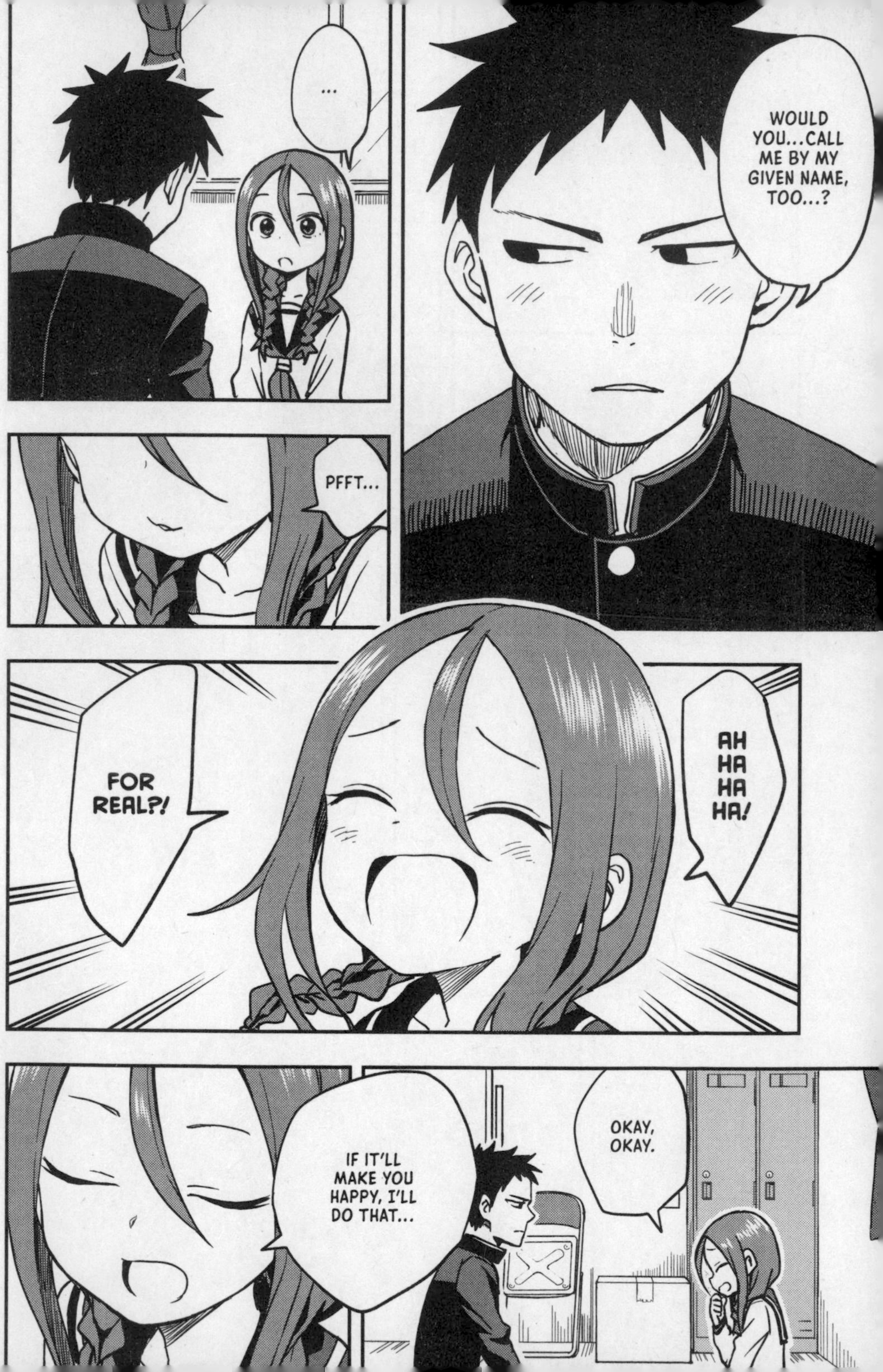
WOULD YOU...CALL ME BY MY GIVEN NAME, TOO...?
...
PFFT...
AH HA HA HA!
FOR REAL?!
OKAY, OKAY.
IF IT'LL MAKE YOU HAPPY, I'LL DO THAT...

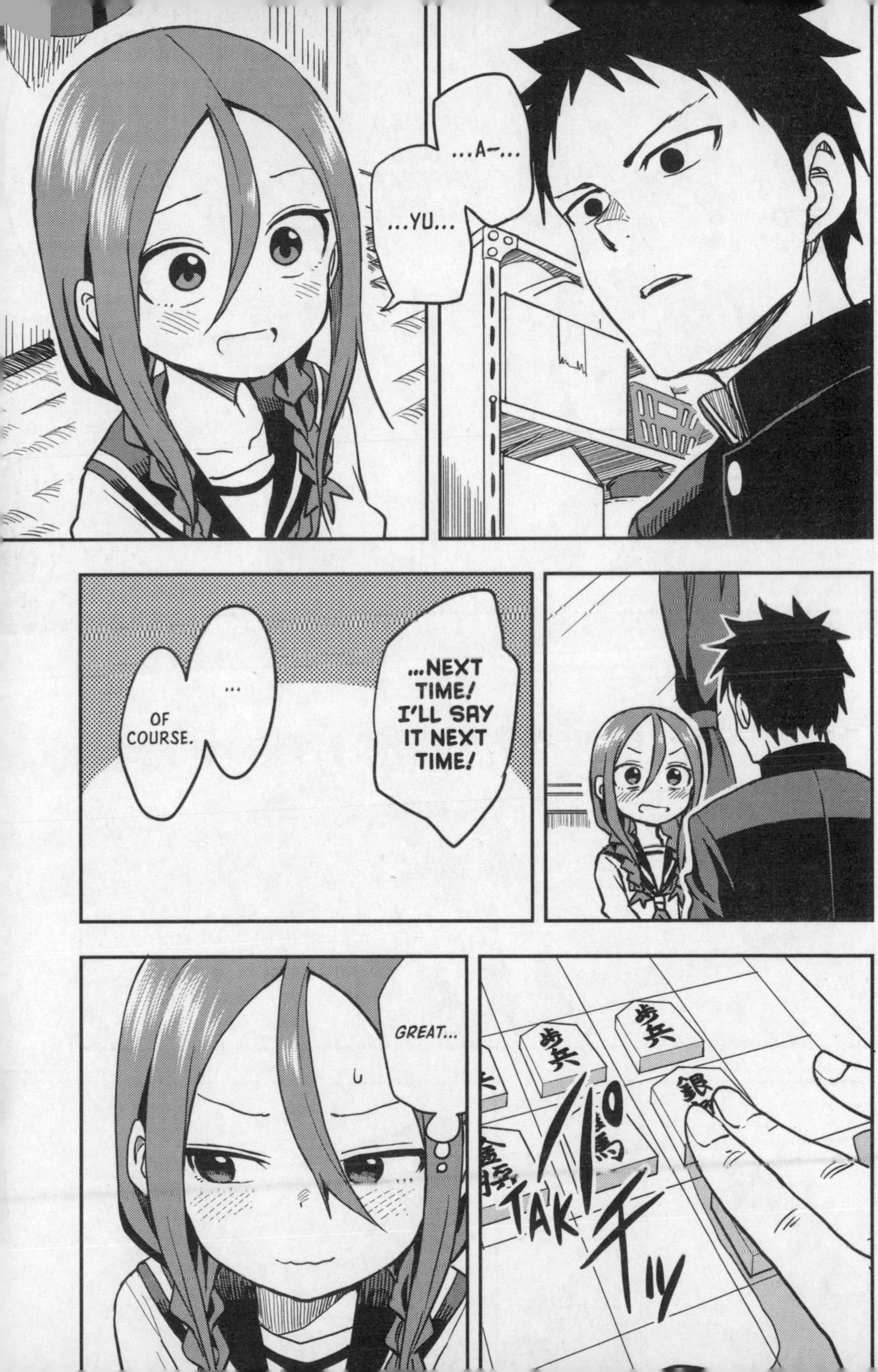
...A-...
...YU...
...NEXT TIME! I'LL SAY IT NEXT TIME!
...
OF COURSE.
TAK
GREAT...
...

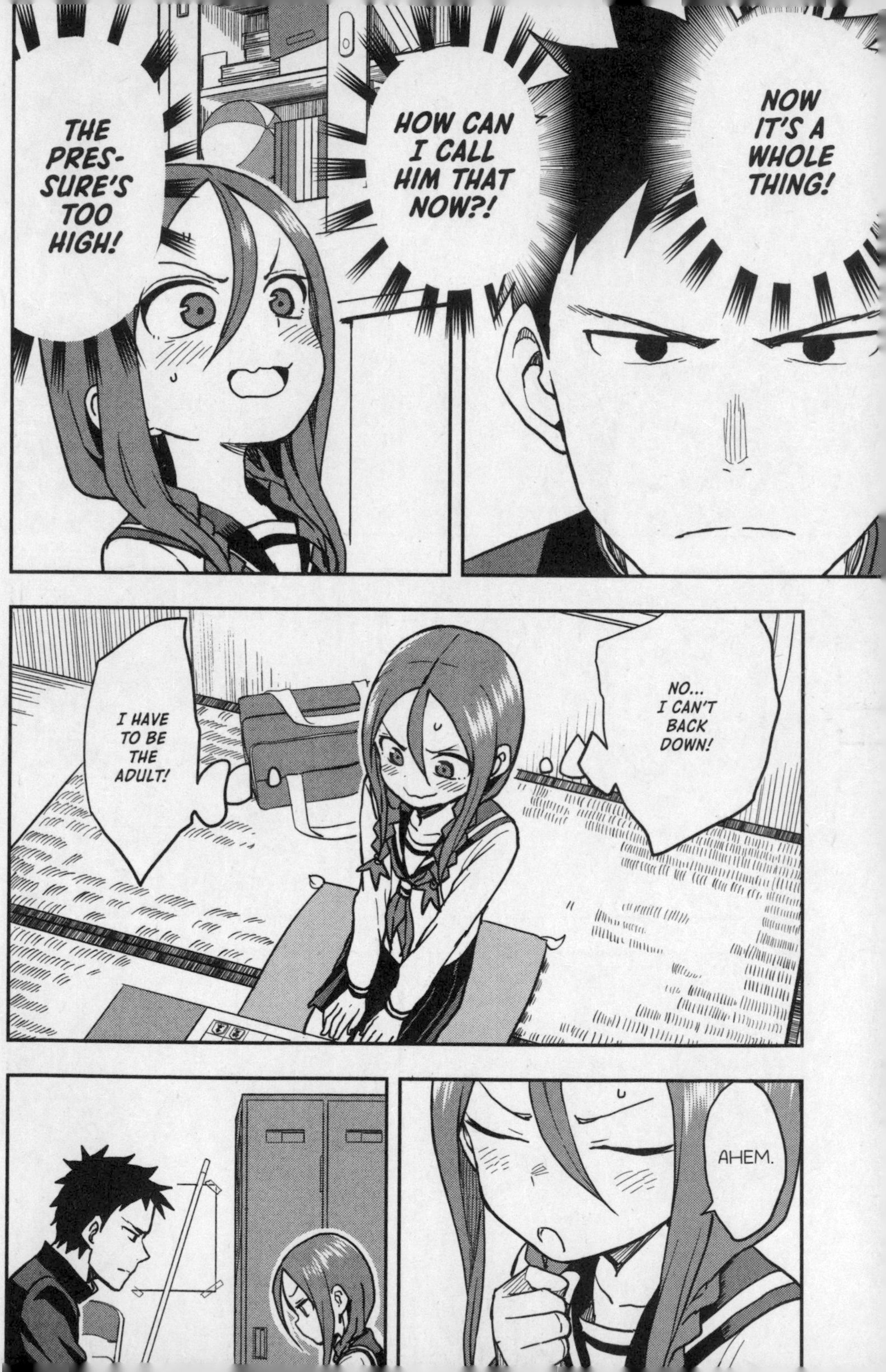
NOW IT'S A WHOLE THING!
HOW CAN I CALL HIM THAT NOW?!
THE PRES-SURE'S TOO HIGH!
NO... I CAN'T BACK DOWN!
I HAVE TO BE THE ADULT!
AHEM.

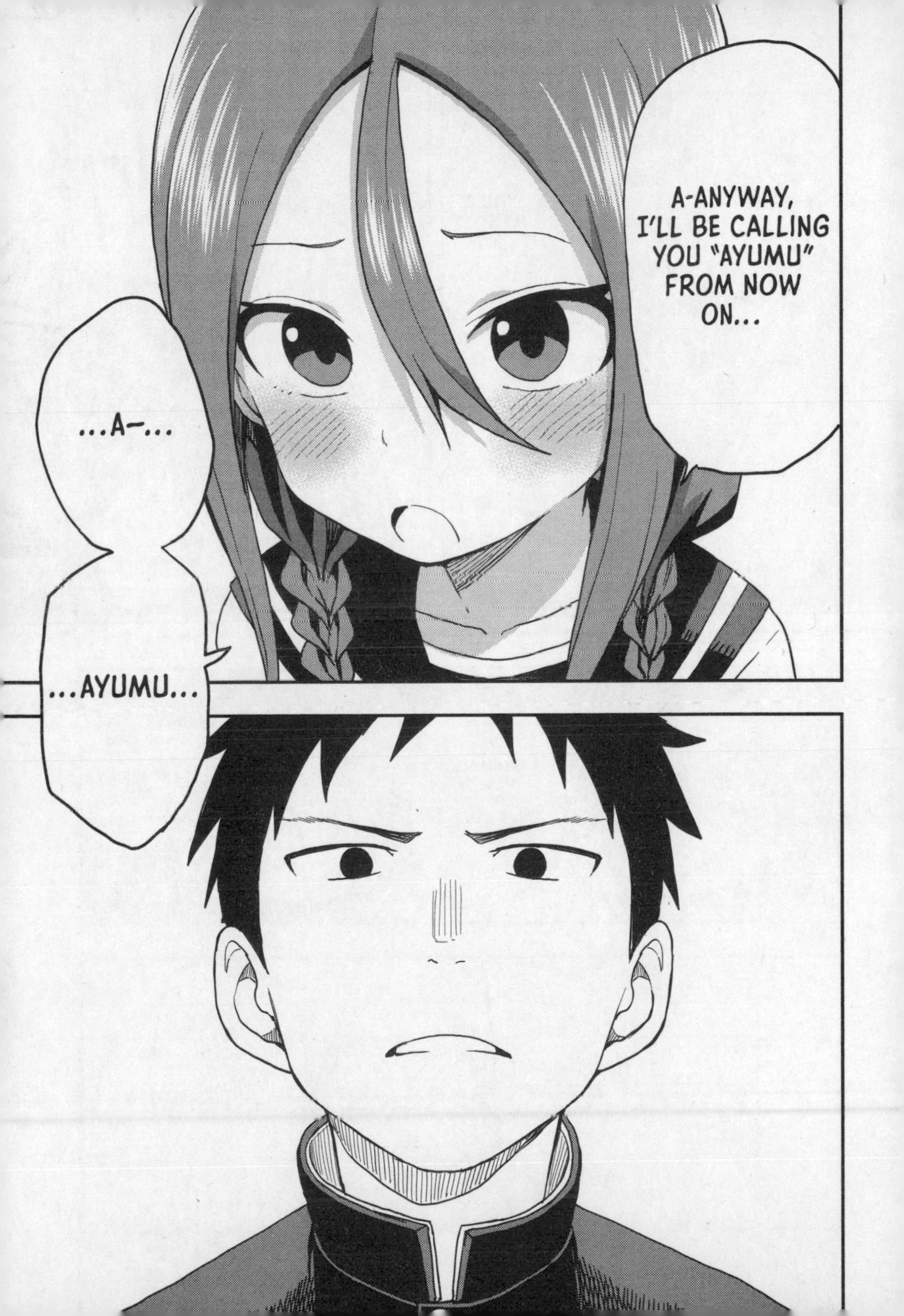
A-ANYWAY, I'LL BE CALLING YOU "AYUMU" FROM NOW ON...
...A-...
...AYUMU...

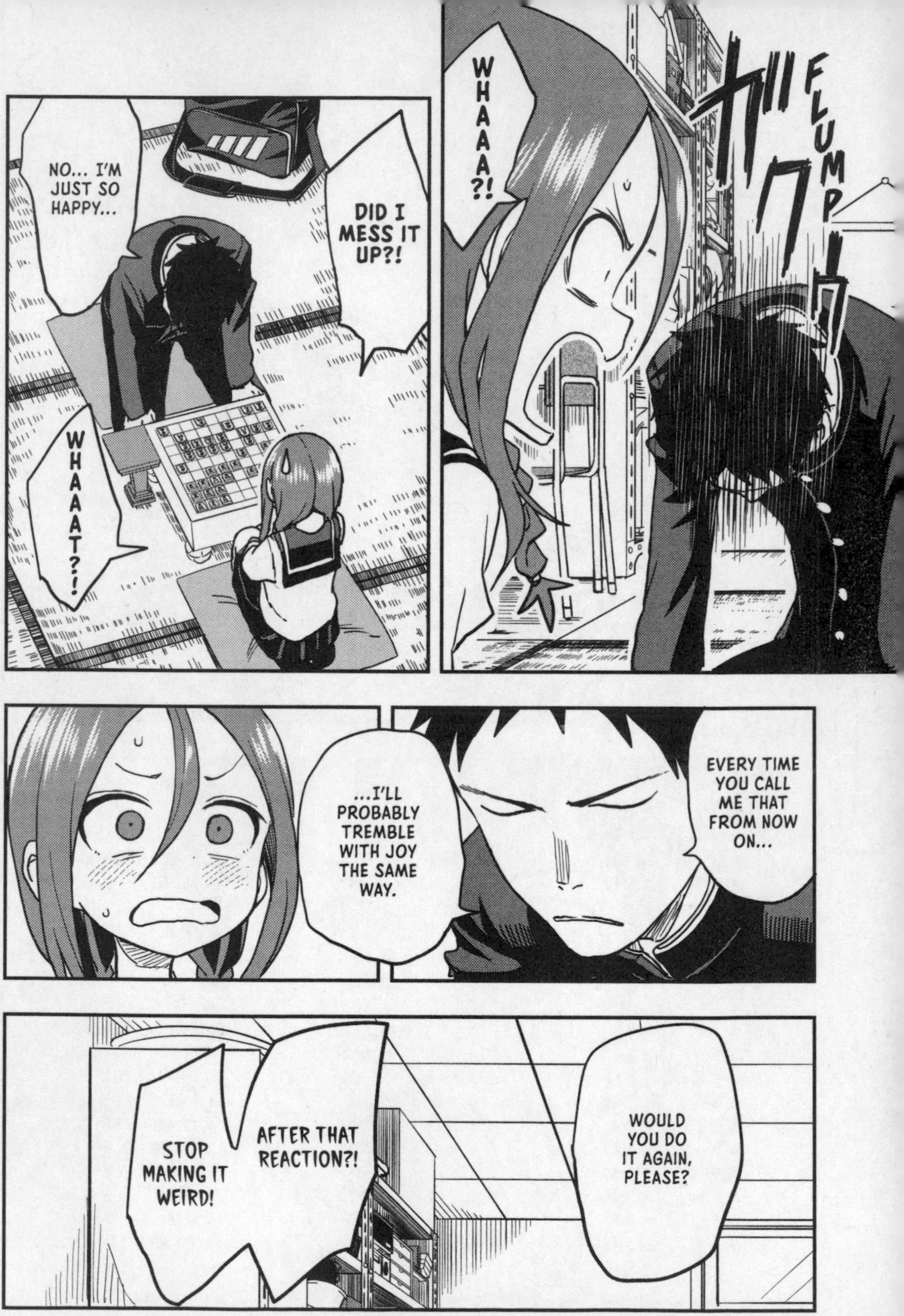
WHAAAA?!
ガク
FLUMP!
DID I MESS IT UP?!
NO... I'M JUST SO HAPPY...
WHAAAAT?!
EVERY TIME YOU CALL ME THAT FROM NOW ON...
...I'LL PROBABLY TREMBLE WITH JOY THE SAME WAY.
WOULD YOU DO IT AGAIN, PLEASE?
AFTER THAT REACTION?!
STOP MAKING IT WEIRD!

GAME 36 RECORD

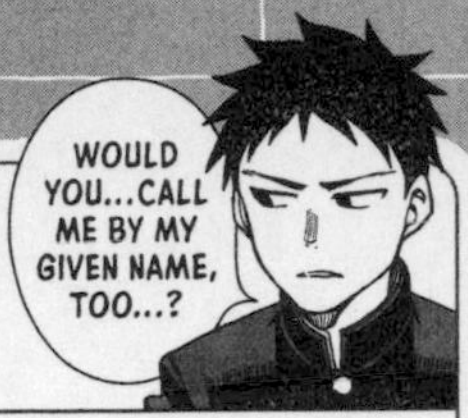
WOULD YOU...CALL ME BY MY GIVEN NAME, TOO...?

▲ BLACK (SENTE): AYUMU TANAKA △ WHITE (GOTE): URUSHI YAOTOME

(DIAGRAM SHOWS BOARD AFTER MOVE 41, ▲ S-2G)

◁URUSHI:

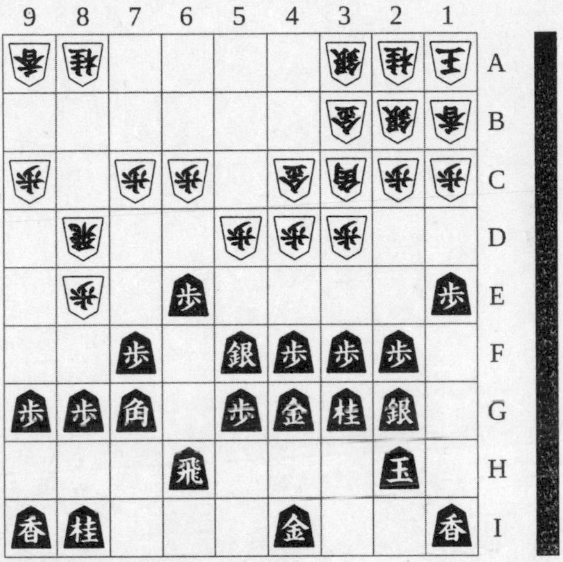
9 8 7 6 5 4 3 2 1
A
B
C
D
E
F
G
H
I

▲ P-7F △ P-3D
▲ P-6F △ P-8D
▲ R-6H △ P-8E
▲ B-7G △ S-6B
▲ G6I-5H △ K-4B
▲ K-4H 1△ K-3B
▲ K-3H △ G6A-5B
▲ K-2H △ P-5D
▲ S-7H △ S-5C
▲ S-3H △ B-3C
▲ P-1F △ K-2B
▲ P-1E △ L-1B
▲ S-6G △ K-1A
▲ S-5F △ P-4D
▲ P-4F △ S-2B
▲ G-4G △ G-4C
▲ P-6E △ G-3B
▲ P-3F △ R-8D
▲ N-3G △ S-4B

▲ P-2F △ S4B-3A
▲ S-2G △ R-7D
▲ R-6F △ P-4E
▲ R-6H △ P×4F
▲ G×4F △ B×7G+
▲ N×7G △ R×7F
▲ P×7H △ B×7I
▲ R-6G △ B-8H+
▲ P-6D 56. △ +B×7H
▲ R-6E △ R×7G+
▲ P×6C+ △ +R-6H
▲ R×6H △ +B×6H
▲ G-3H △ R×6I
▲ R×6A △ P×4E
▲ N×4E △ P*4D
▲ N-5C+ △ +B×5G
▲ S-4G △ G×5C
▲ R×8A+ △ P-4E
▲ G×4E △ N×3C

▲ G-4F △ P×4E
▲ G-5F △ +B×4G
▲ G×4G △ N×4D
▲ G5F-5G 84. △ R-6H+
▲ P×5H △ S×4F
▲ +P×5C △ S×4G+
▲ GX4G △ +R×5H
▲ G×4H △ +R-6H
▲ S×4C △ P-4F
▲ S×3B+ △ S×3B
▲ G×5H △ +R-6I
▲ G×4F △ S*3I
▲ K-3G △ P×4E
▲ +P-4B △ P×4F
▲ +PX×3B △ G×4G
▲ G5H×4G △ P×4G+
▲ G×4G △ N-4E
▲ K-4F △ G×5E

(WHITE WINS AT MOVE 112)

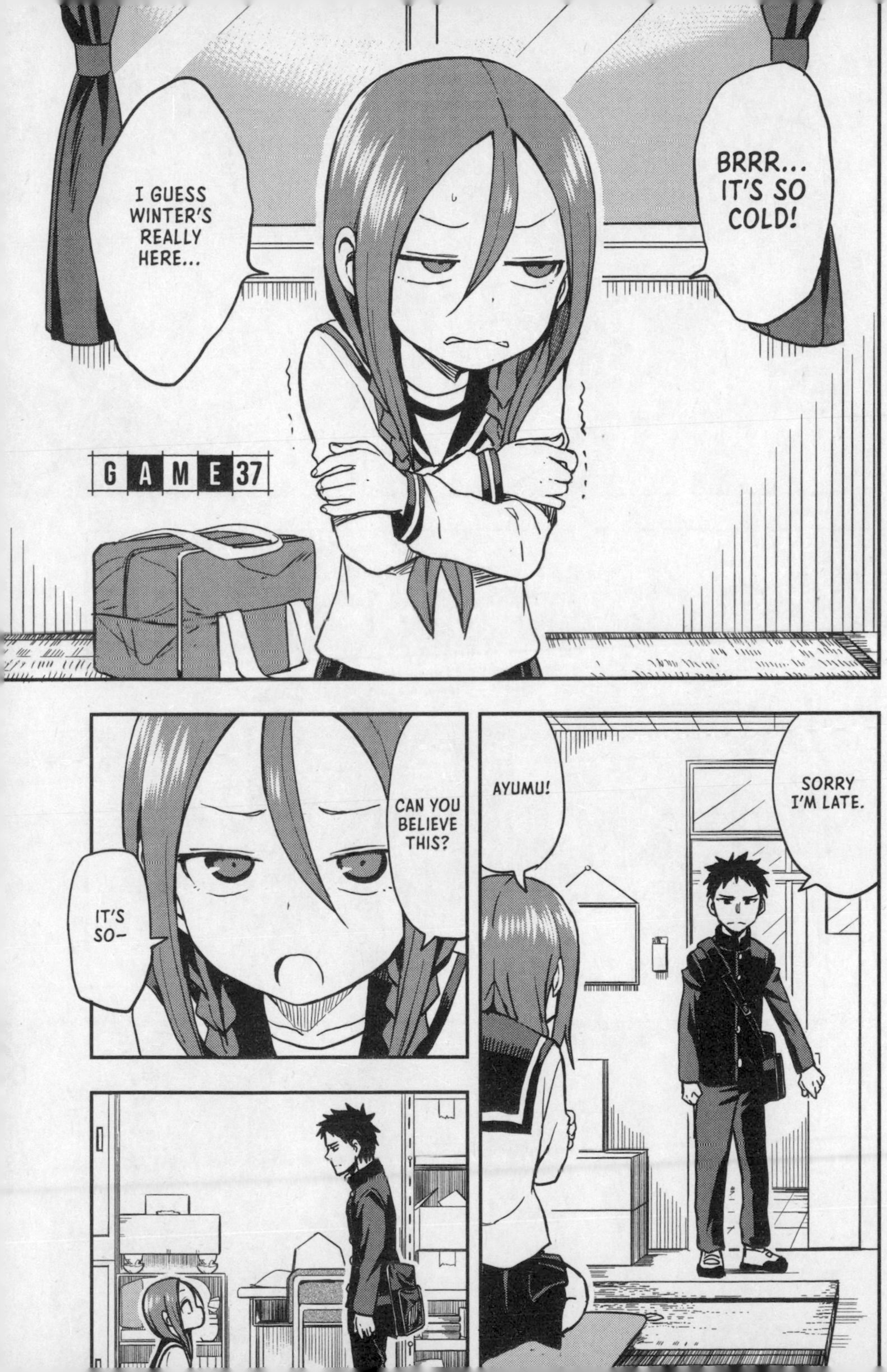
BRRR... IT'S SO COLD!
I GUESS WINTER'S REALLY HERE...
GAME 37
SORRY I'M LATE.
AYUMU!
CAN YOU BELIEVE THIS?
IT'S SO–

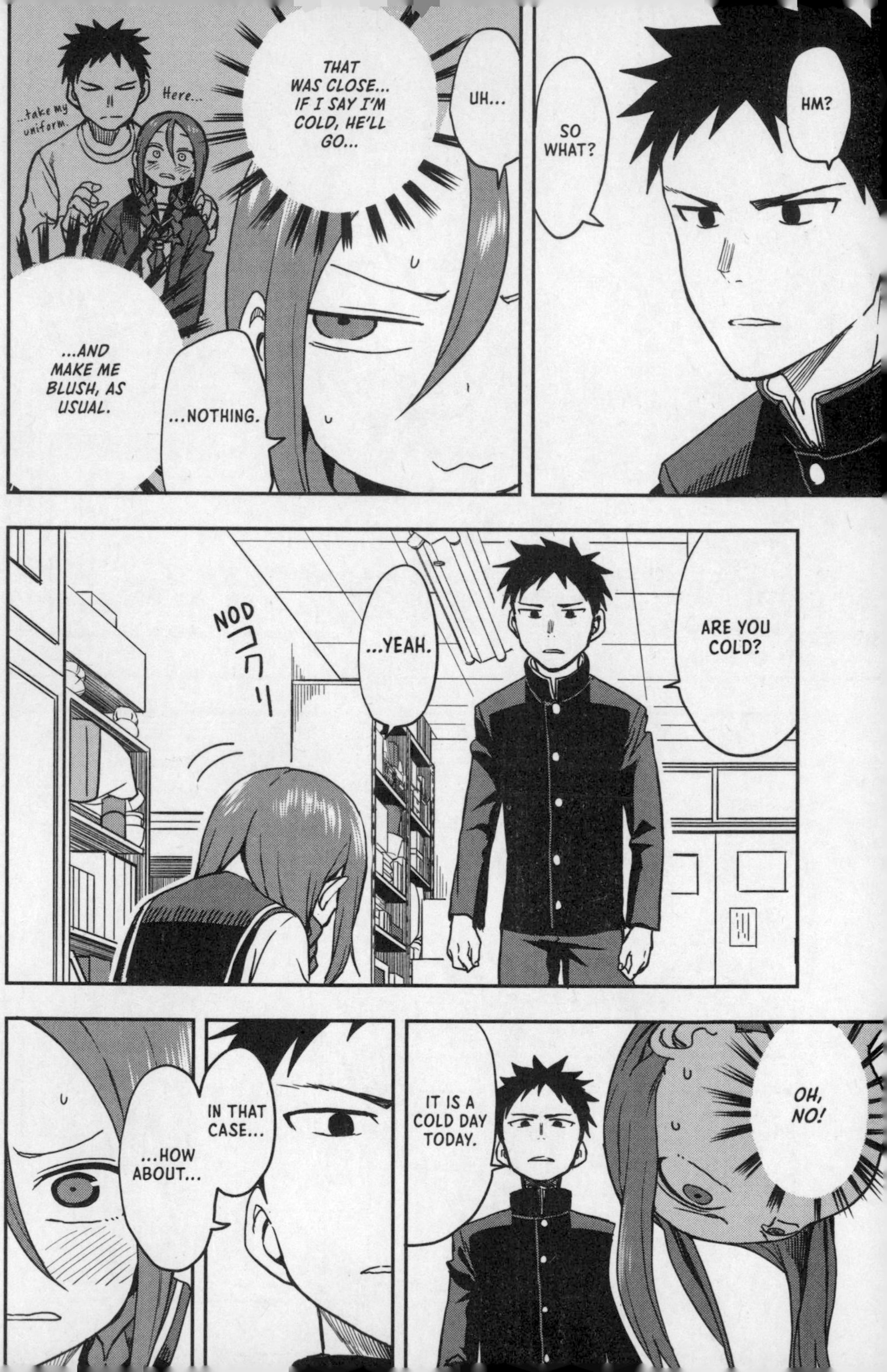
HM?
SO WHAT?
UH...
THAT WAS CLOSE... IF I SAY I'M COLD, HE'LL GO...
Here...
...take my uniform.
...AND MAKE ME BLUSH, AS USUAL.
...NOTHING.
ARE YOU COLD?
...YEAH.
NOD コクリ
OH, NO!
IT IS A COLD DAY TODAY.
IN THAT CASE...
...HOW ABOUT...

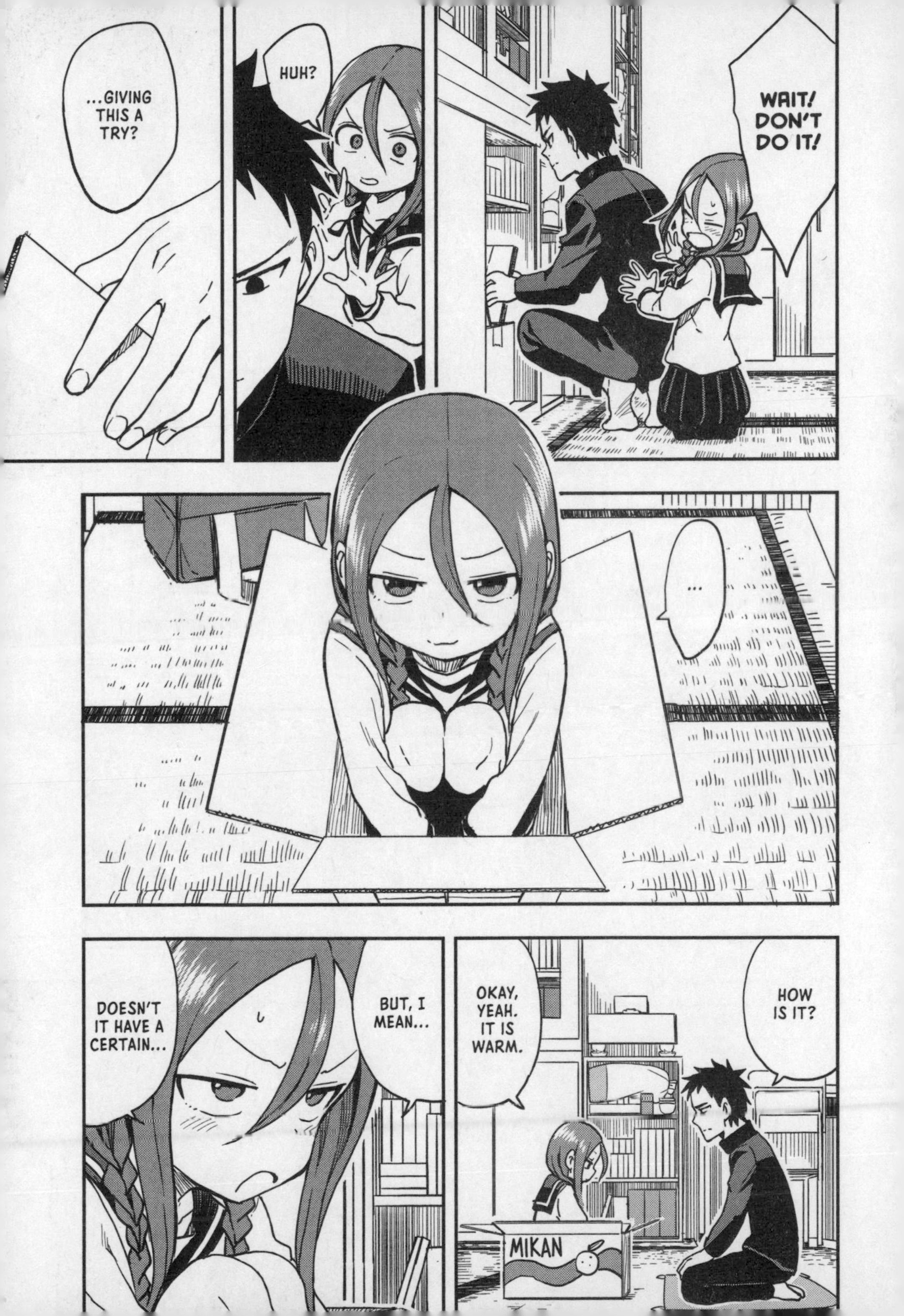
WAIT! DON'T DO IT!
HUH?
...GIVING THIS A TRY?
...
HOW IS IT?
OKAY, YEAH. IT IS WARM.
MIKAN
BUT, I MEAN...
DOESN'T IT HAVE A CERTAIN...

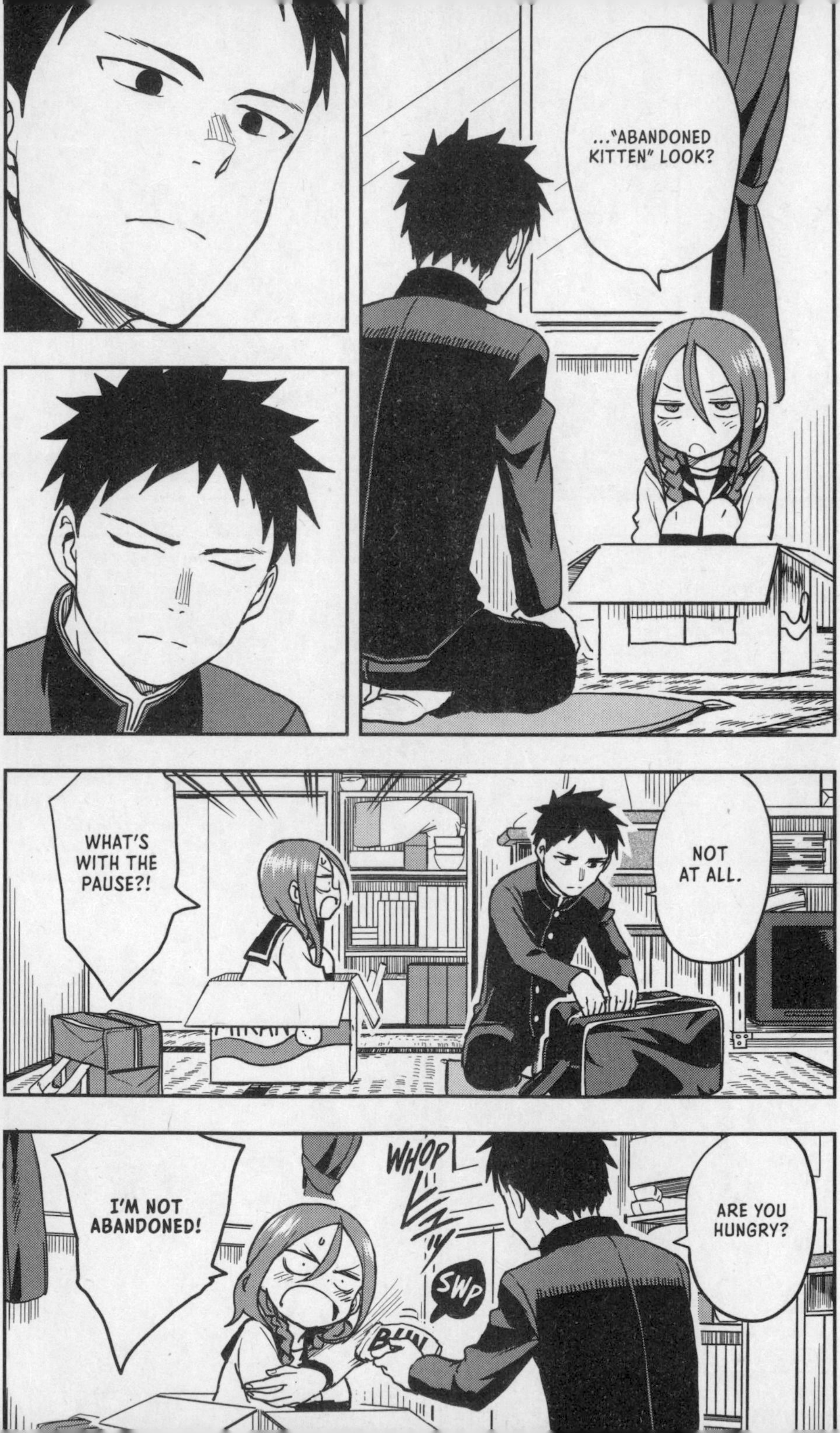
..."ABANDONED KITTEN" LOOK?
NOT AT ALL.
WHAT'S WITH THE PAUSE?!
ARE YOU HUNGRY?
WHOP
SWP
BUN
I'M NOT ABANDONED!

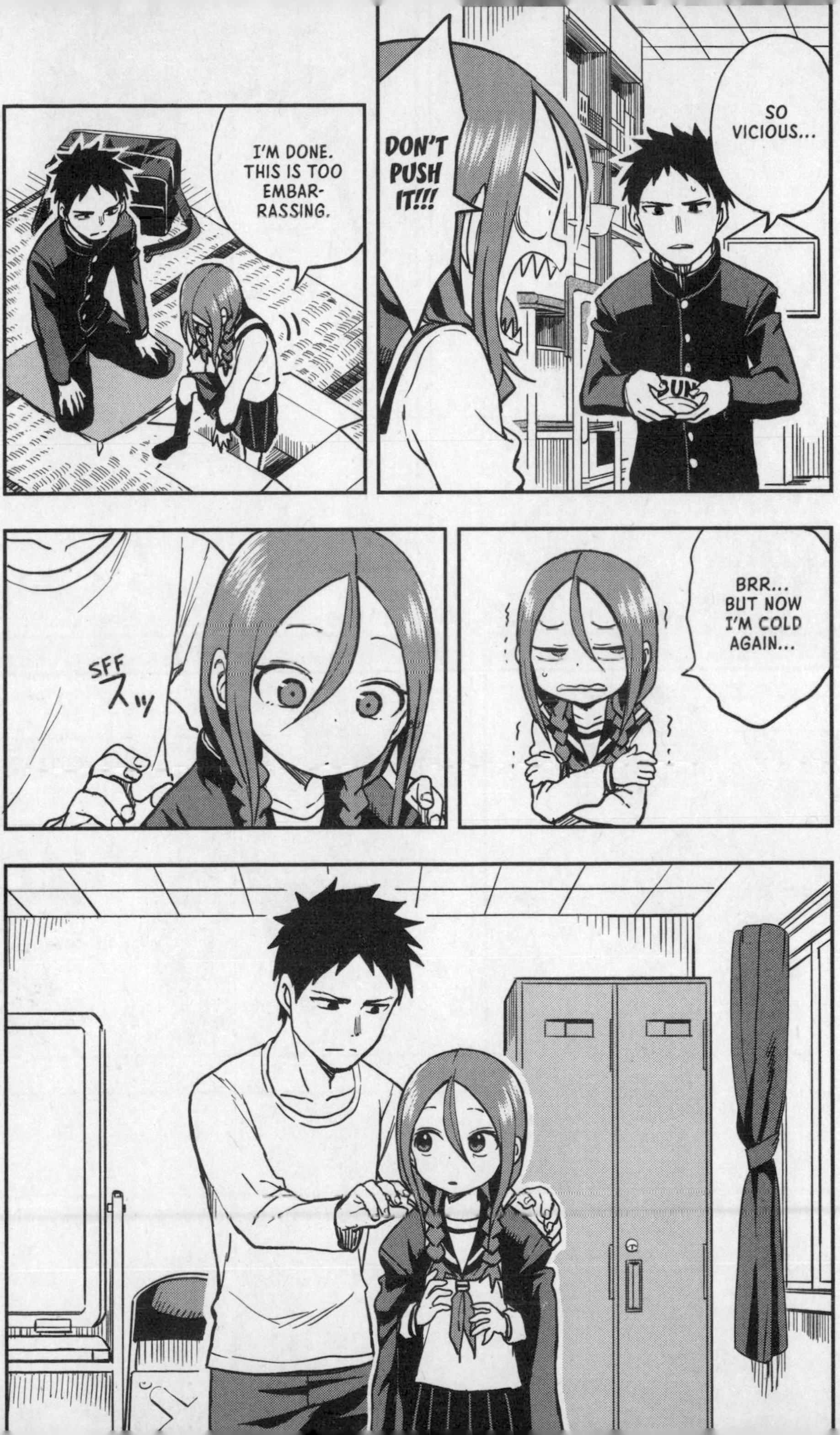
SO VICIOUS...
DON'T PUSH IT!!!
I'M DONE. THIS IS TOO EMBARRASSING.
BRR... BUT NOW I'M COLD AGAIN...
SFF スッ

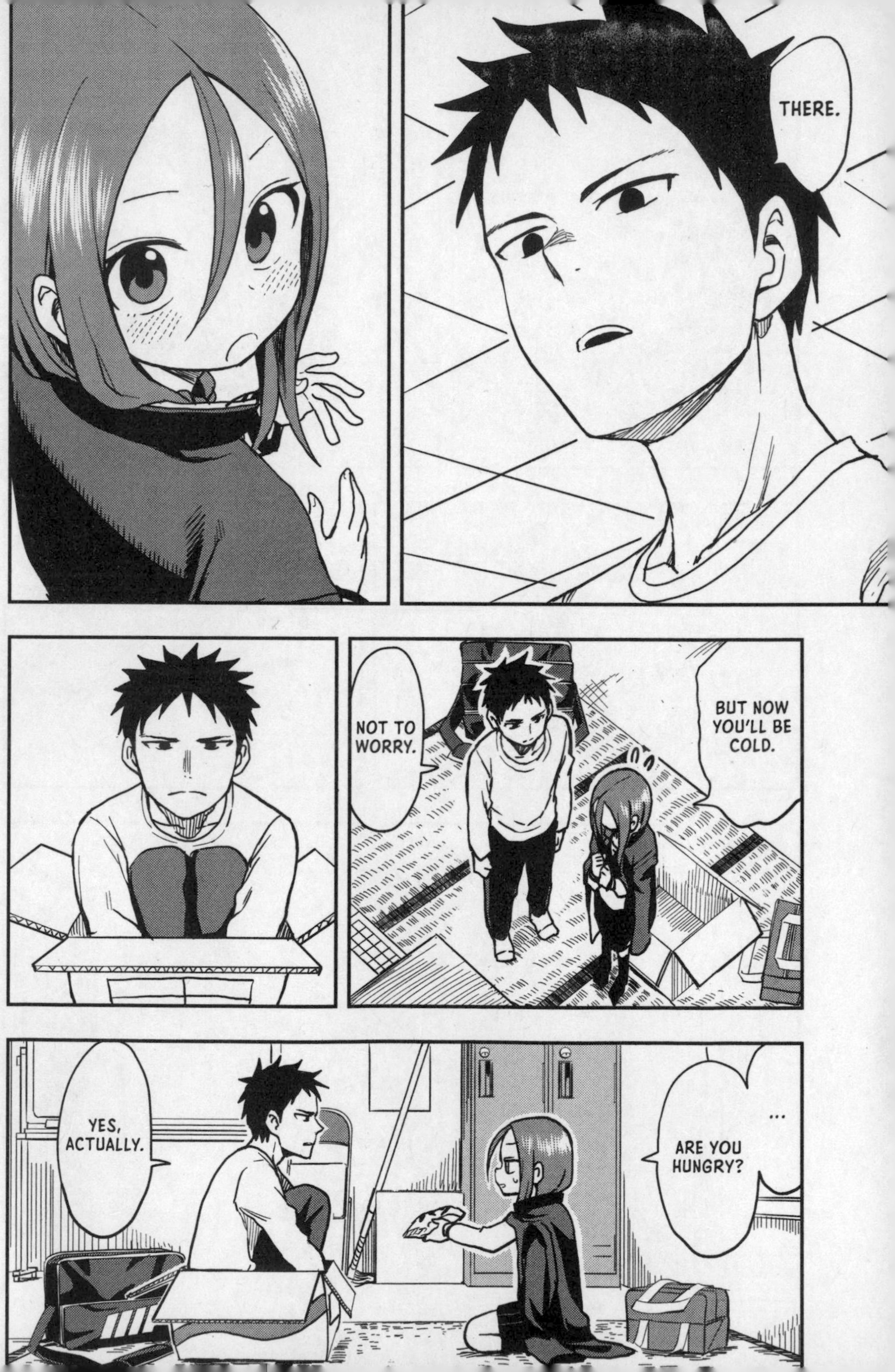
THERE.
BUT NOW YOU'LL BE COLD.
NOT TO WORRY.
...
ARE YOU HUNGRY?
YES, ACTUALLY.

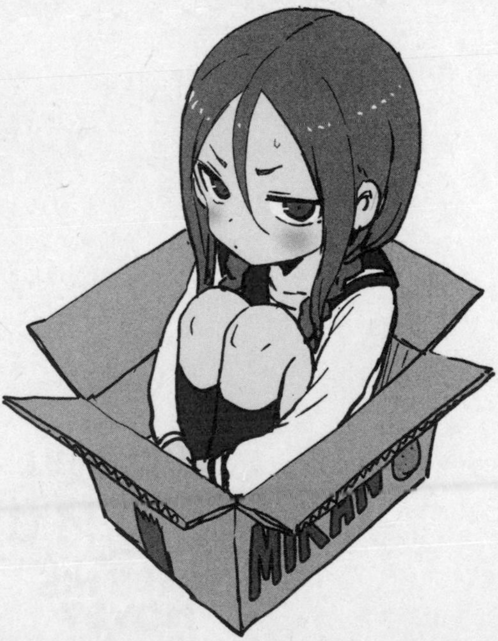
MIKAN

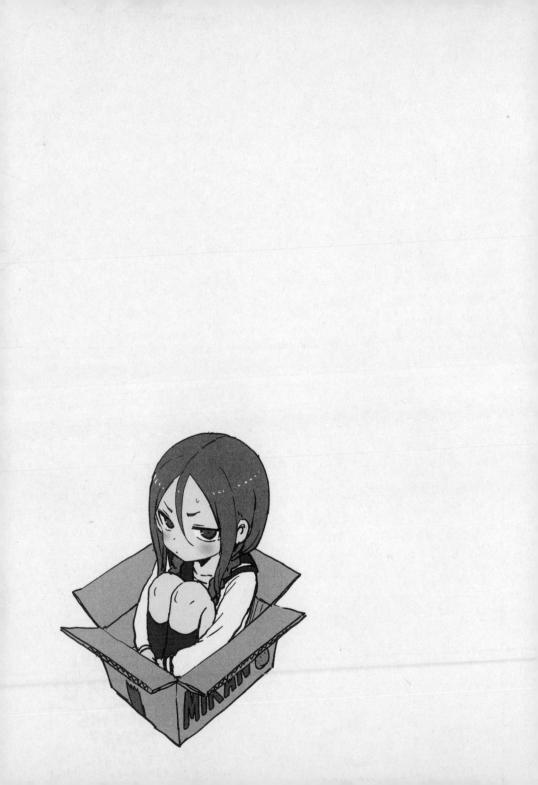

WHEN WILL AYUMU MAKE HIS MOVE?

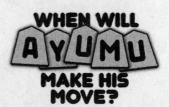

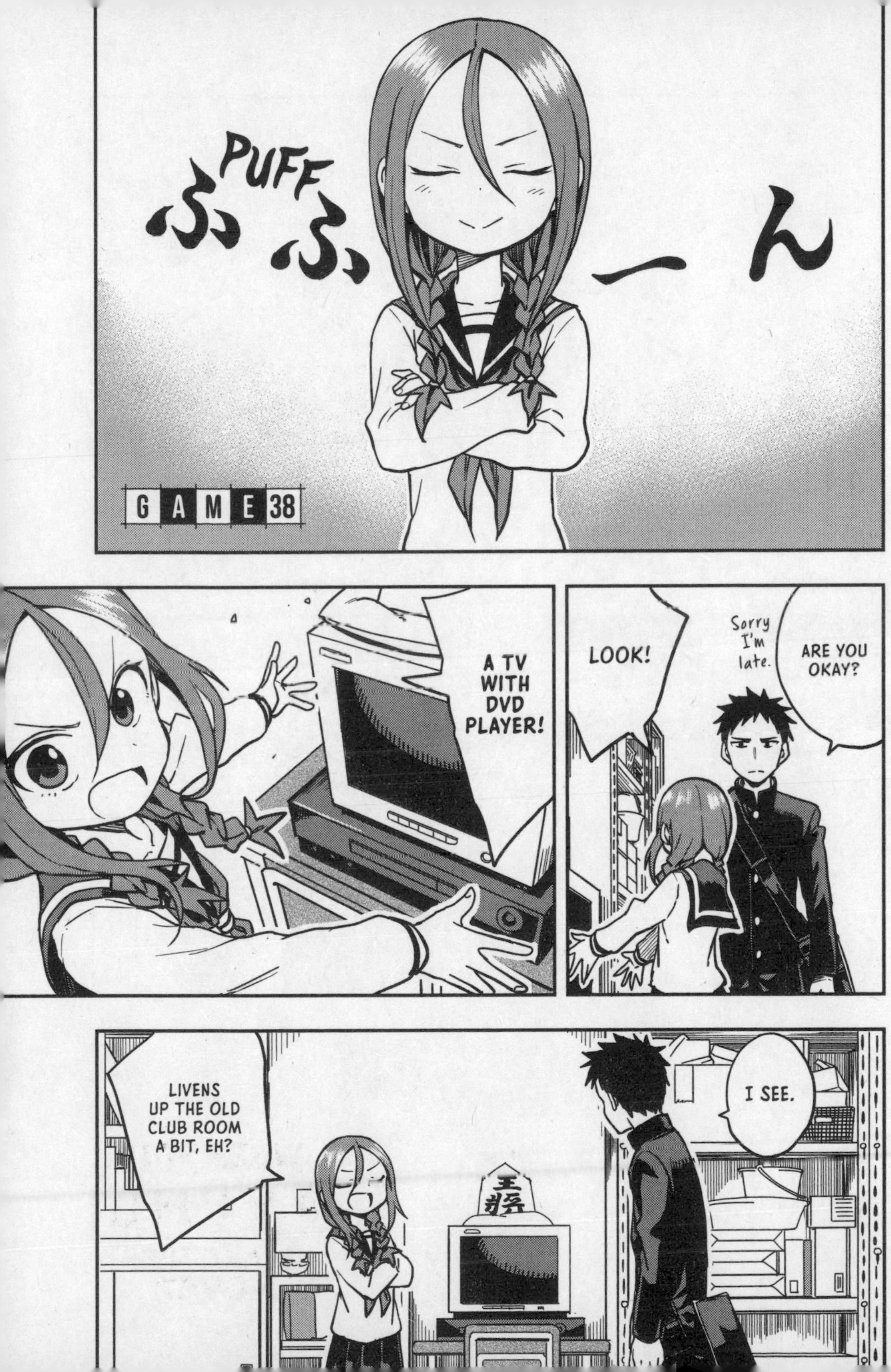
PUFF
ふふーん
GAME 38
ARE YOU OKAY?
Sorry I'm late.
LOOK!
A TV WITH DVD PLAYER!
I SEE.
LIVENS UP THE OLD CLUB ROOM A BIT, EH?

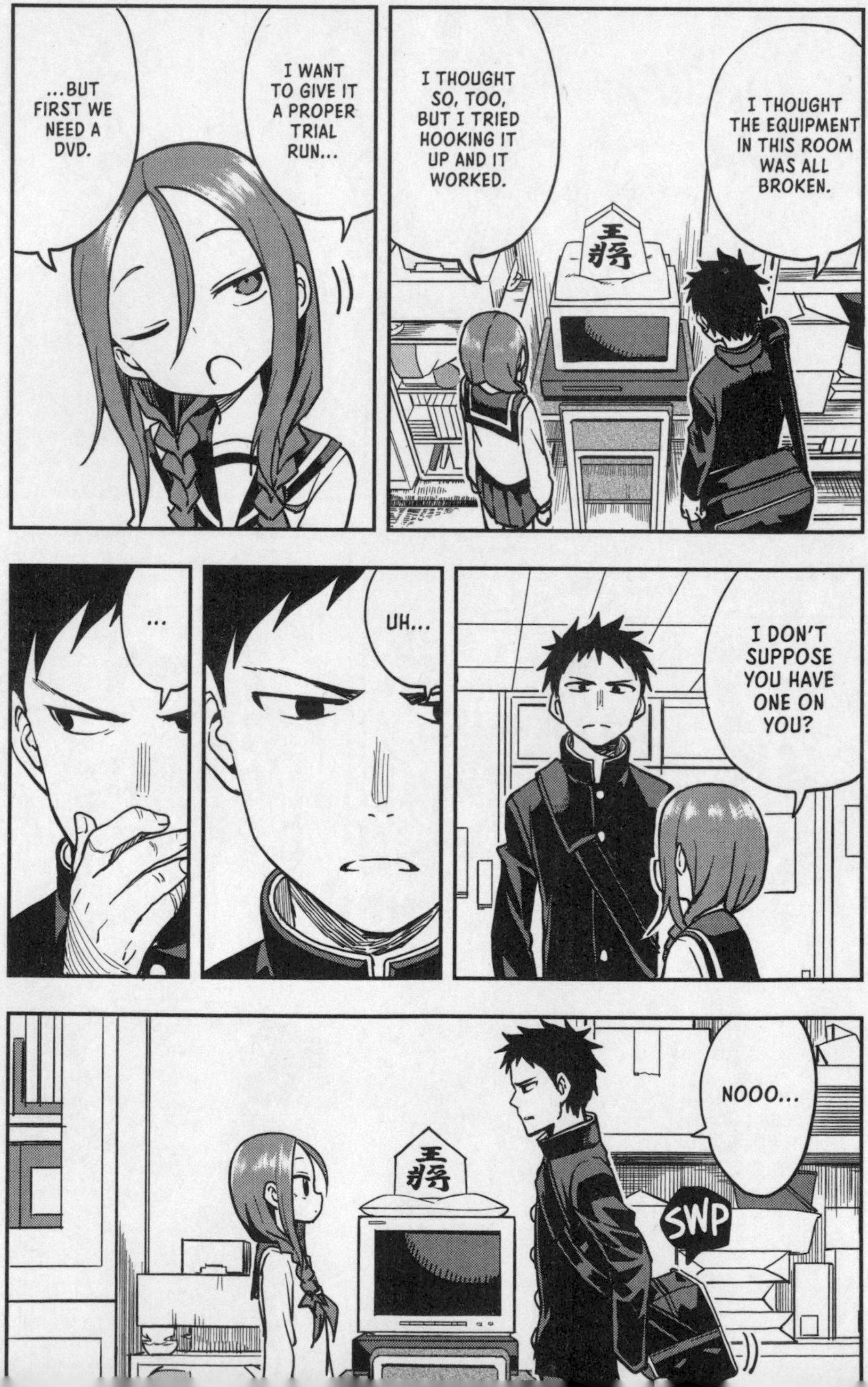
I THOUGHT THE EQUIPMENT IN THIS ROOM WAS ALL BROKEN.
I THOUGHT SO, TOO, BUT I TRIED HOOKING IT UP AND IT WORKED.
王将
I WANT TO GIVE IT A PROPER TRIAL RUN...
...BUT FIRST WE NEED A DVD.
I DON'T SUPPOSE YOU HAVE ONE ON YOU?
UH...
...
NOOO...
SWP
王将

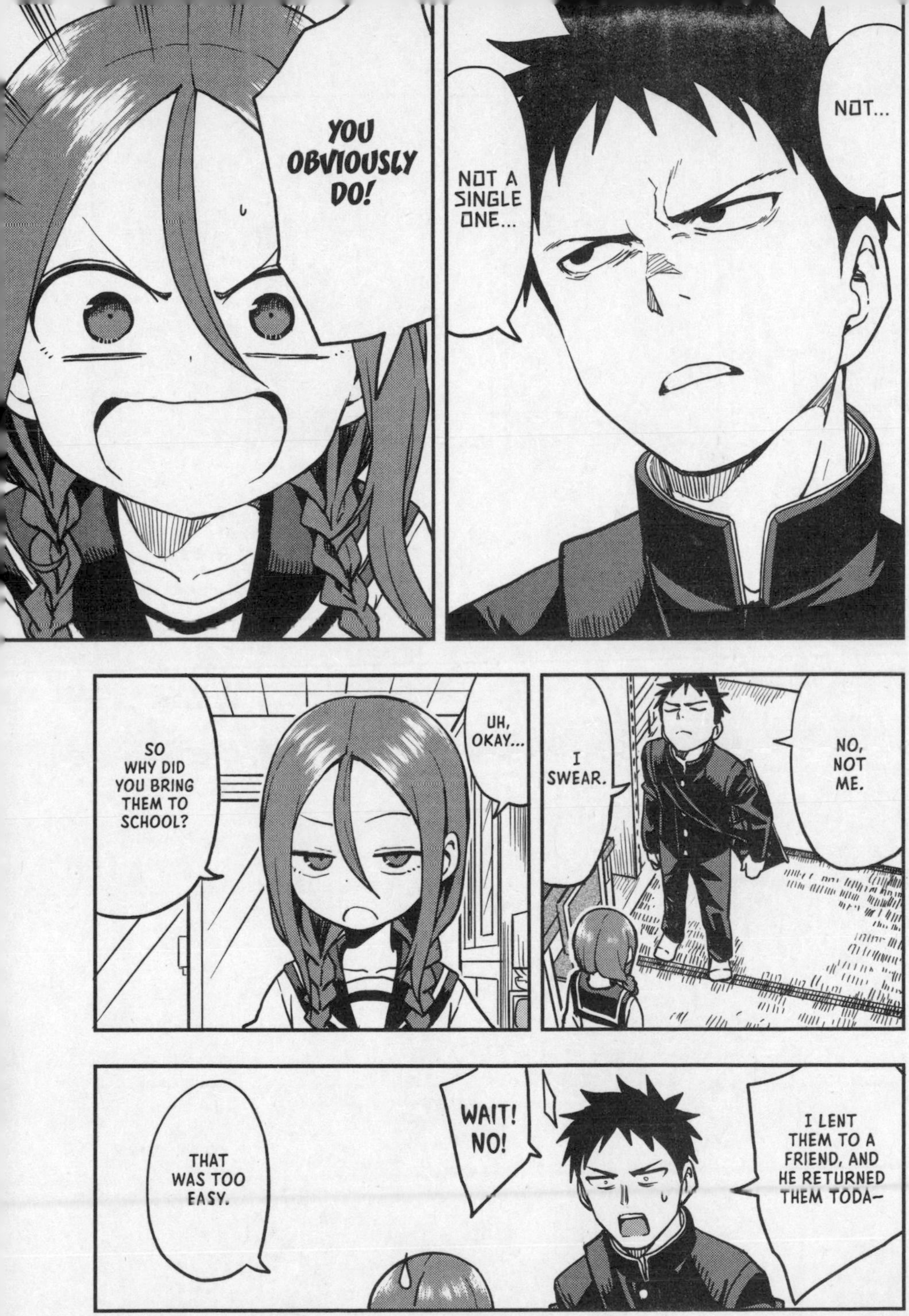
NOT...
NOT A SINGLE ONE...
YOU OBVIOUSLY DO!
NO, NOT ME.
I SWEAR.
UH, OKAY...
SO WHY DID YOU BRING THEM TO SCHOOL?
I LENT THEM TO A FRIEND, AND HE RETURNED THEM TODA—
WAIT! NO!
THAT WAS TOO EASY.

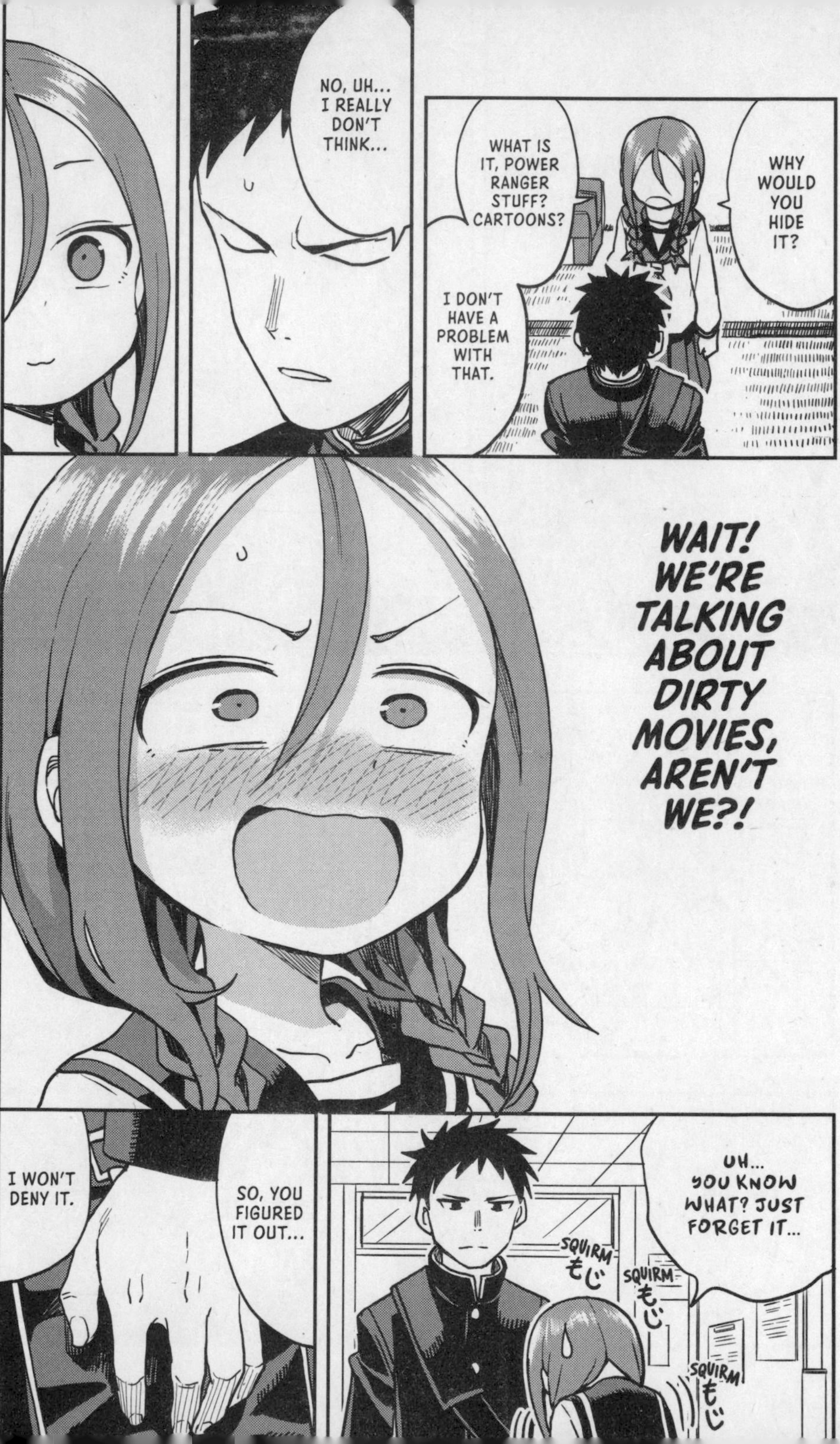
WHY WOULD YOU HIDE IT?
WHAT IS IT, POWER RANGER STUFF? CARTOONS?
I DON'T HAVE A PROBLEM WITH THAT.
NO, UH... I REALLY DON'T THINK...
WAIT! WE'RE TALKING ABOUT DIRTY MOVIES, AREN'T WE?!
UH... YOU KNOW WHAT? JUST FORGET IT...
SQUIRM もじ
SQUIRM もじ
SQUIRM もじ
SO, YOU FIGURED IT OUT...
I WON'T DENY IT.

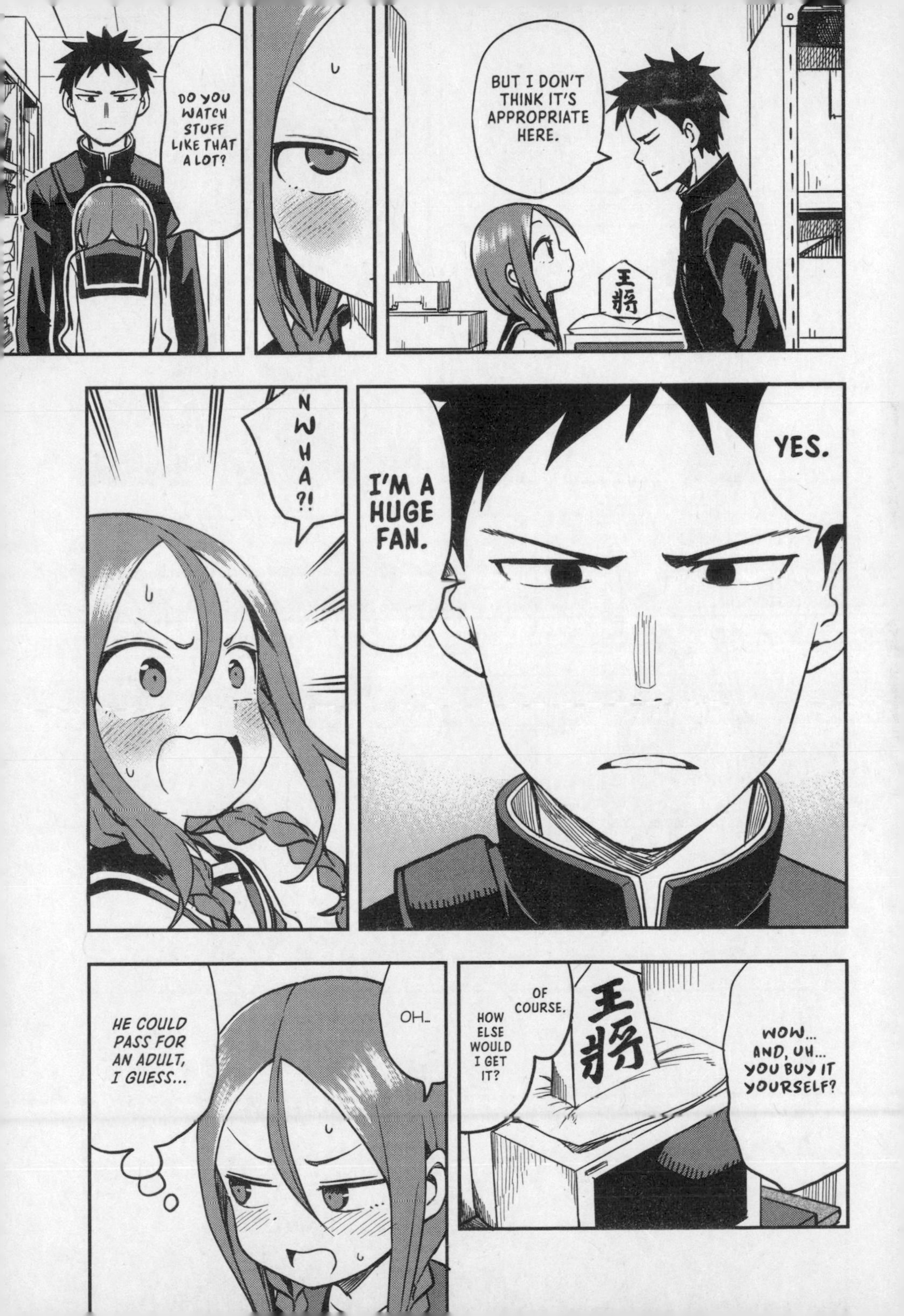
BUT I DON'T THINK IT'S APPROPRIATE HERE.
王将
DO YOU WATCH STUFF LIKE THAT A LOT?
YES.
I'M A HUGE FAN.
NWHA?!
WOW... AND, UH... YOU BUY IT YOURSELF?
OF COURSE.
HOW ELSE WOULD I GET IT?
王将
OH...
HE COULD PASS FOR AN ADULT, I GUESS...

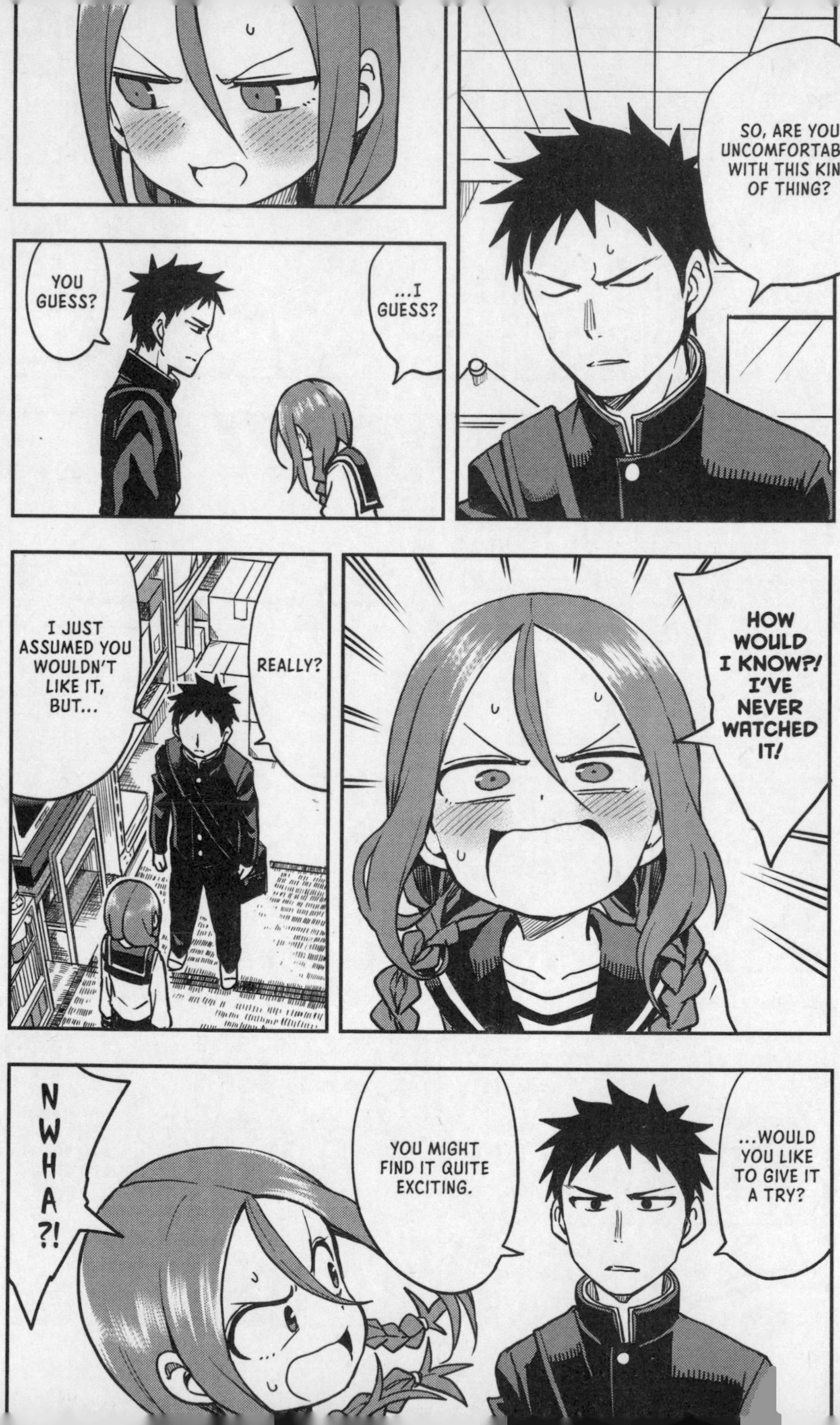
SO, ARE YOU UNCOMFORTABLE WITH THIS KIND OF THING?
...I GUESS?
YOU GUESS?
HOW WOULD I KNOW?! I'VE NEVER WATCHED IT!
REALLY?
I JUST ASSUMED YOU WOULDN'T LIKE IT, BUT...
...WOULD YOU LIKE TO GIVE IT A TRY?
YOU MIGHT FIND IT QUITE EXCITING.
NWHA?!

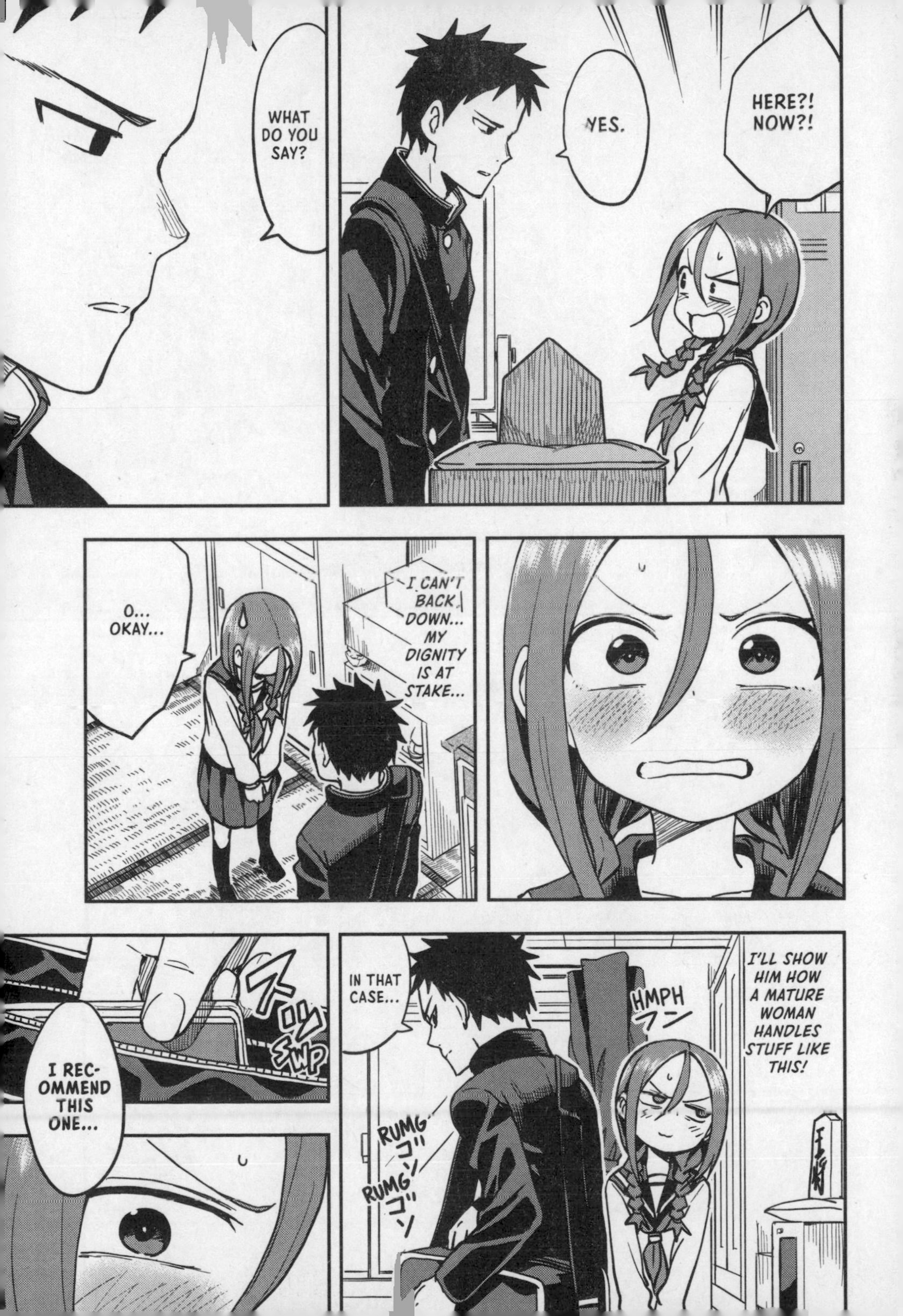
HERE?! NOW?!
YES.
WHAT DO YOU SAY?
I CAN'T BACK DOWN... MY DIGNITY IS AT STAKE...
O... OKAY...
I'LL SHOW HIM HOW A MATURE WOMAN HANDLES STUFF LIKE THIS!
HMPH フン
IN THAT CASE...
RUMG ゴソ
RUMG ゴソ
SWP
I REC-OMMEND THIS ONE...

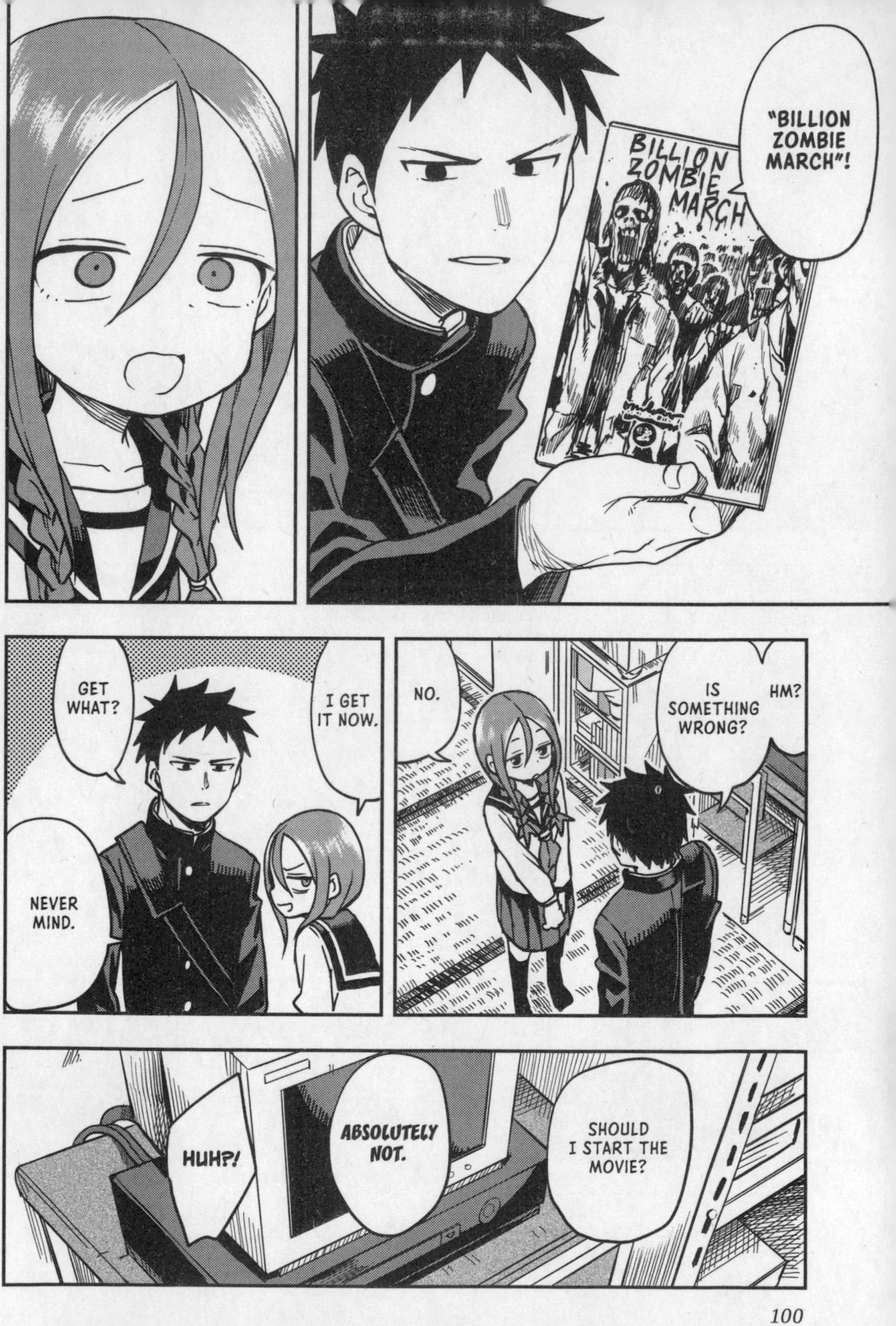
BILLION ZOMBIE MARCH
"BILLION ZOMBIE MARCH"!
HM?
IS SOMETHING WRONG?
NO.
I GET IT NOW.
GET WHAT?
NEVER MIND.
SHOULD I START THE MOVIE?
ABSOLUTELY NOT.
HUH?!

WHEN WILL
AYUMU
MAKE HIS
MOVE?

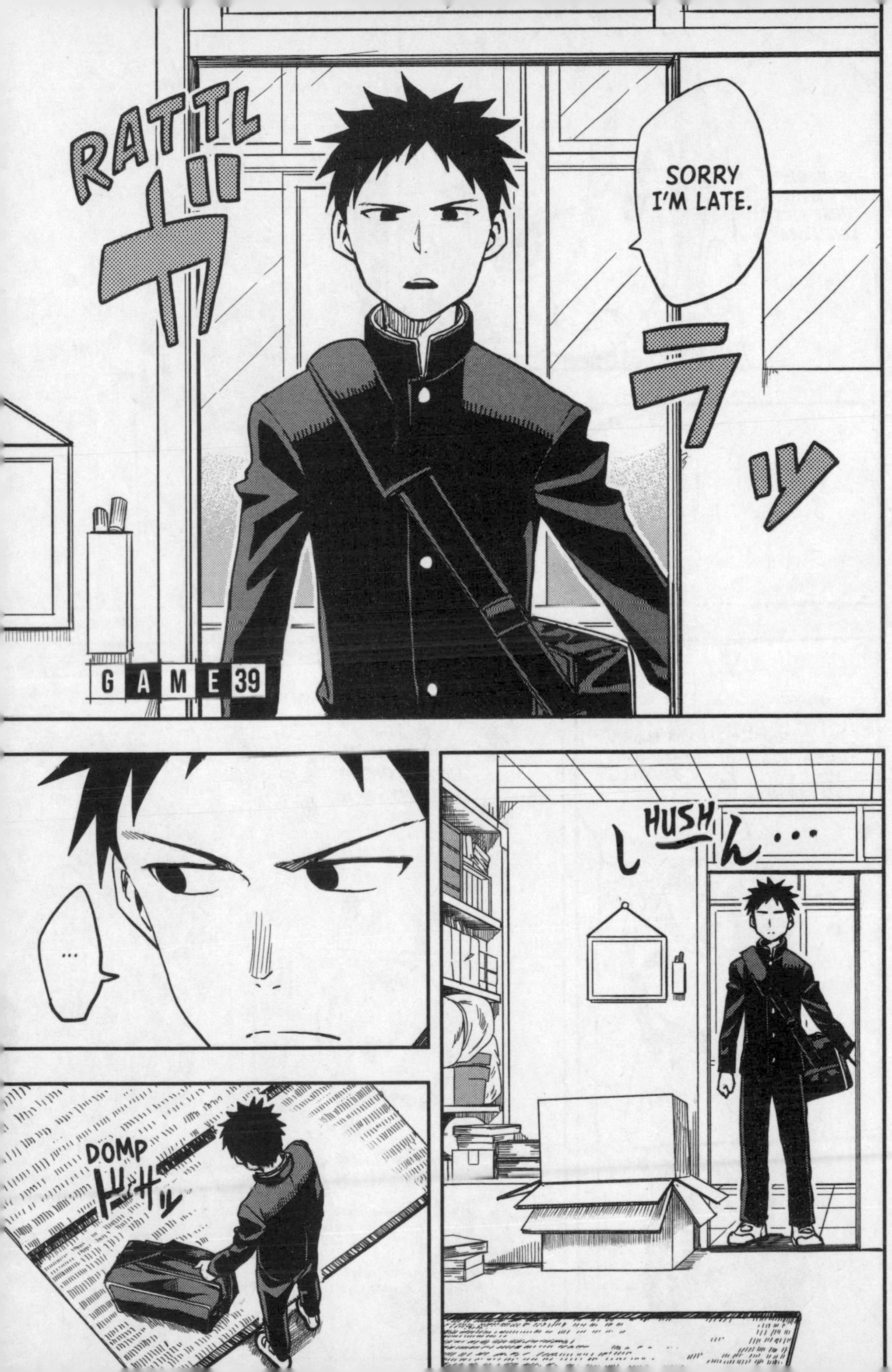
SORRY I'M LATE.
RATTL
ガラッ
GAME 39
HUSH
しーん…
...
DOMP
ドサッ

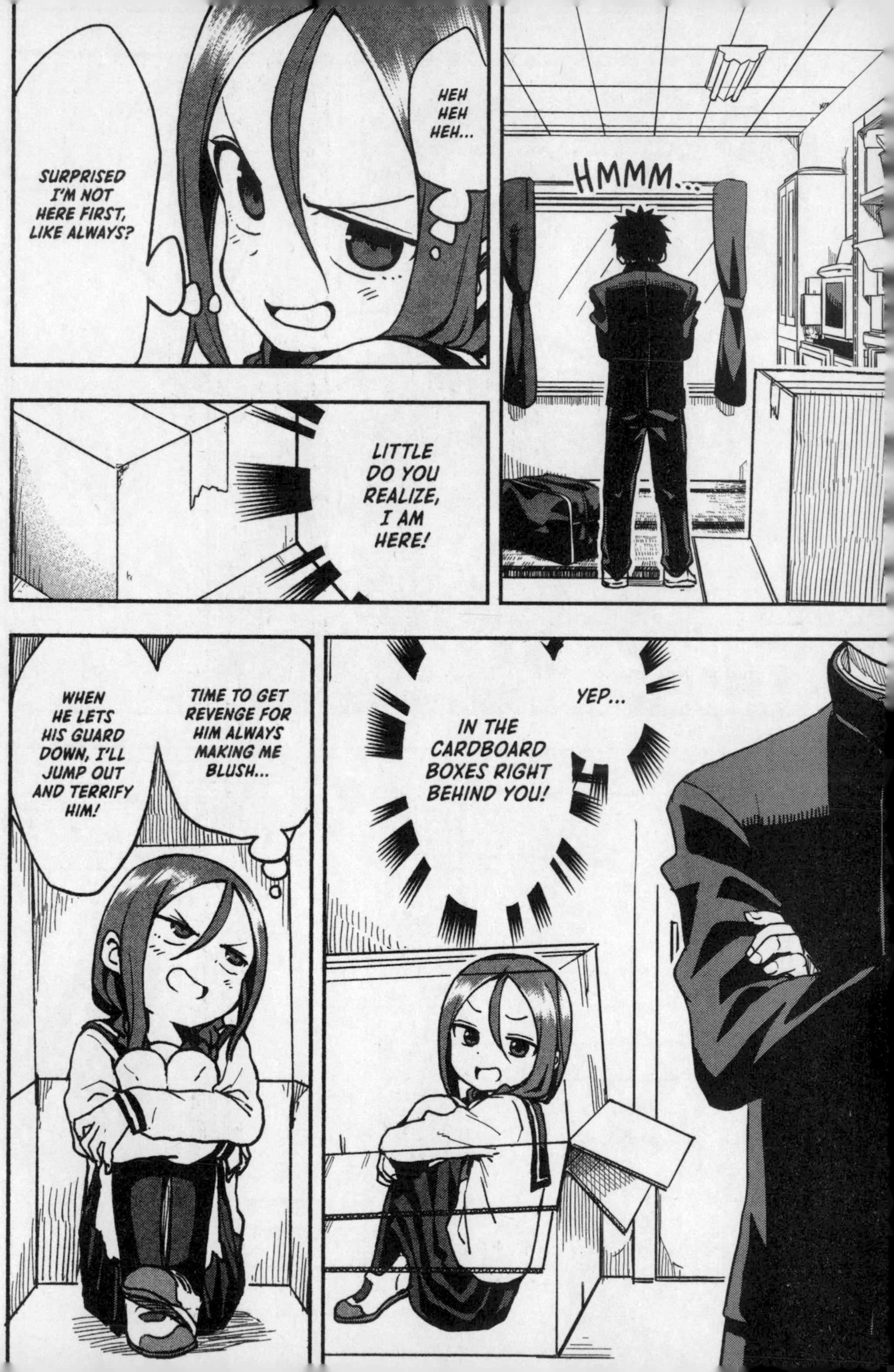
HMMM...
HEH HEH HEH...
SURPRISED I'M NOT HERE FIRST, LIKE ALWAYS?
LITTLE DO YOU REALIZE, I AM HERE!
YEP...
IN THE CARDBOARD BOXES RIGHT BEHIND YOU!
TIME TO GET REVENGE FOR HIM ALWAYS MAKING ME BLUSH...
WHEN HE LETS HIS GUARD DOWN, I'LL JUMP OUT AND TERRIFY HIM!

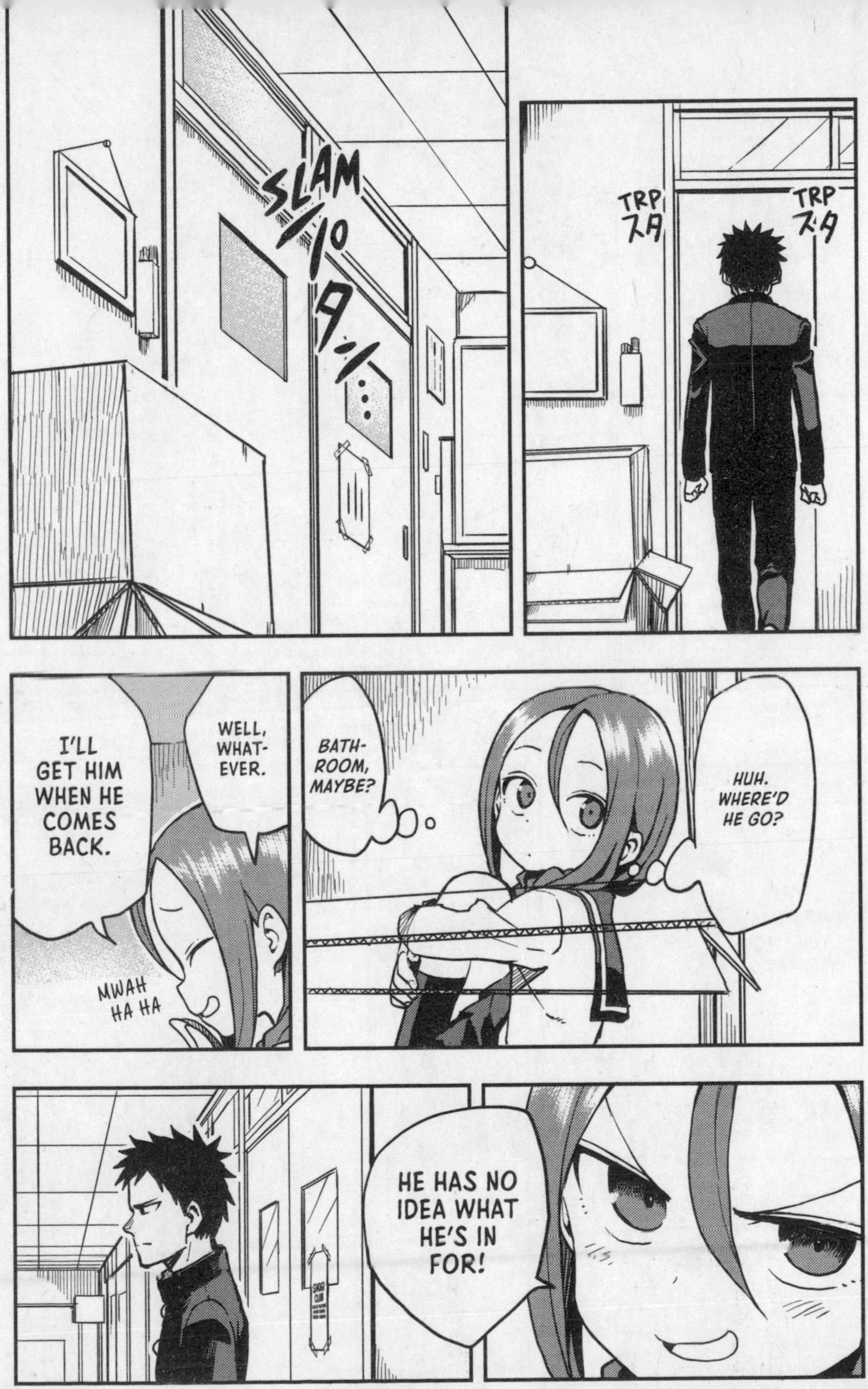
TRP
スタ
TRP
スタ
SLAM
パタン
...
HUH. WHERE'D HE GO?
BATH-ROOM, MAYBE?
WELL, WHAT-EVER.
I'LL GET HIM WHEN HE COMES BACK.
MWAH HA HA
HE HAS NO IDEA WHAT HE'S IN FOR!

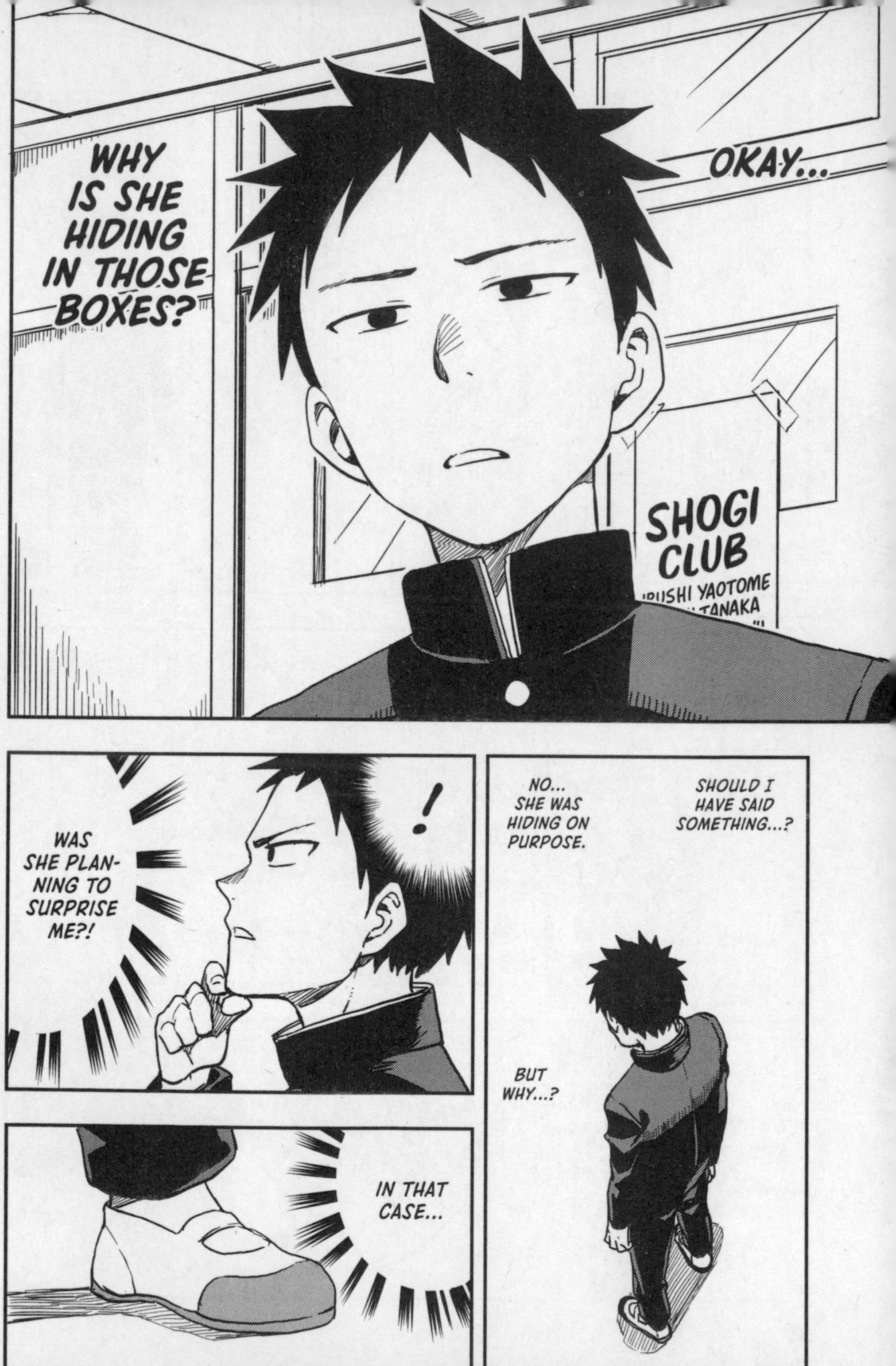
OKAY...
WHY IS SHE HIDING IN THOSE BOXES?
SHOGI CLUB
SHOULD I HAVE SAID SOMETHING...?
NO... SHE WAS HIDING ON PURPOSE.
BUT WHY...?
!
WAS SHE PLAN-NING TO SURPRISE ME?!
IN THAT CASE...

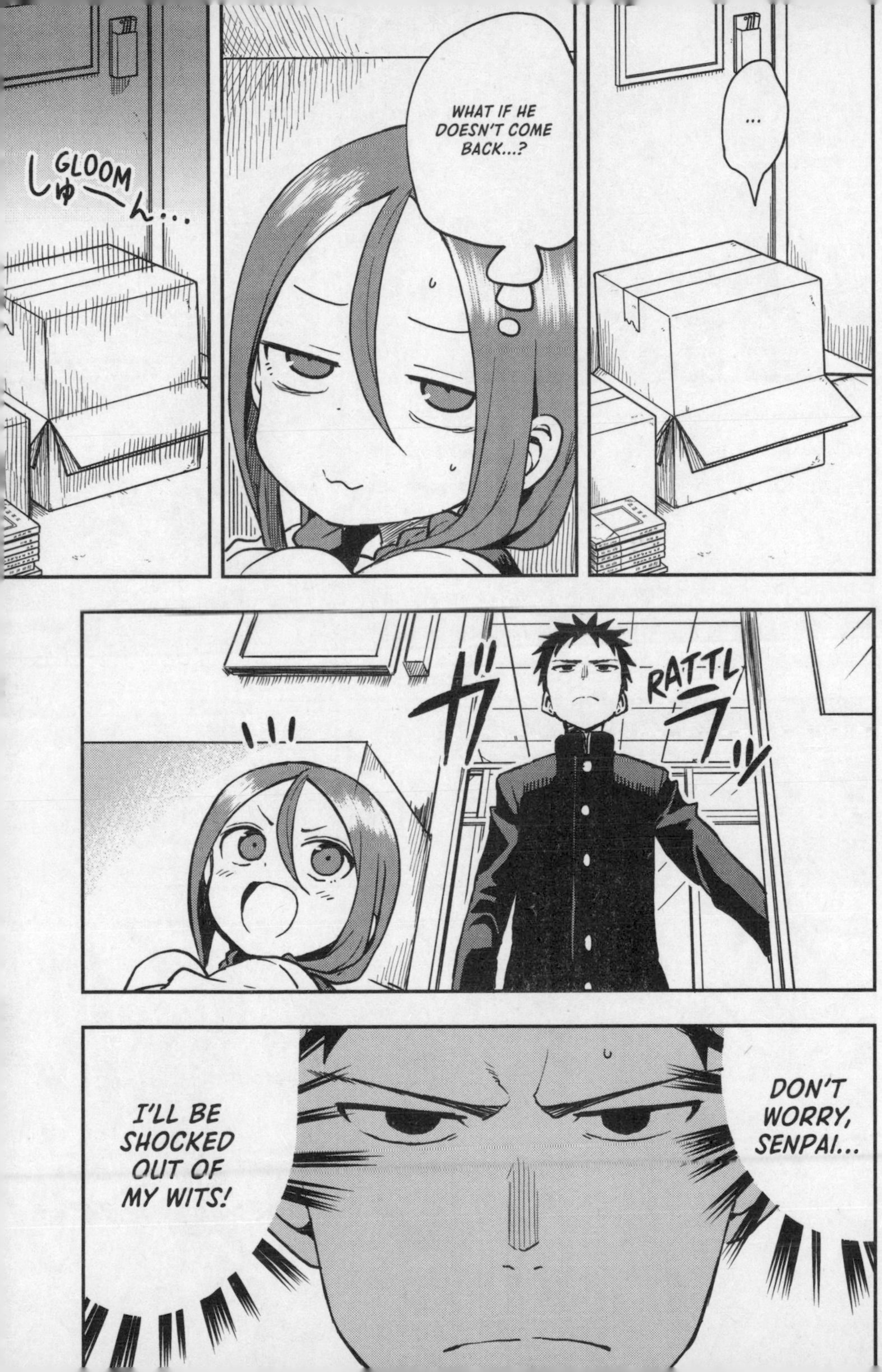
...
WHAT IF HE DOESN'T COME BACK...?
GLOOM
しゅーん...
RATTL
ガラッ
DON'T WORRY, SENPAI...
I'LL BE SHOCKED OUT OF MY WITS!

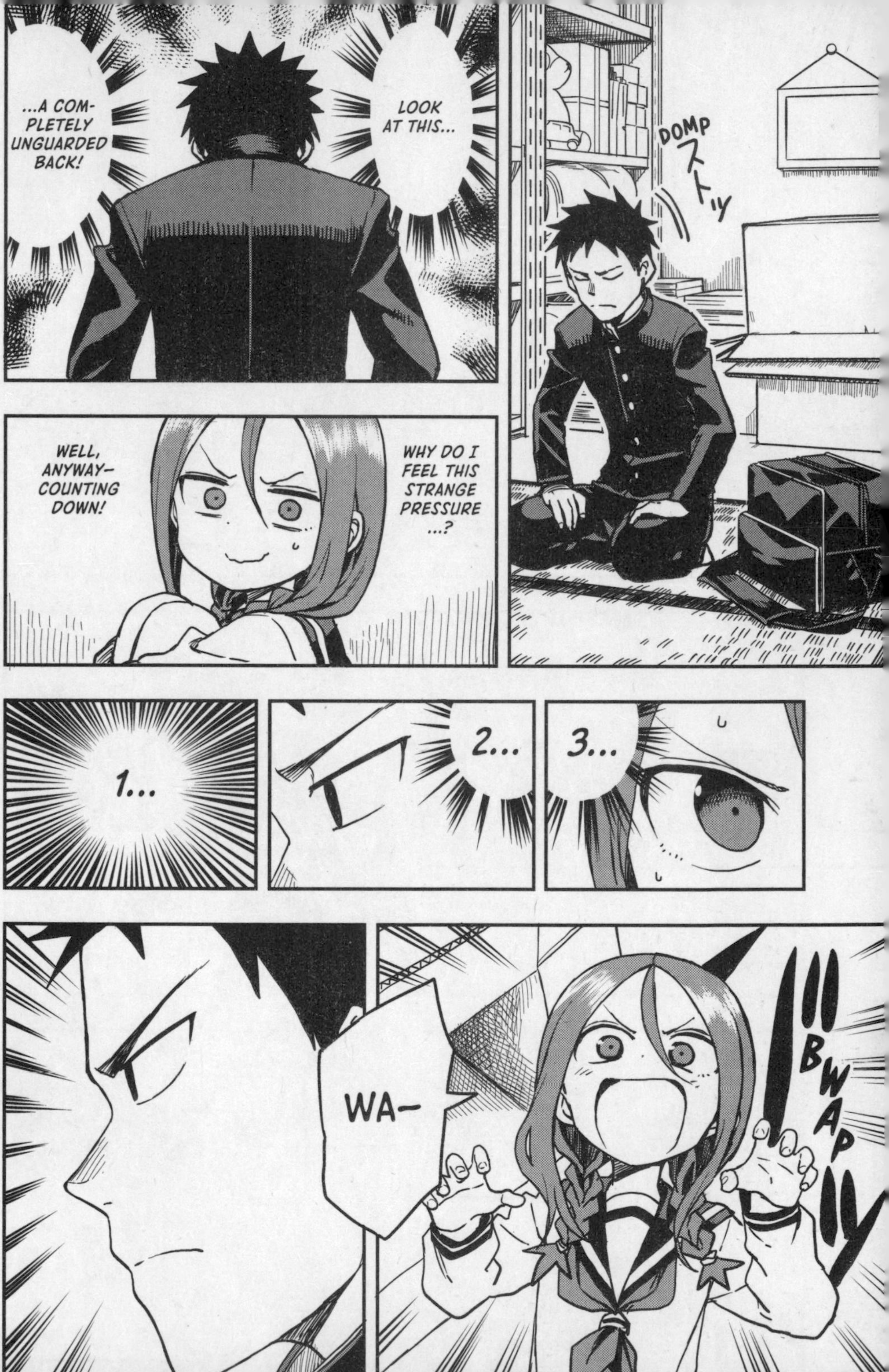
DOMP
ストッ
LOOK AT THIS...
...A COM-PLETELY UNGUARDED BACK!
WHY DO I FEEL THIS STRANGE PRESSURE ...?
WELL, ANYWAY— COUNTING DOWN!
3...
2...
1...
BWAP!!
WA-

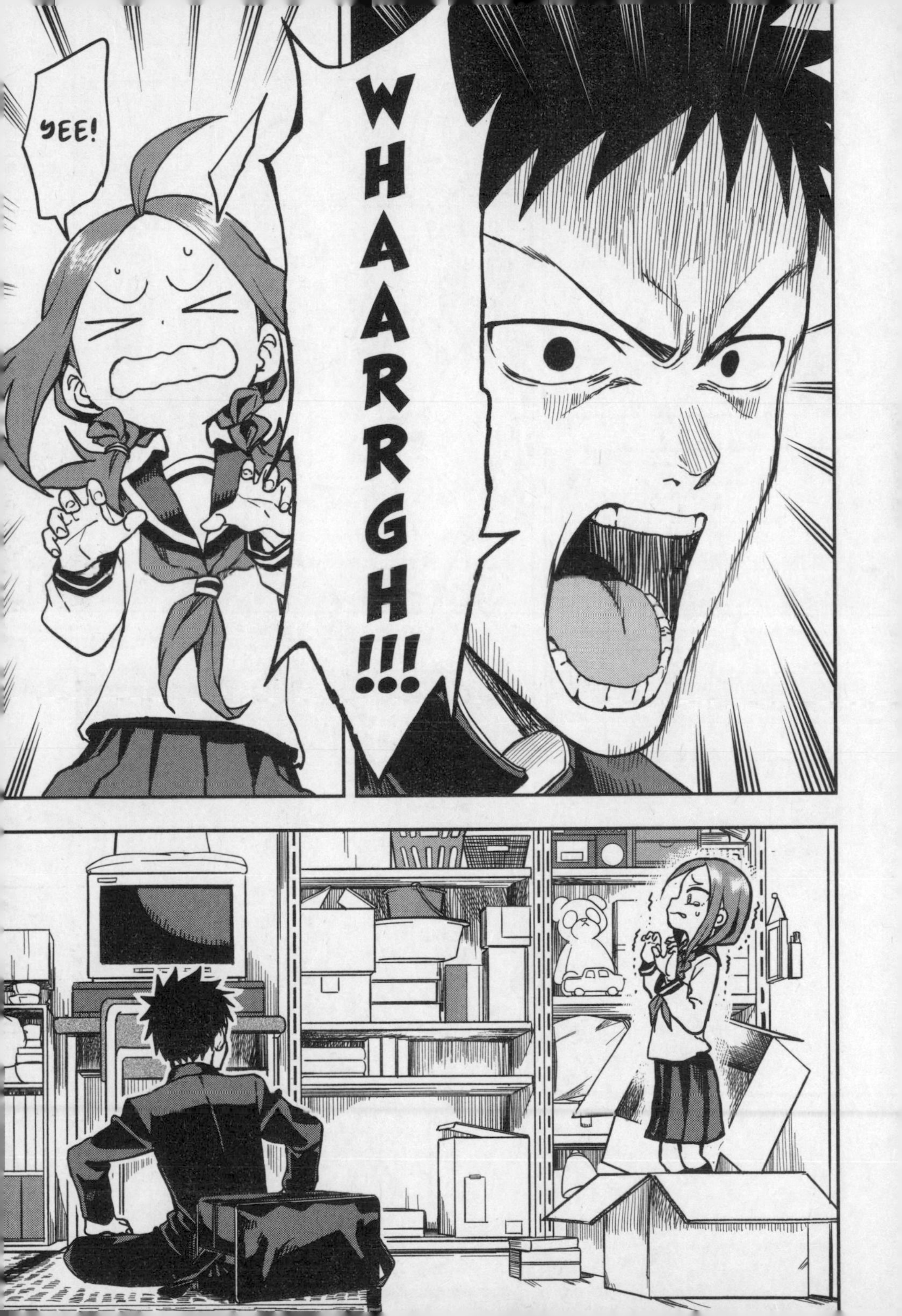
WHARRGH!!!
YEE!

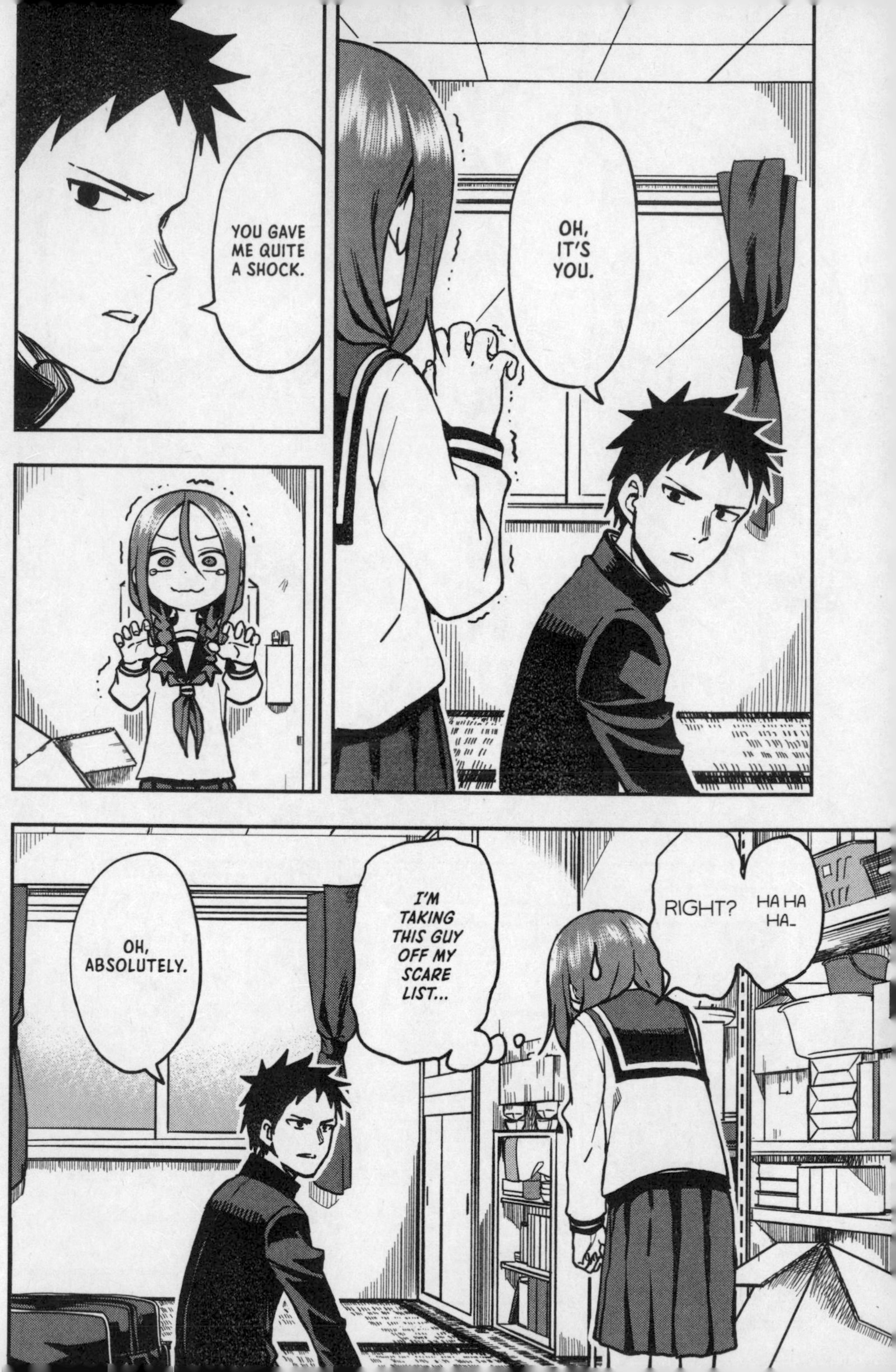
OH, IT'S YOU.
YOU GAVE ME QUITE A SHOCK.
RIGHT? HA HA HA_
I'M TAKING THIS GUY OFF MY SCARE LIST...
OH, ABSOLUTELY.

WHEN WILL
AYUMU
MAKE HIS
MOVE?

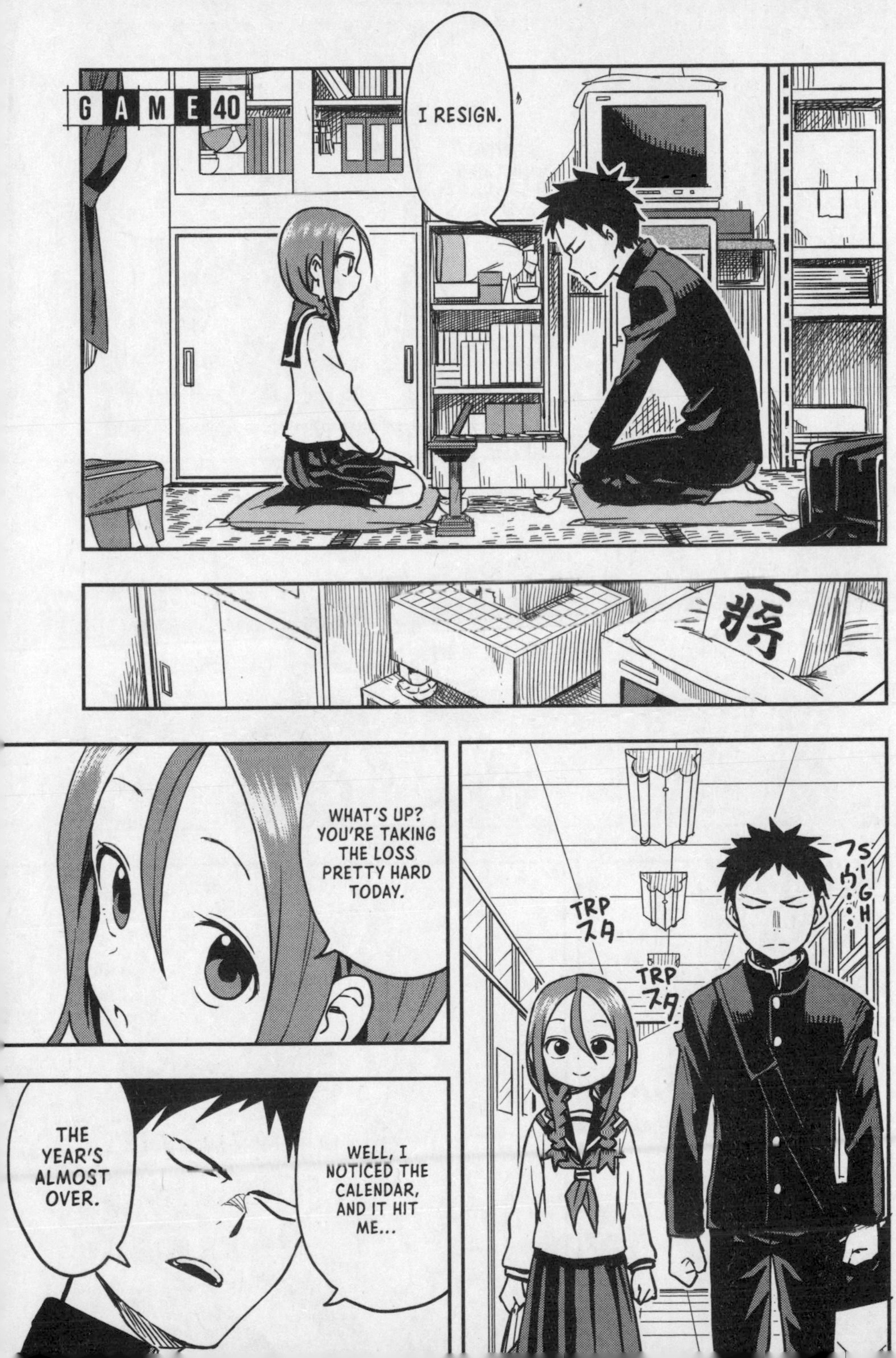
GAME 40
I RESIGN.
SIGH
フウ…
TRP
スタ
TRP
スタ
WHAT'S UP? YOU'RE TAKING THE LOSS PRETTY HARD TODAY.
WELL, I NOTICED THE CALENDAR, AND IT HIT ME...
THE YEAR'S ALMOST OVER.

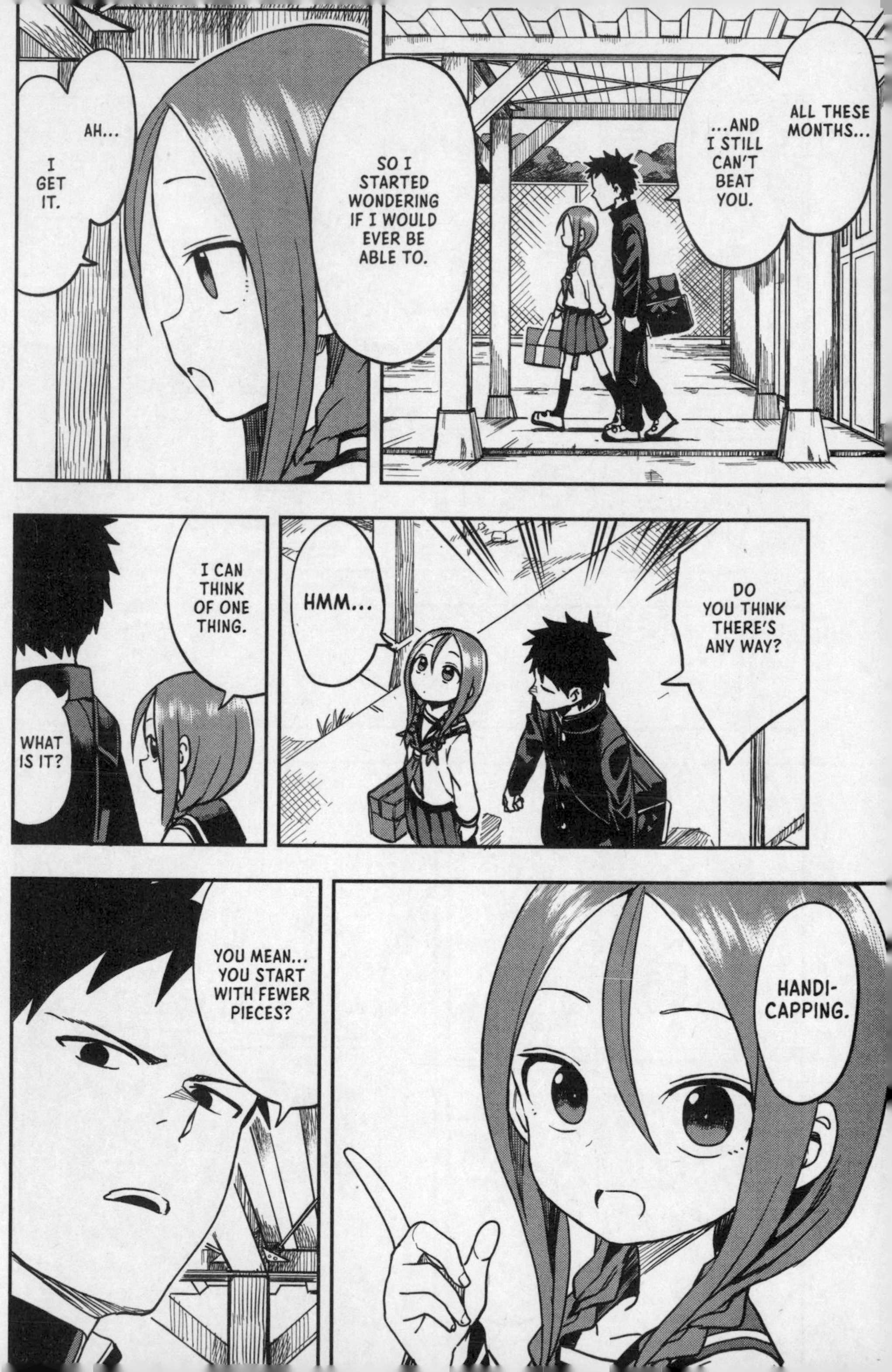
ALL THESE MONTHS...
...AND I STILL CAN'T BEAT YOU.
SO I STARTED WONDERING IF I WOULD EVER BE ABLE TO.
AH...
I GET IT.
DO YOU THINK THERE'S ANY WAY?
HMM...
I CAN THINK OF ONE THING.
WHAT IS IT?
HANDI-CAPPING.
YOU MEAN... YOU START WITH FEWER PIECES?

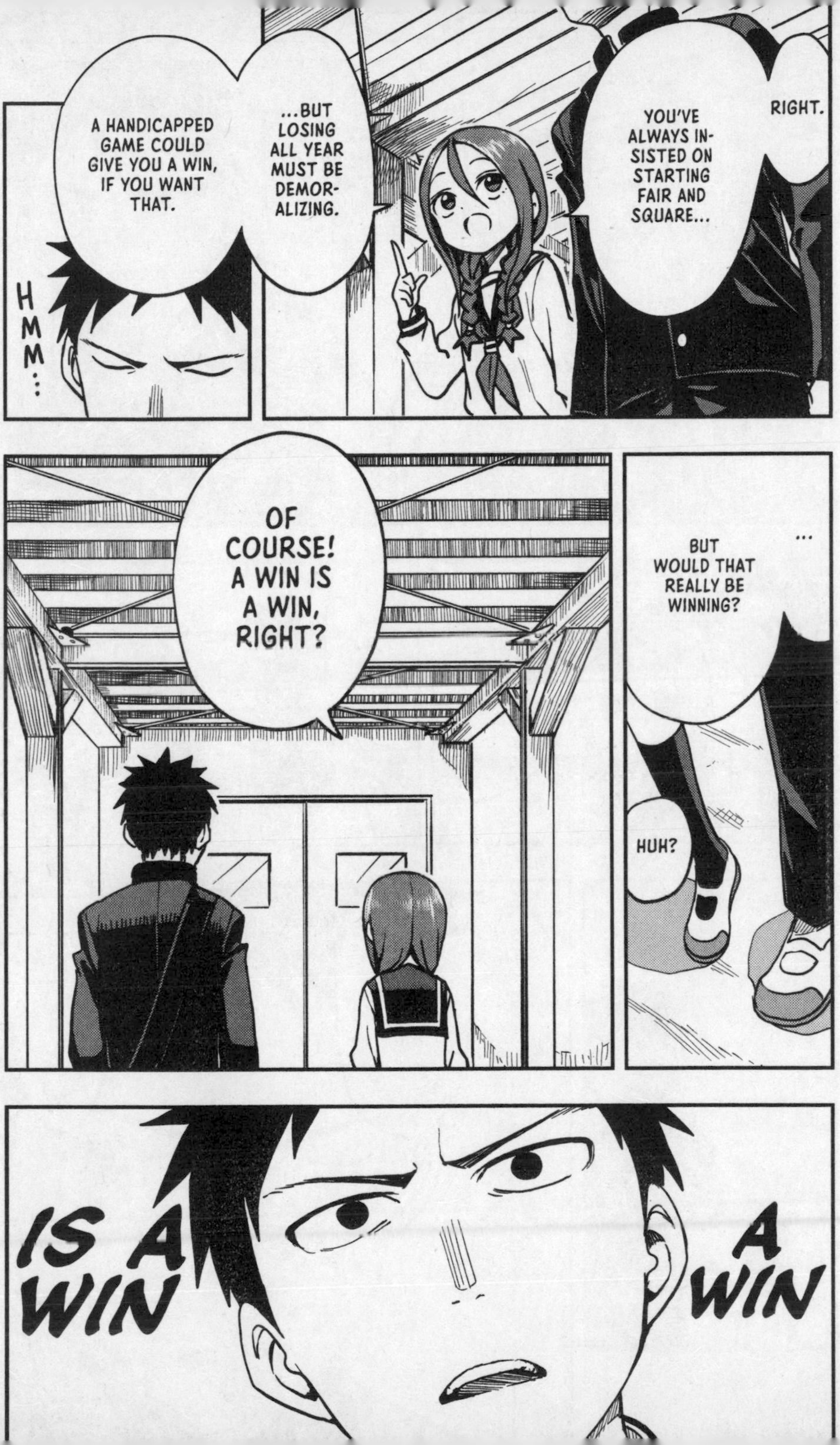
RIGHT.
YOU'VE ALWAYS IN-SISTED ON STARTING FAIR AND SQUARE...
...BUT LOSING ALL YEAR MUST BE DEMOR-ALIZING.
A HANDICAPPED GAME COULD GIVE YOU A WIN, IF YOU WANT THAT.
HMM...
...
BUT WOULD THAT REALLY BE WINNING?
HUH?
OF COURSE! A WIN IS A WIN, RIGHT?
A WIN
IS A WIN

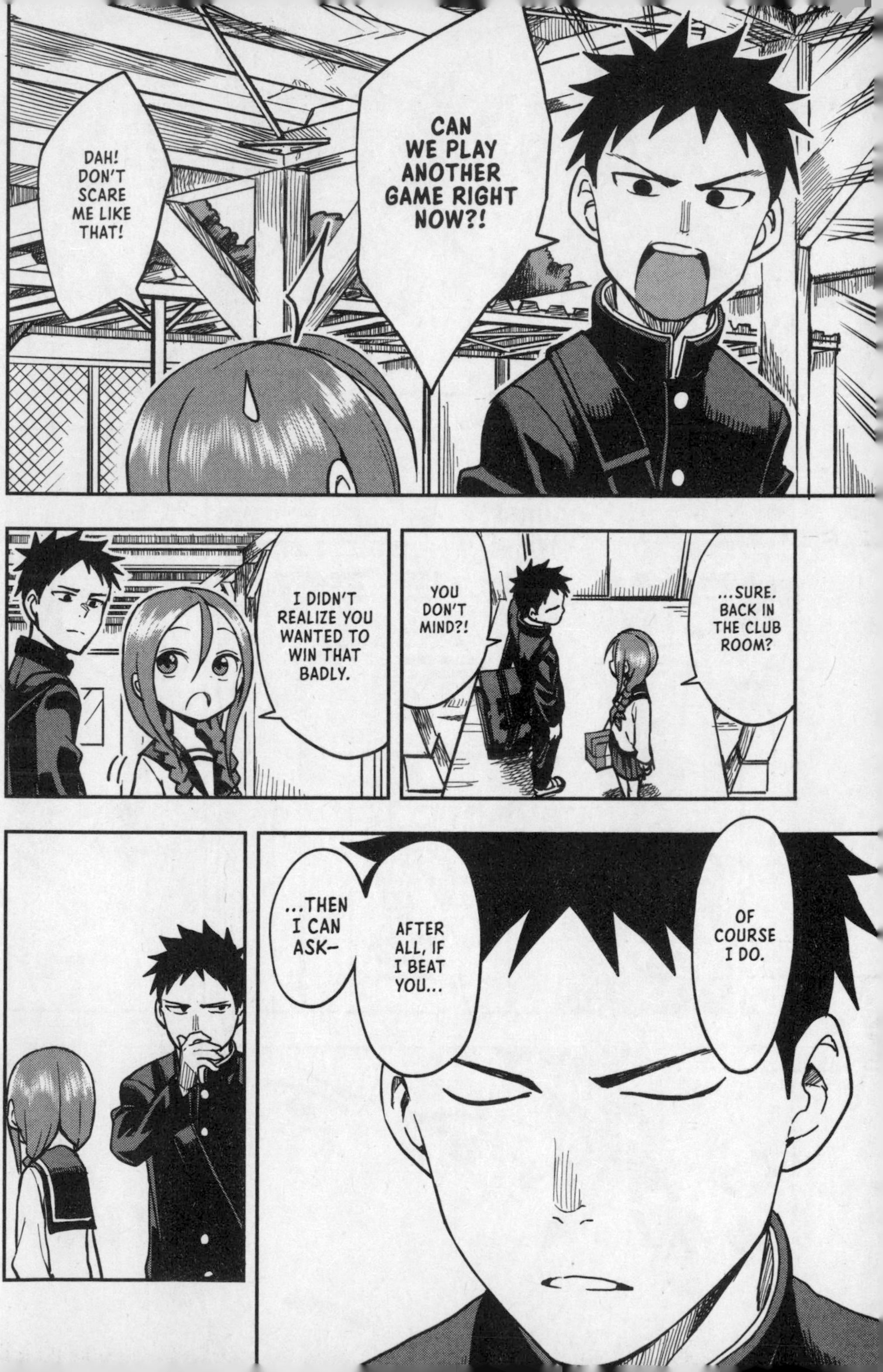
CAN WE PLAY ANOTHER GAME RIGHT NOW?!
DAH! DON'T SCARE ME LIKE THAT!
...SURE. BACK IN THE CLUB ROOM?
YOU DON'T MIND?!
I DIDN'T REALIZE YOU WANTED TO WIN THAT BADLY.
OF COURSE I DO.
AFTER ALL, IF I BEAT YOU...
...THEN I CAN ASK–

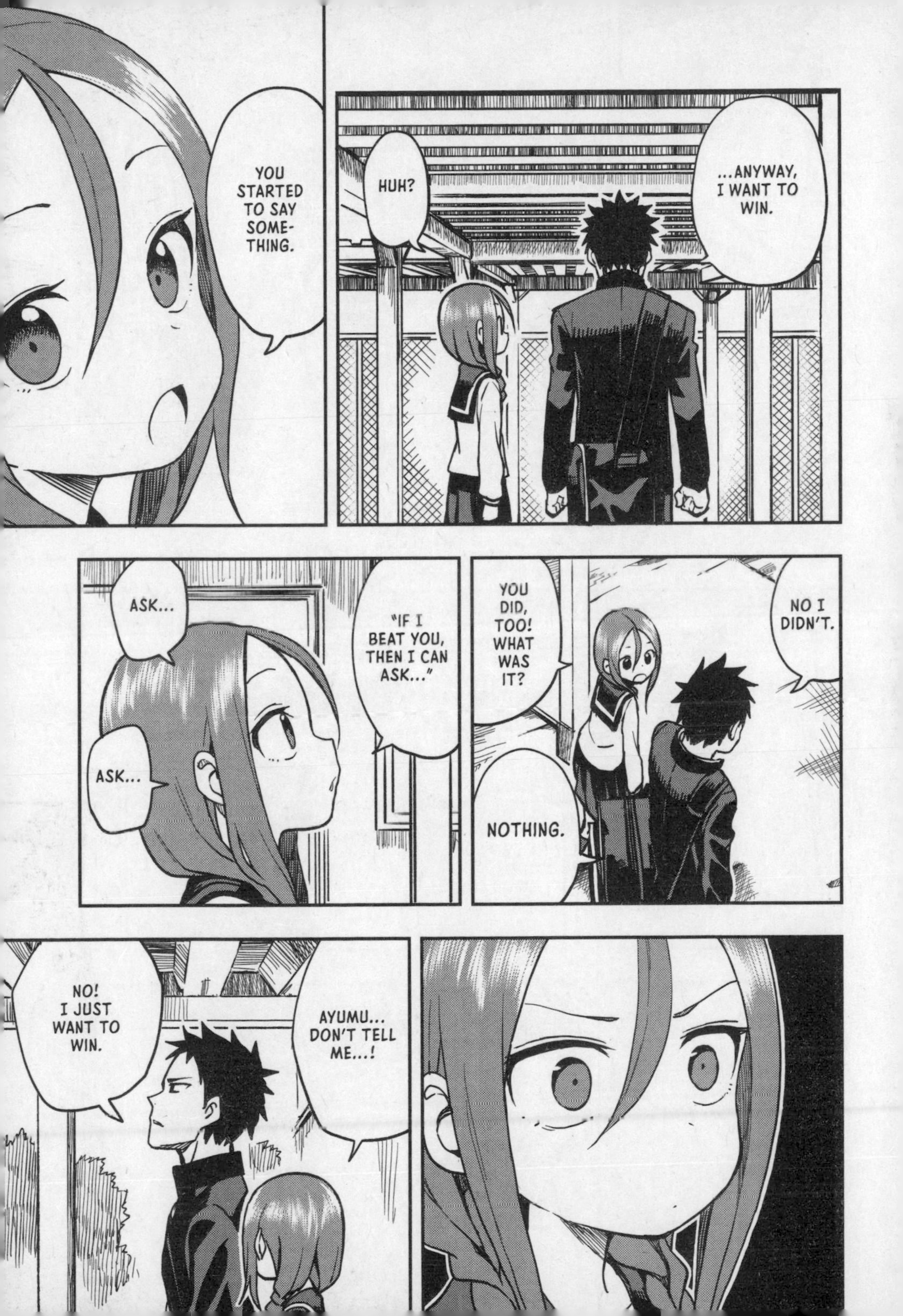
...ANYWAY, I WANT TO WIN.
HUH?
YOU STARTED TO SAY SOME-THING.
NO I DIDN'T.
YOU DID, TOO! WHAT WAS IT?
NOTHING.
"IF I BEAT YOU, THEN I CAN ASK..."
ASK...
ASK...
AYUMU... DON'T TELL ME...!
NO! I JUST WANT TO WIN.

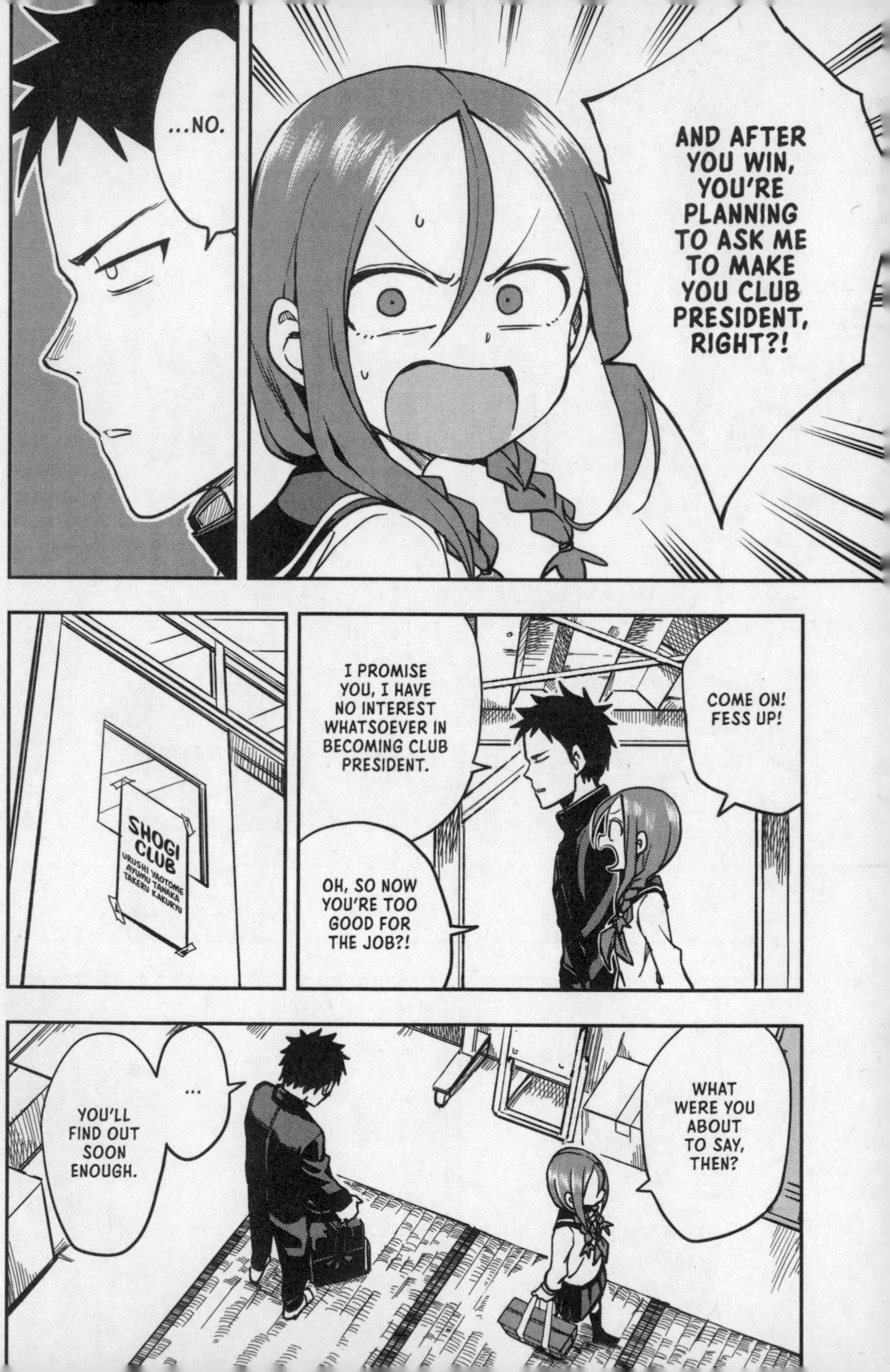
AND AFTER YOU WIN, YOU'RE PLANNING TO ASK ME TO MAKE YOU CLUB PRESIDENT, RIGHT?!
...NO.
COME ON! FESS UP!
I PROMISE YOU, I HAVE NO INTEREST WHATSOEVER IN BECOMING CLUB PRESIDENT.
OH, SO NOW YOU'RE TOO GOOD FOR THE JOB?!
SHOGI CLUB
URUSHI YAOTOME
AYUMU TANAKA
TAKERU KAKURYU
WHAT WERE YOU ABOUT TO SAY, THEN?
...
YOU'LL FIND OUT SOON ENOUGH.

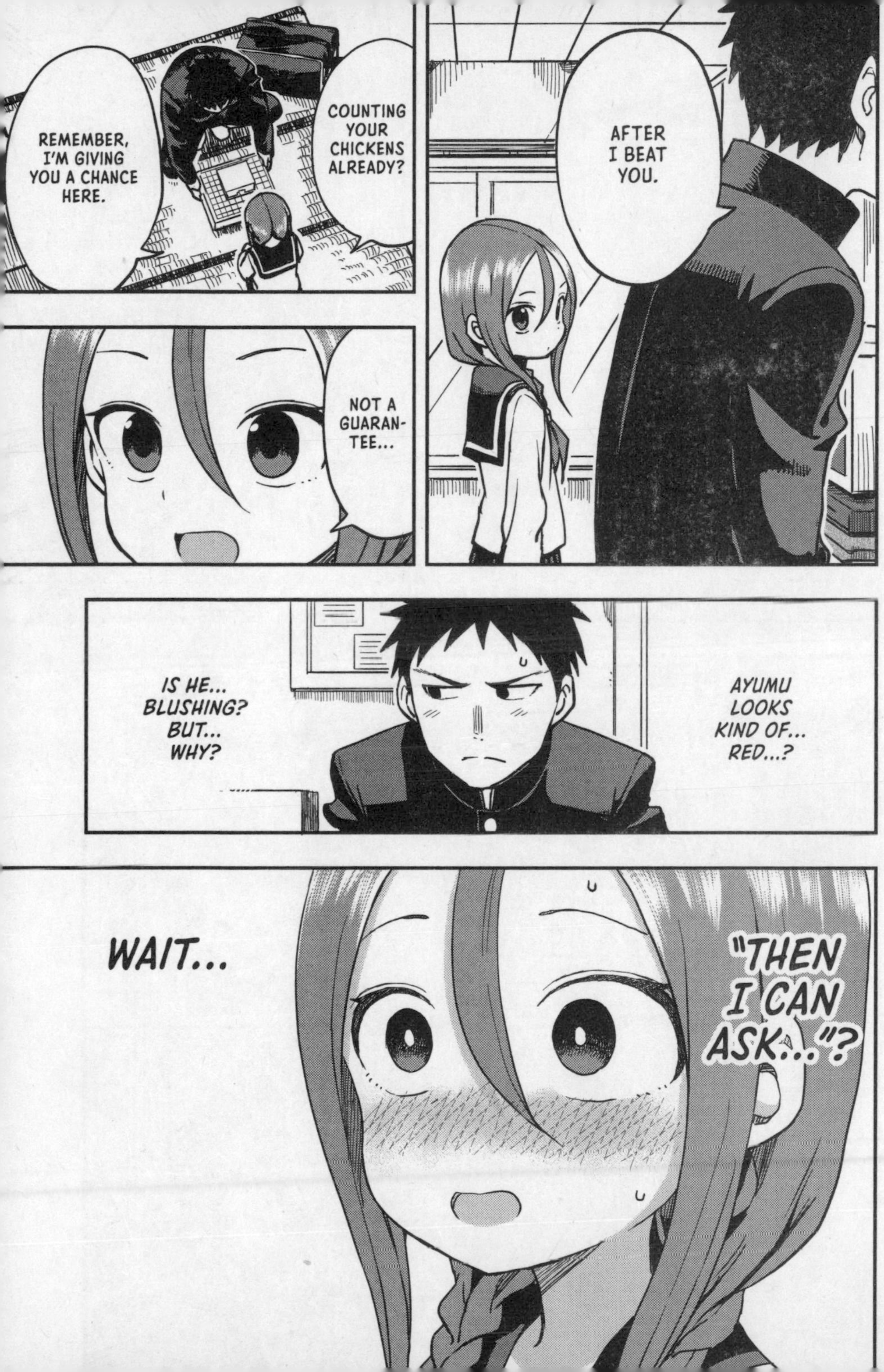
AFTER I BEAT YOU.
COUNTING YOUR CHICKENS ALREADY?
REMEMBER, I'M GIVING YOU A CHANCE HERE.
NOT A GUARANTEE...
AYUMU LOOKS KIND OF... RED...?
IS HE... BLUSHING? BUT... WHY?
"THEN I CAN ASK..."?
WAIT...

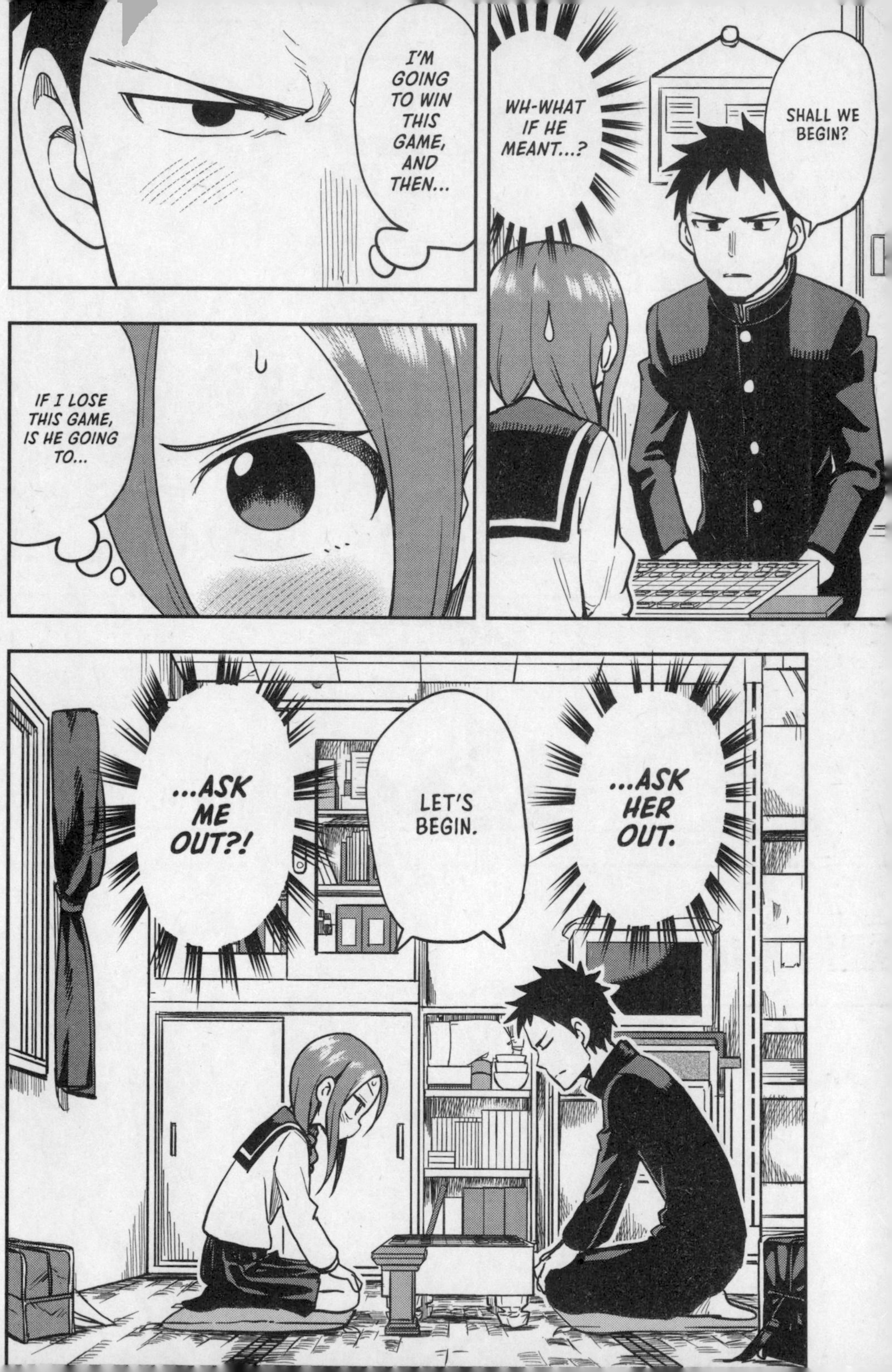
SHALL WE BEGIN?
WH-WHAT IF HE MEANT...?
I'M GOING TO WIN THIS GAME, AND THEN...
IF I LOSE THIS GAME, IS HE GOING TO...
...ASK HER OUT.
LET'S BEGIN.
...ASK ME OUT?!

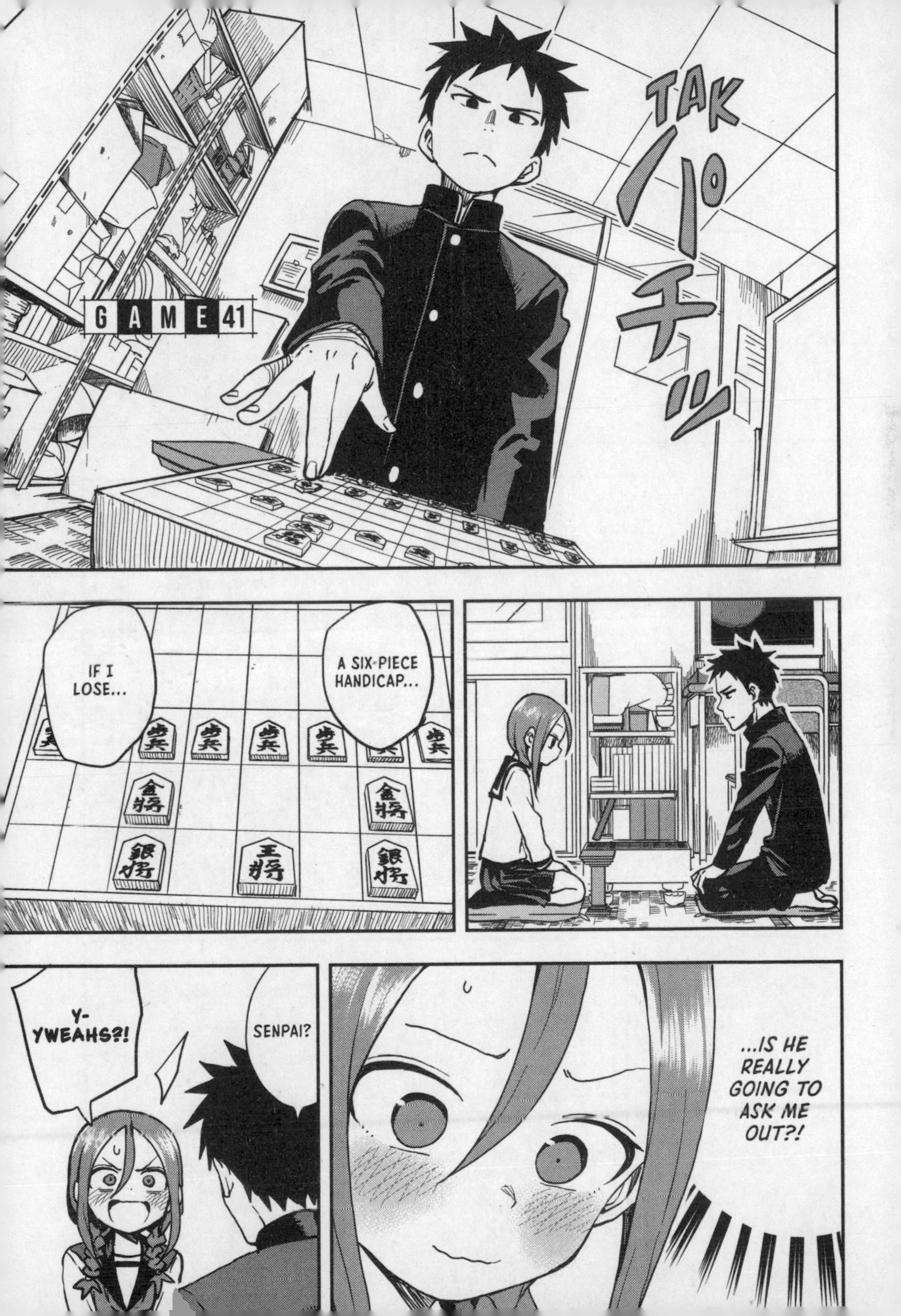
GAME 41
TAK
パチッ
A SIX-PIECE HANDICAP...
IF I LOSE...
...IS HE REALLY GOING TO ASK ME OUT?!
SENPAI?
Y-YWEAHS?!

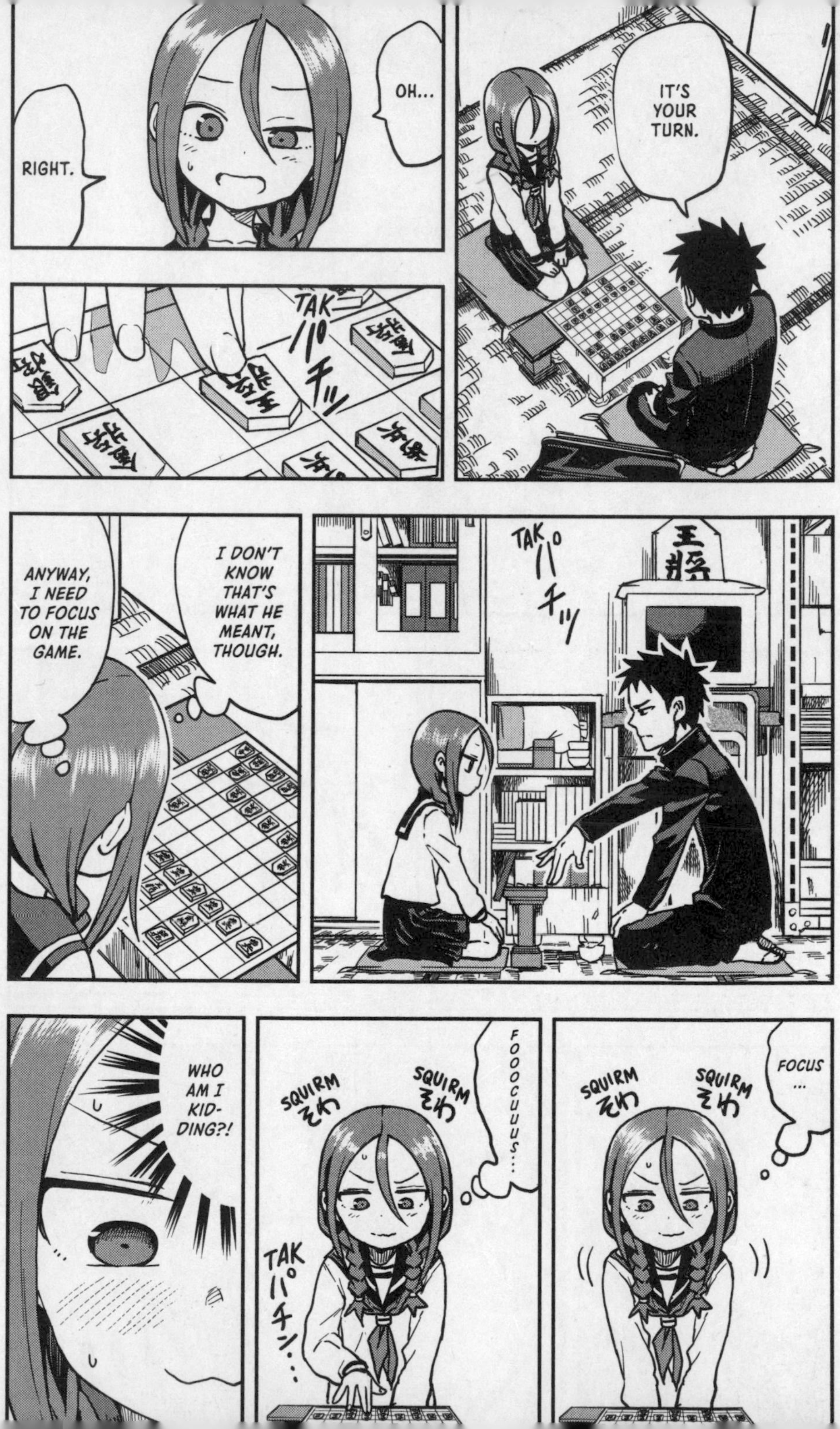
IT'S YOUR TURN.
OH...
RIGHT.
TAK
パチッ
TAK
パチッ
I DON'T KNOW THAT'S WHAT HE MEANT, THOUGH.
ANYWAY, I NEED TO FOCUS ON THE GAME.
FOCUS...
SQUIRM そわ
SQUIRM そわ
FOOOCUUUS...
SQUIRM そわ
SQUIRM そわ
TAK
パチン...
WHO AM I KID-DING?!

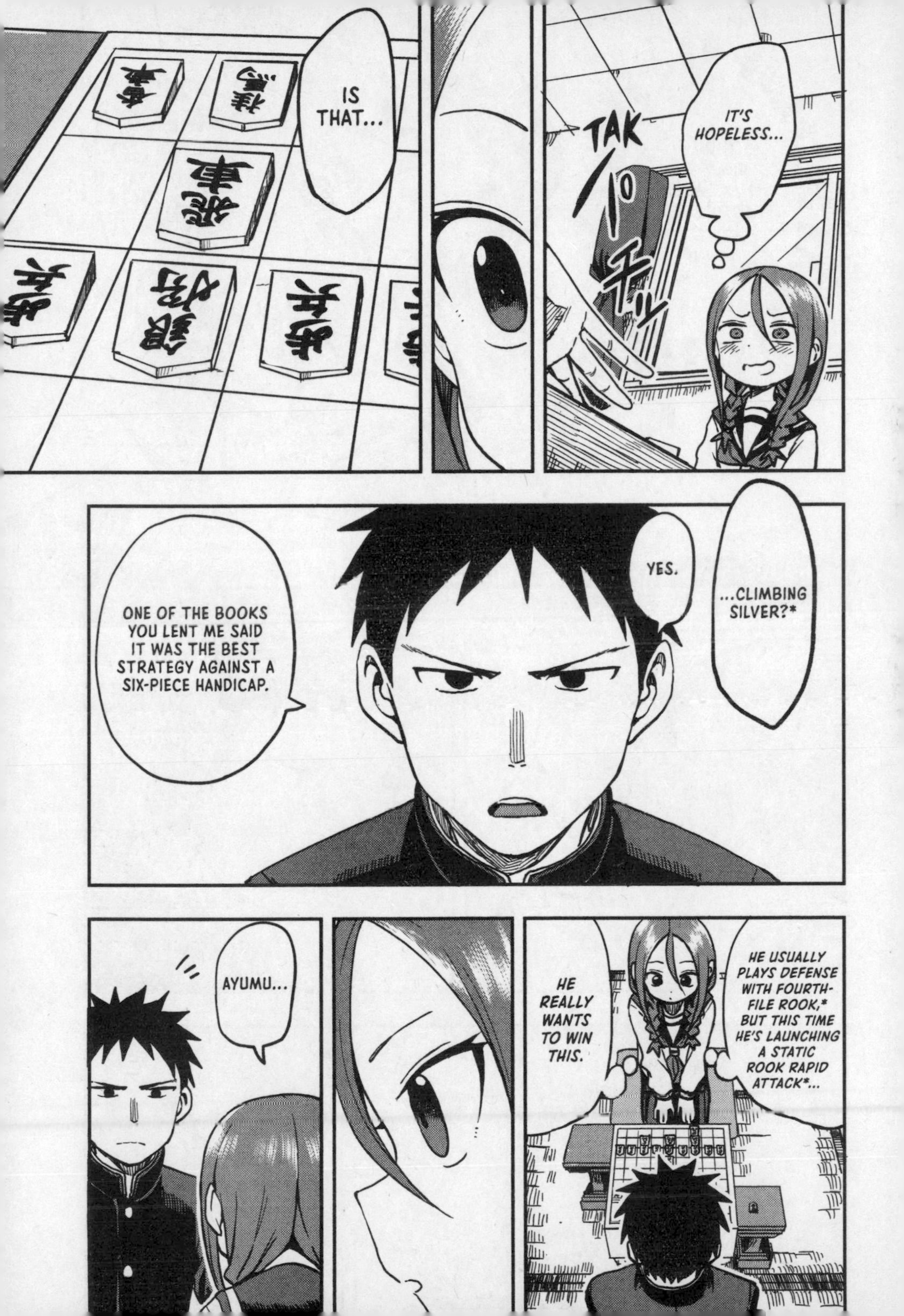
IT'S HOPELESS...
TAK
IS THAT...
...CLIMBING SILVER?*
YES.
ONE OF THE BOOKS YOU LENT ME SAID IT WAS THE BEST STRATEGY AGAINST A SIX-PIECE HANDICAP.
HE USUALLY PLAYS DEFENSE WITH FOURTH-FILE ROOK,* BUT THIS TIME HE'S LAUNCHING A STATIC ROOK RAPID ATTACK*...
HE REALLY WANTS TO WIN THIS.
AYUMU...

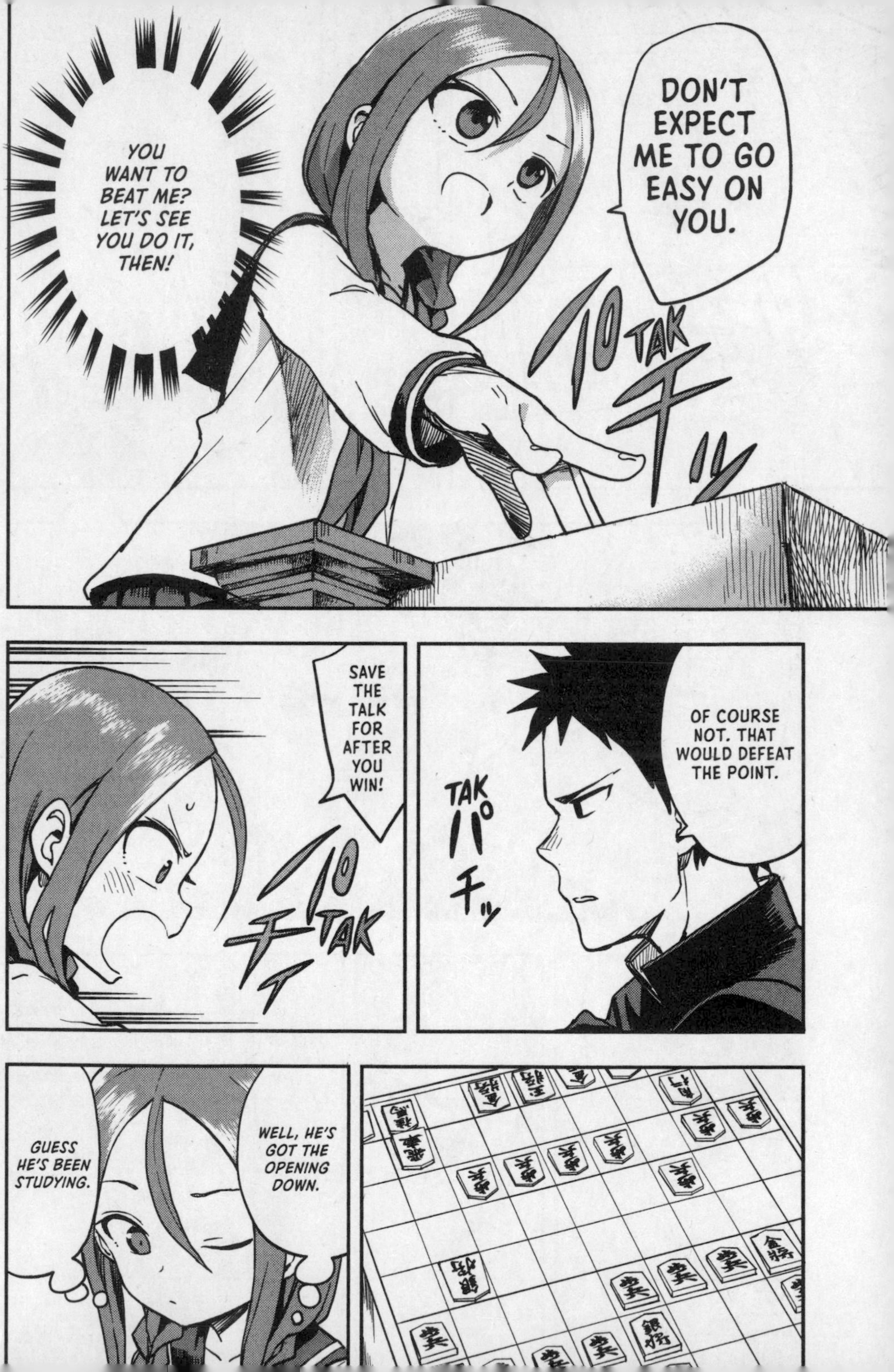
DON'T EXPECT ME TO GO EASY ON YOU.
YOU WANT TO BEAT ME? LET'S SEE YOU DO IT, THEN!
TAK
OF COURSE NOT. THAT WOULD DEFEAT THE POINT.
TAK
SAVE THE TALK FOR AFTER YOU WIN!
TAK
WELL, HE'S GOT THE OPENING DOWN.
GUESS HE'S BEEN STUDYING.

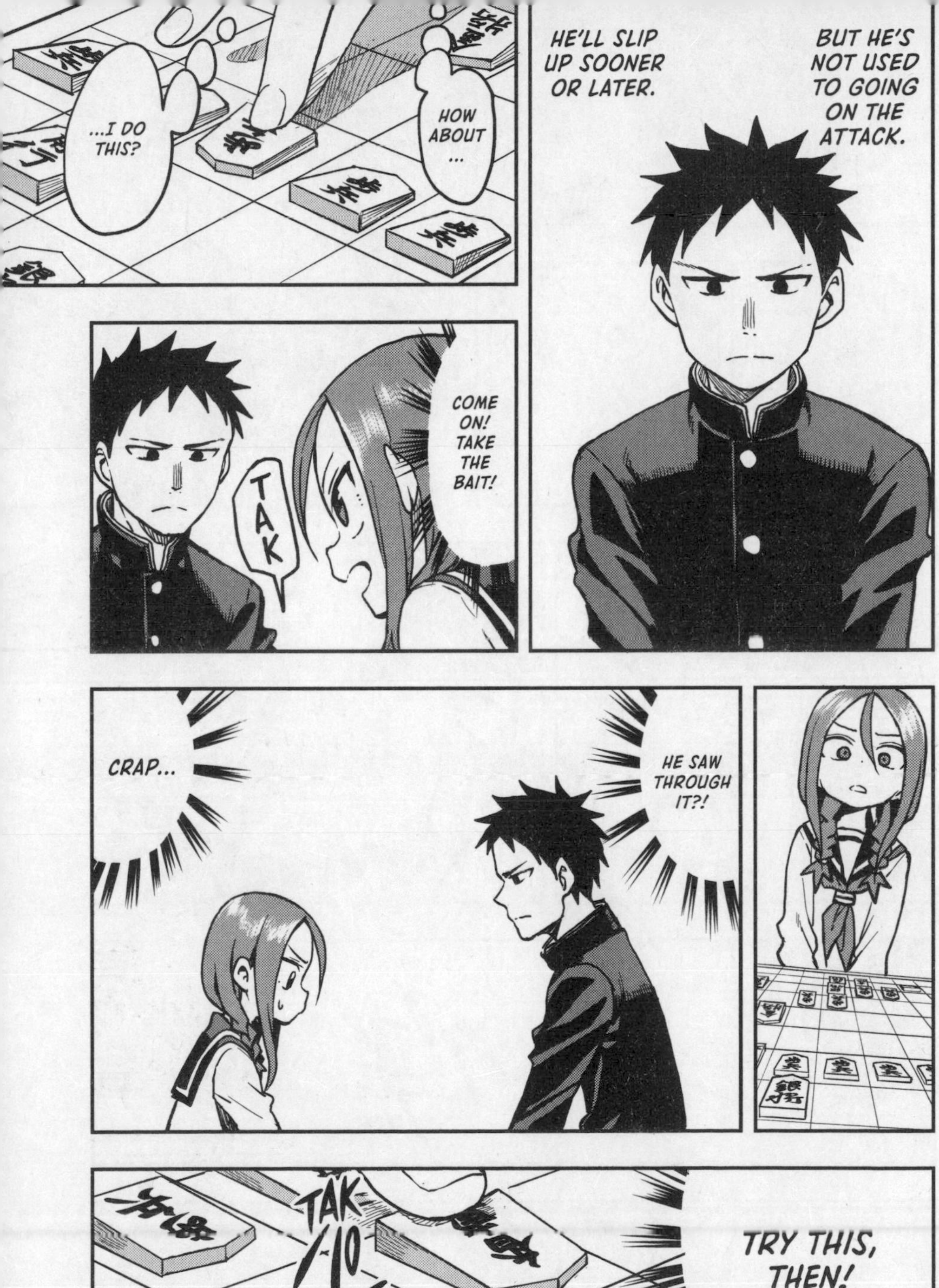
BUT HE'S NOT USED TO GOING ON THE ATTACK.
HE'LL SLIP UP SOONER OR LATER.
HOW ABOUT ...
...I DO THIS?
COME ON! TAKE THE BAIT!
TAK
HE SAW THROUGH IT?!
CRAP...
TRY THIS, THEN!
TAK
チッ

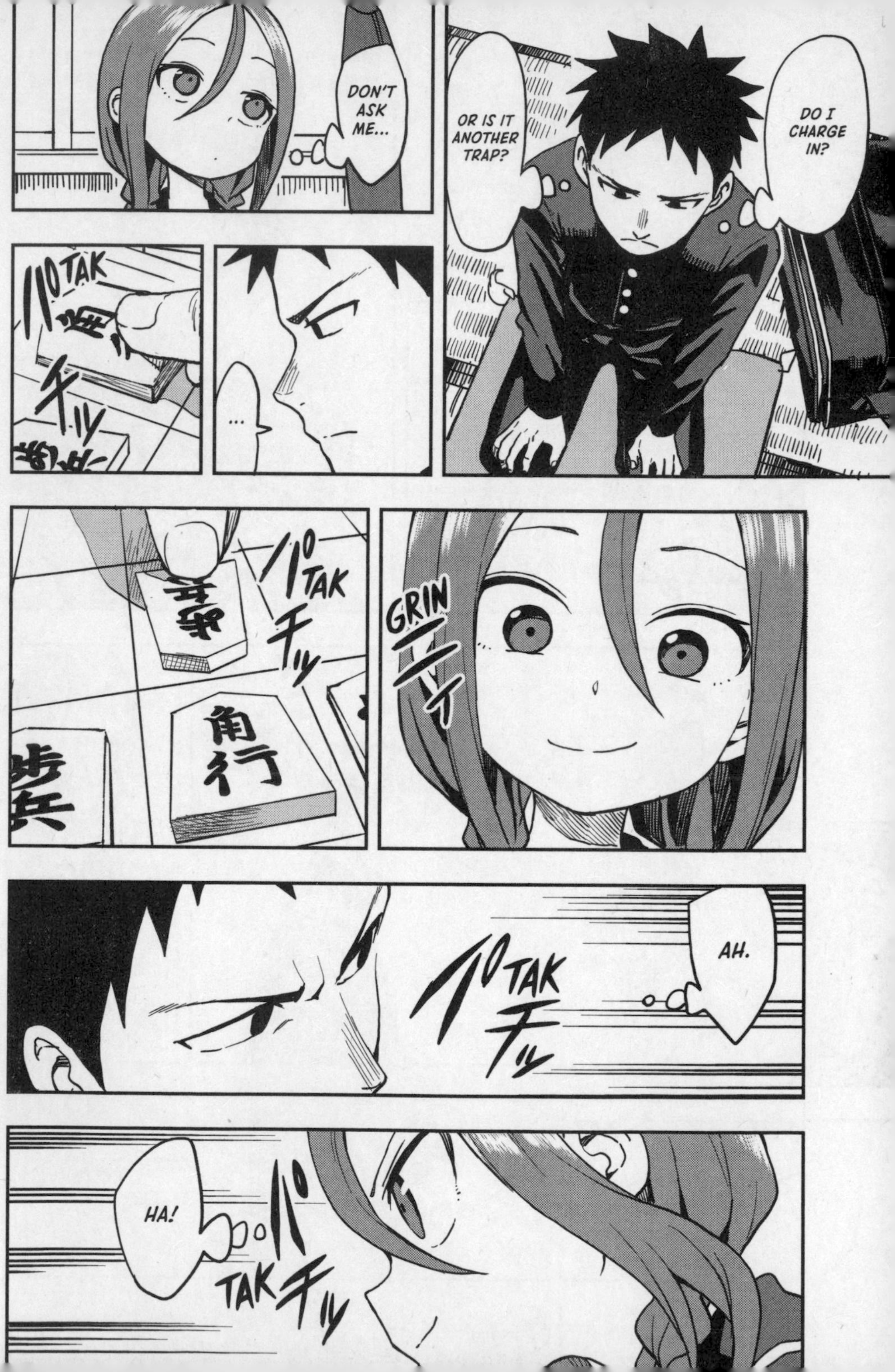
DO I CHARGE IN?
OR IS IT ANOTHER TRAP?
DON'T ASK ME...
...
TAK
GRIN
TAK
AH.
TAK
HA!
TAK

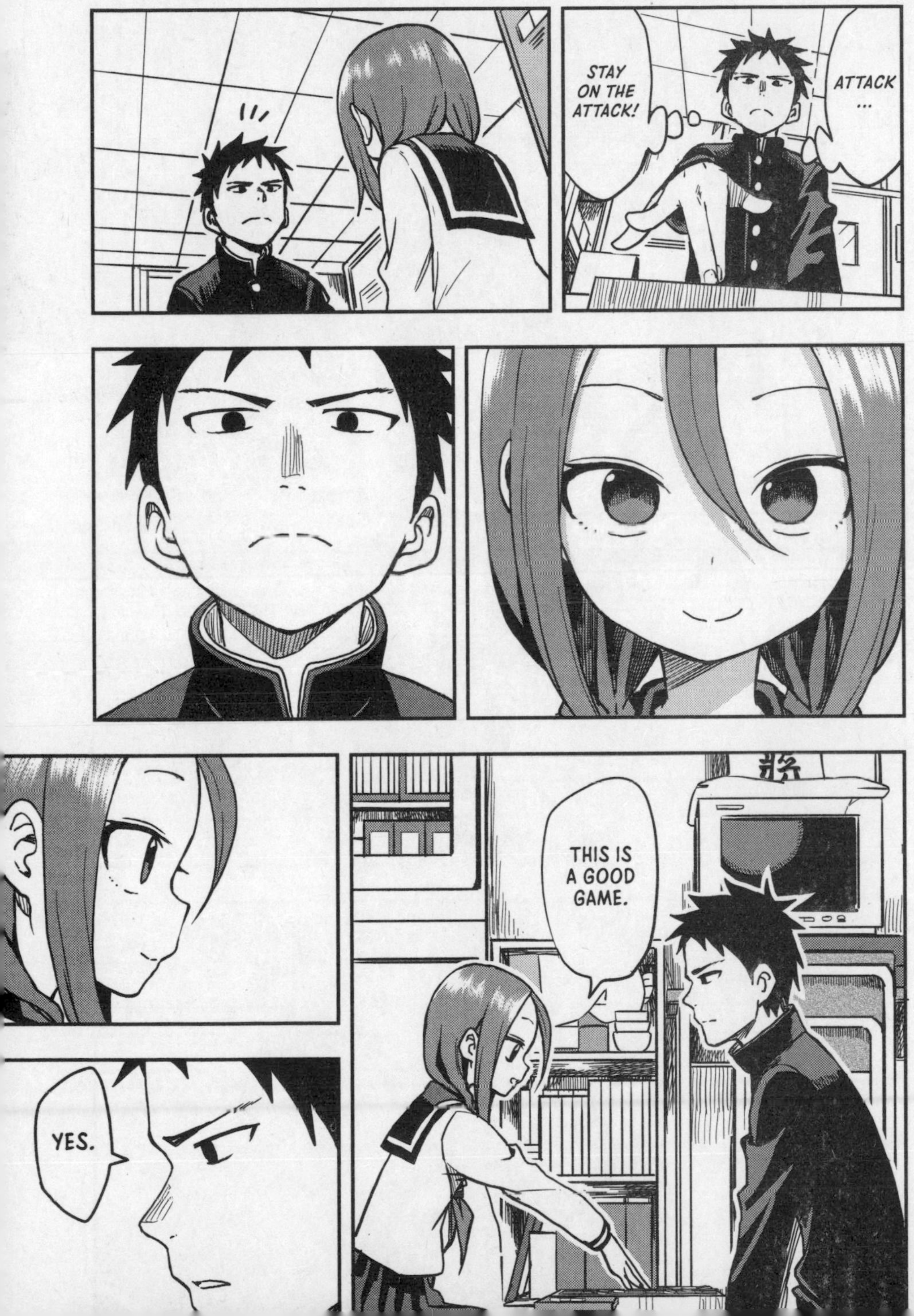
ATTACK ...
STAY ON THE ATTACK!
THIS IS A GOOD GAME.
YES.

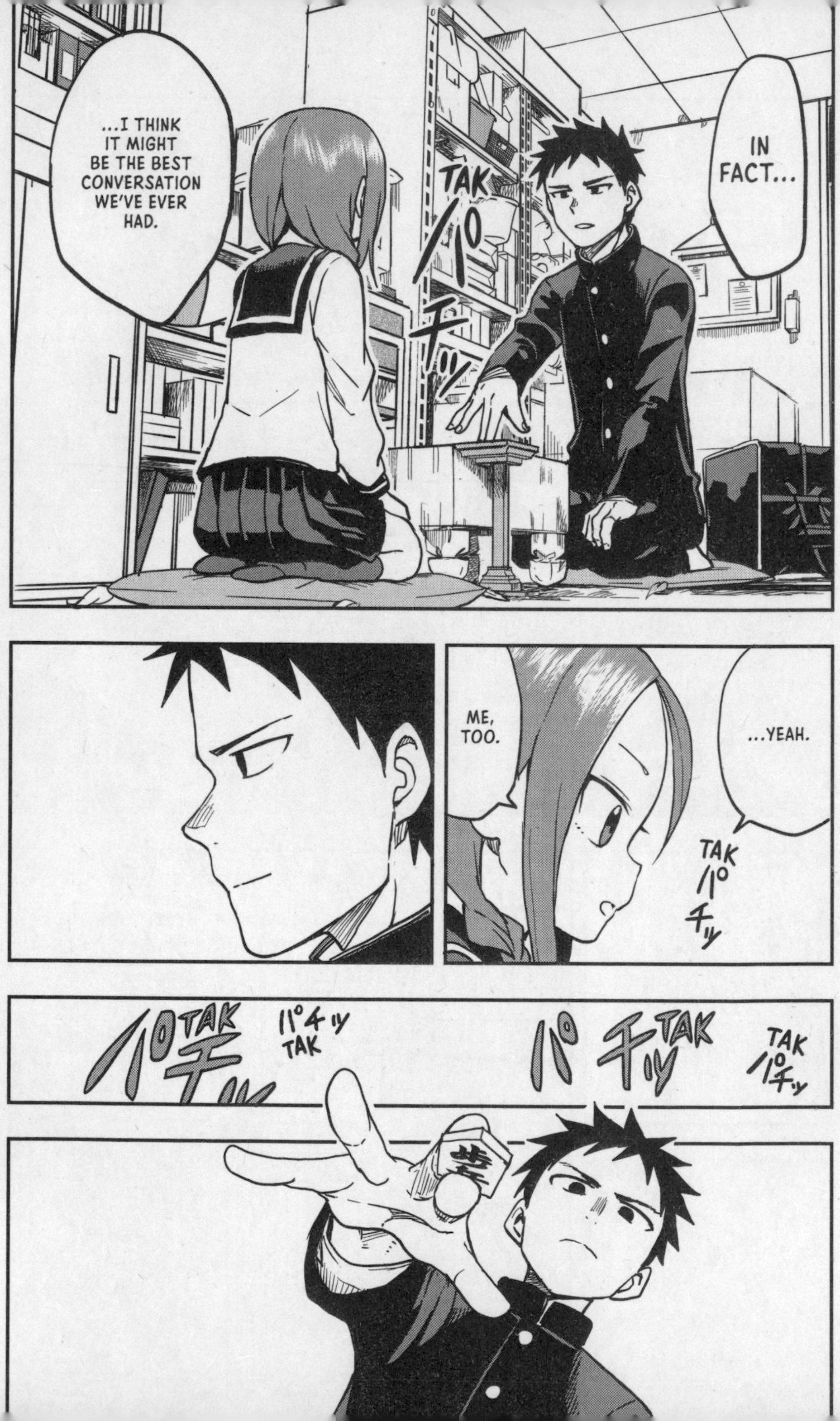
IN FACT...
...I THINK IT MIGHT BE THE BEST CONVERSATION WE'VE EVER HAD.
TAK
パチッ
...YEAH.
ME, TOO.
TAK
パチッ
TAK
パチッ
TAK
パチッ
パチッ
TAK
TAK
パチッ

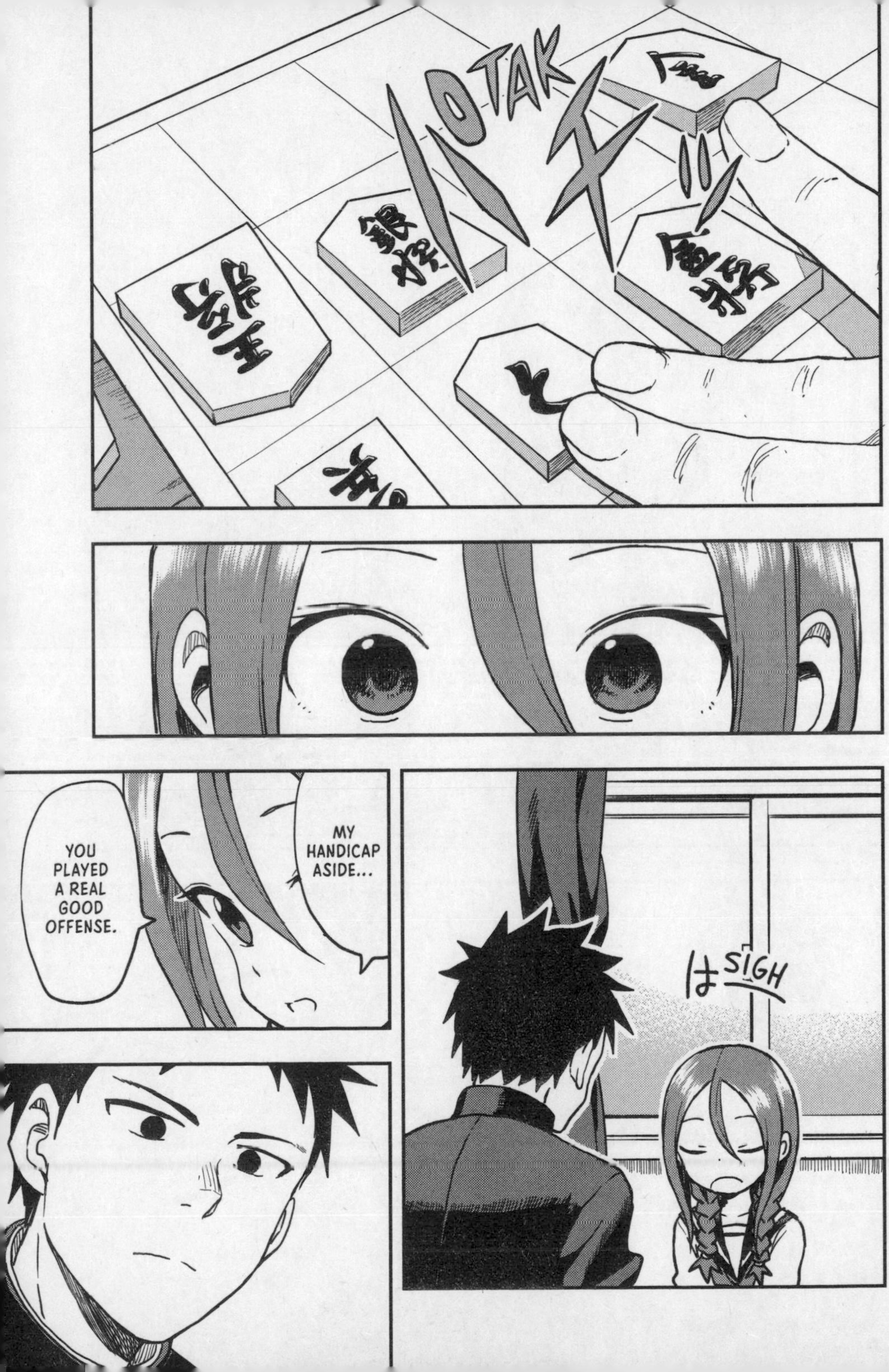
TAK
はSIGH
MY HANDICAP ASIDE...
YOU PLAYED A REAL GOOD OFFENSE.

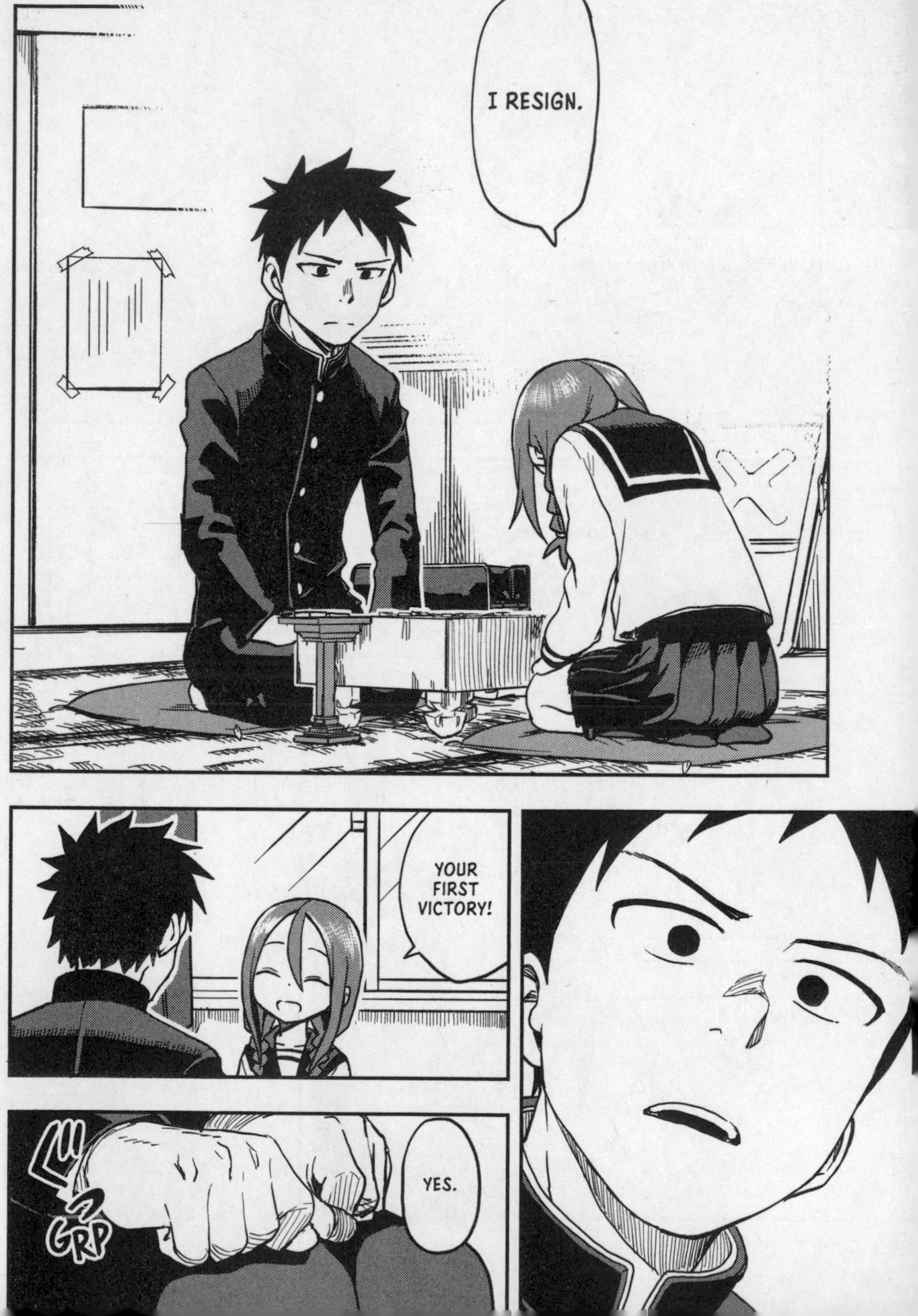
I RESIGN.
YOUR FIRST VICTORY!
YES.
GRP

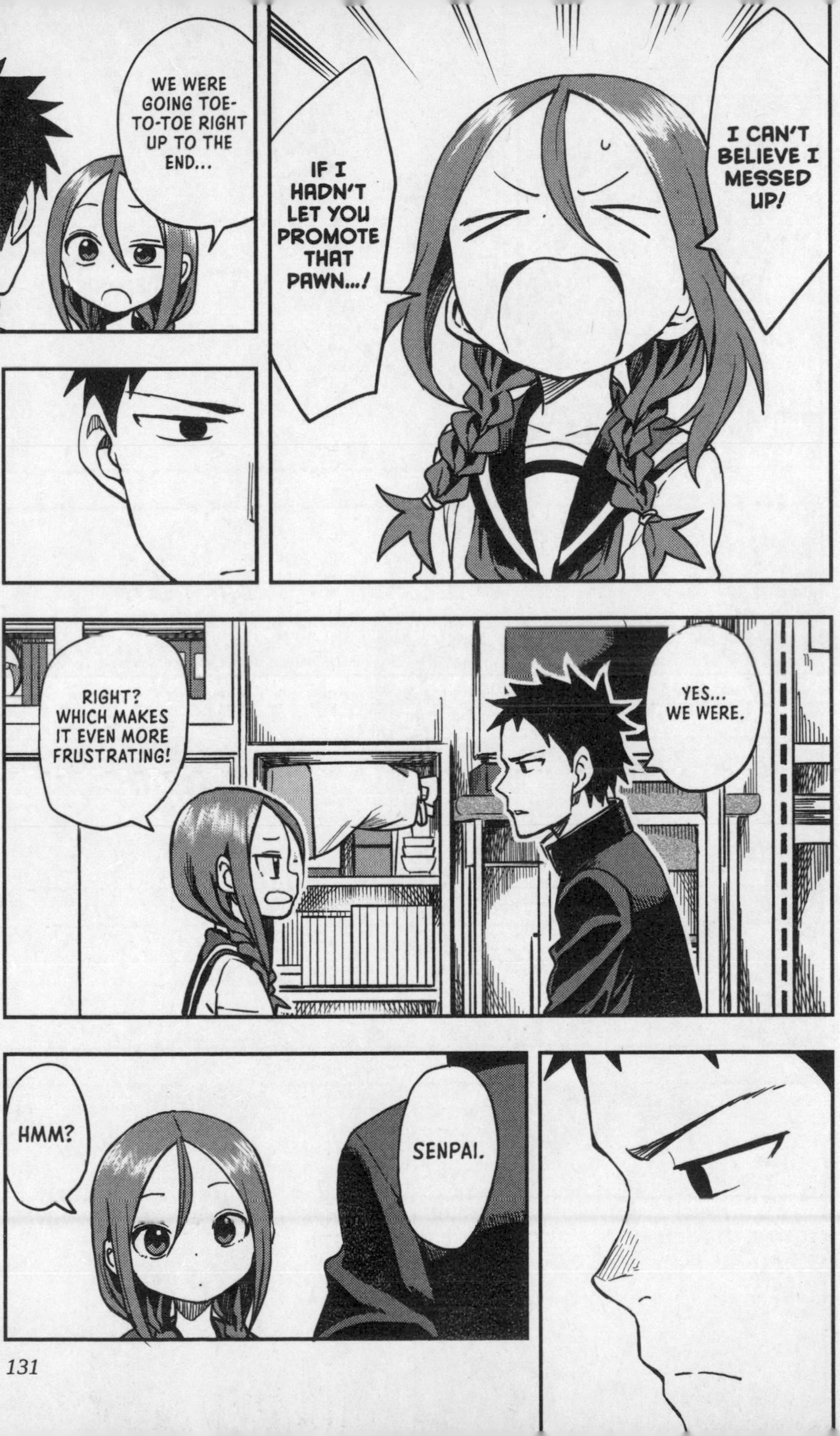
I CAN'T BELIEVE I MESSED UP!
IF I HADN'T LET YOU PROMOTE THAT PAWN...!
WE WERE GOING TOE-TO-TOE RIGHT UP TO THE END...
YES... WE WERE.
RIGHT? WHICH MAKES IT EVEN MORE FRUSTRATING!
SENPAI.
HMM?

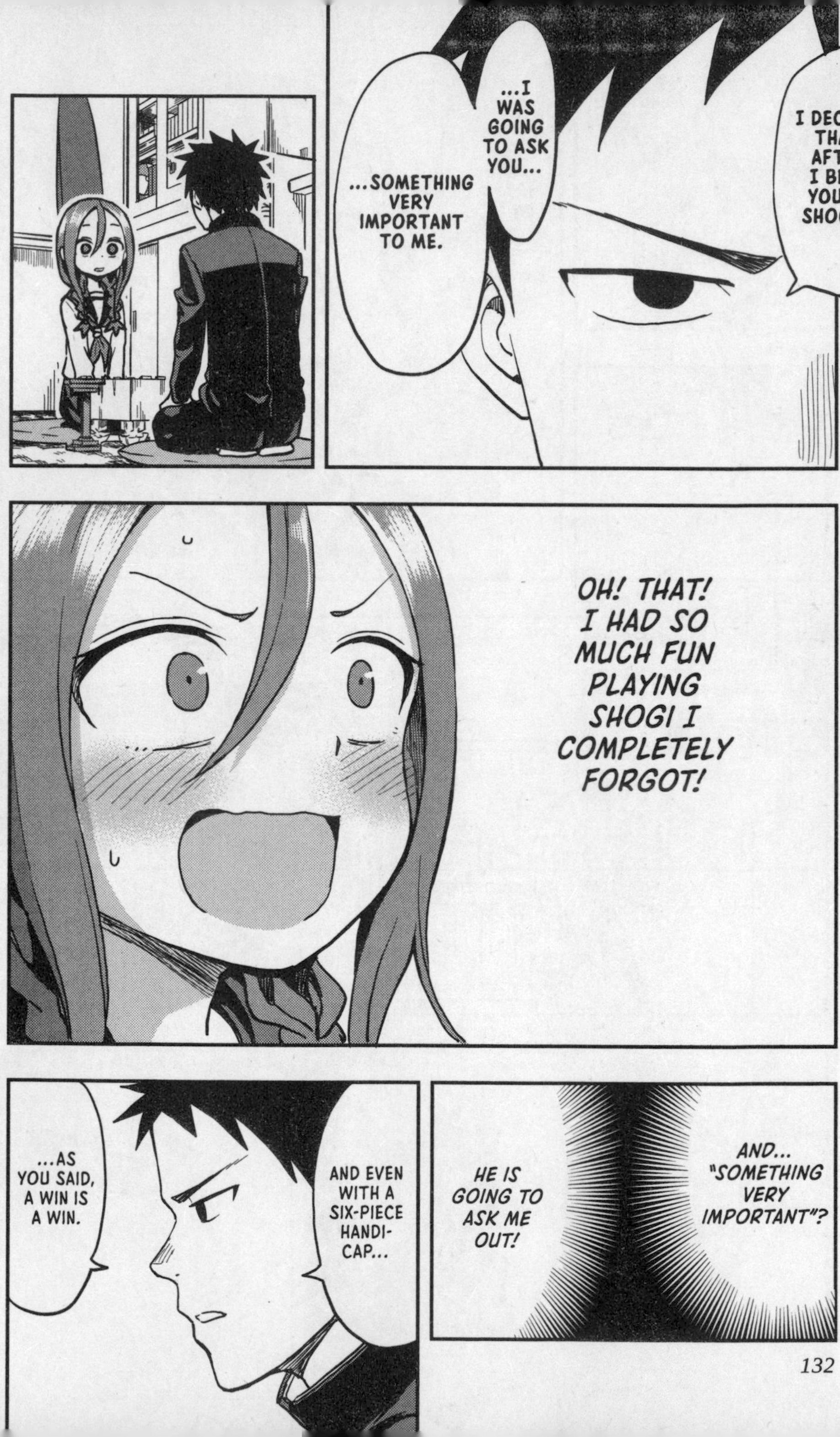
I DECIDED THAT, AFTER I BEAT YOU AT SHOGI...
...I WAS GOING TO ASK YOU...
...SOMETHING VERY IMPORTANT TO ME.
OH! THAT! I HAD SO MUCH FUN PLAYING SHOGI I COMPLETELY FORGOT!
AND... "SOMETHING VERY IMPORTANT"?
HE IS GOING TO ASK ME OUT!
AND EVEN WITH A SIX-PIECE HANDI-CAP...
...AS YOU SAID, A WIN IS A WIN.

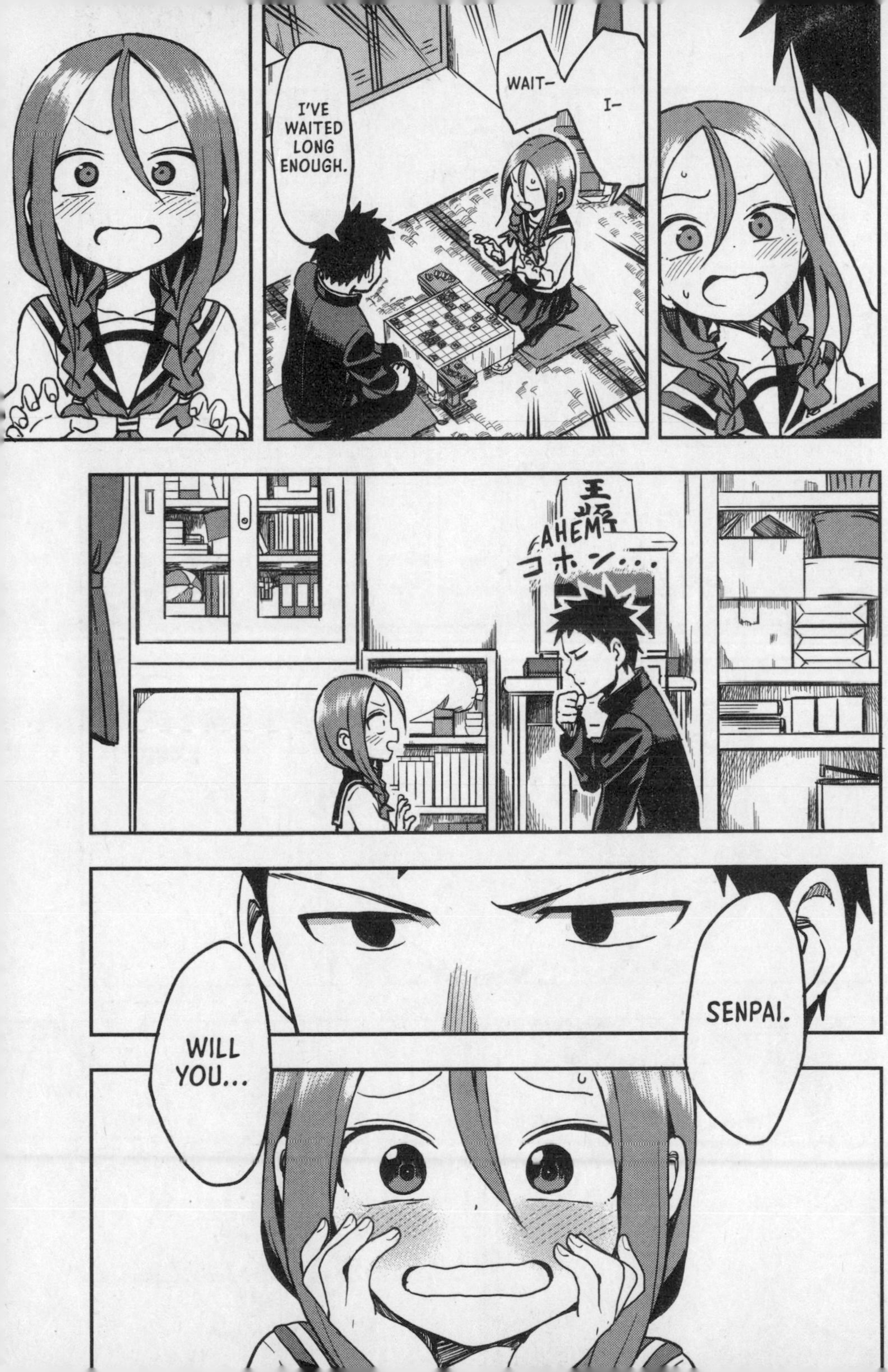
WAIT—
I—
I'VE WAITED LONG ENOUGH.
AHEM
コホン…
SENPAI.
WILL YOU...

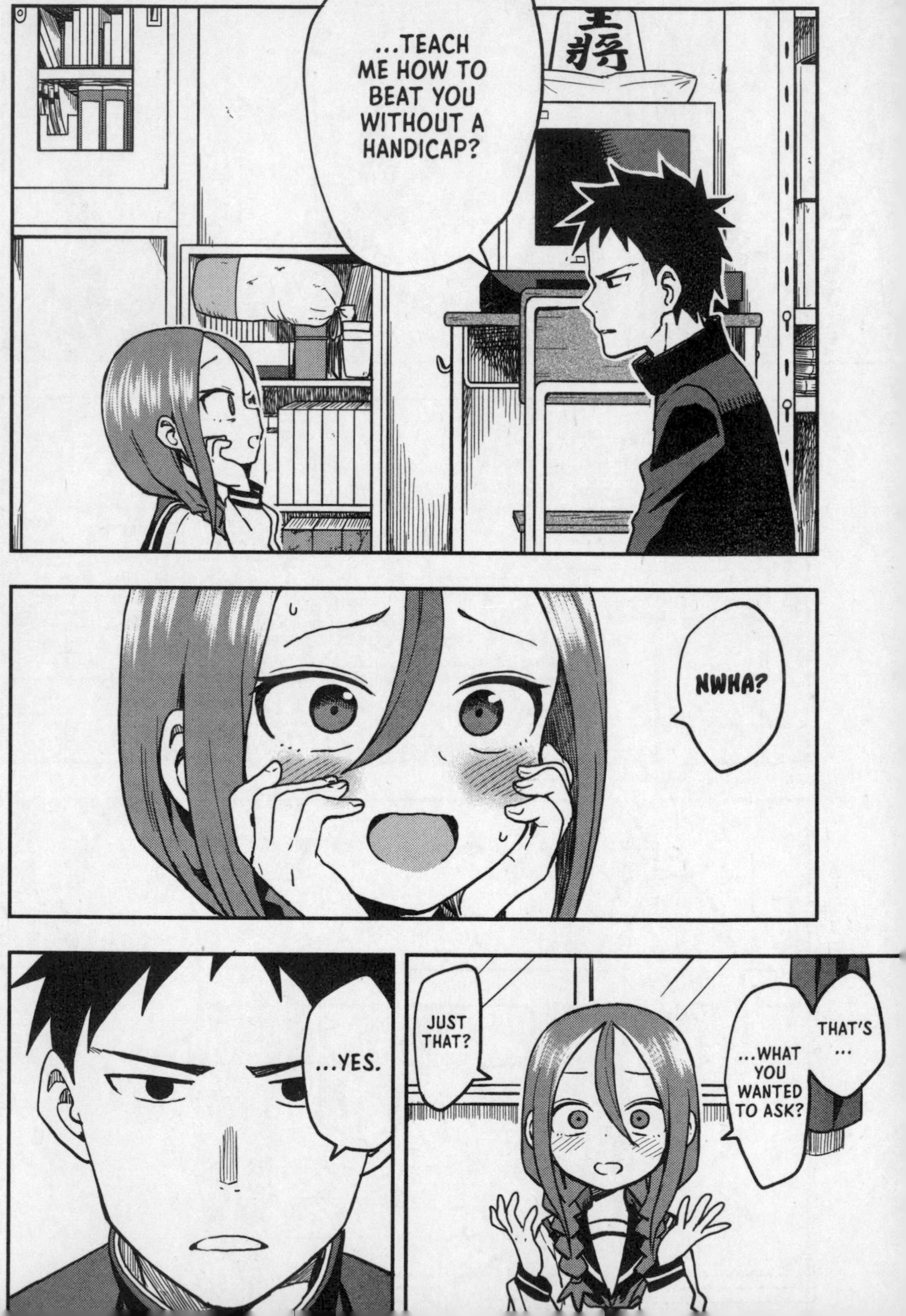
王将
...TEACH ME HOW TO BEAT YOU WITHOUT A HANDICAP?
NWHA?
THAT'S ...
...WHAT YOU WANTED TO ASK?
JUST THAT?
...YES.

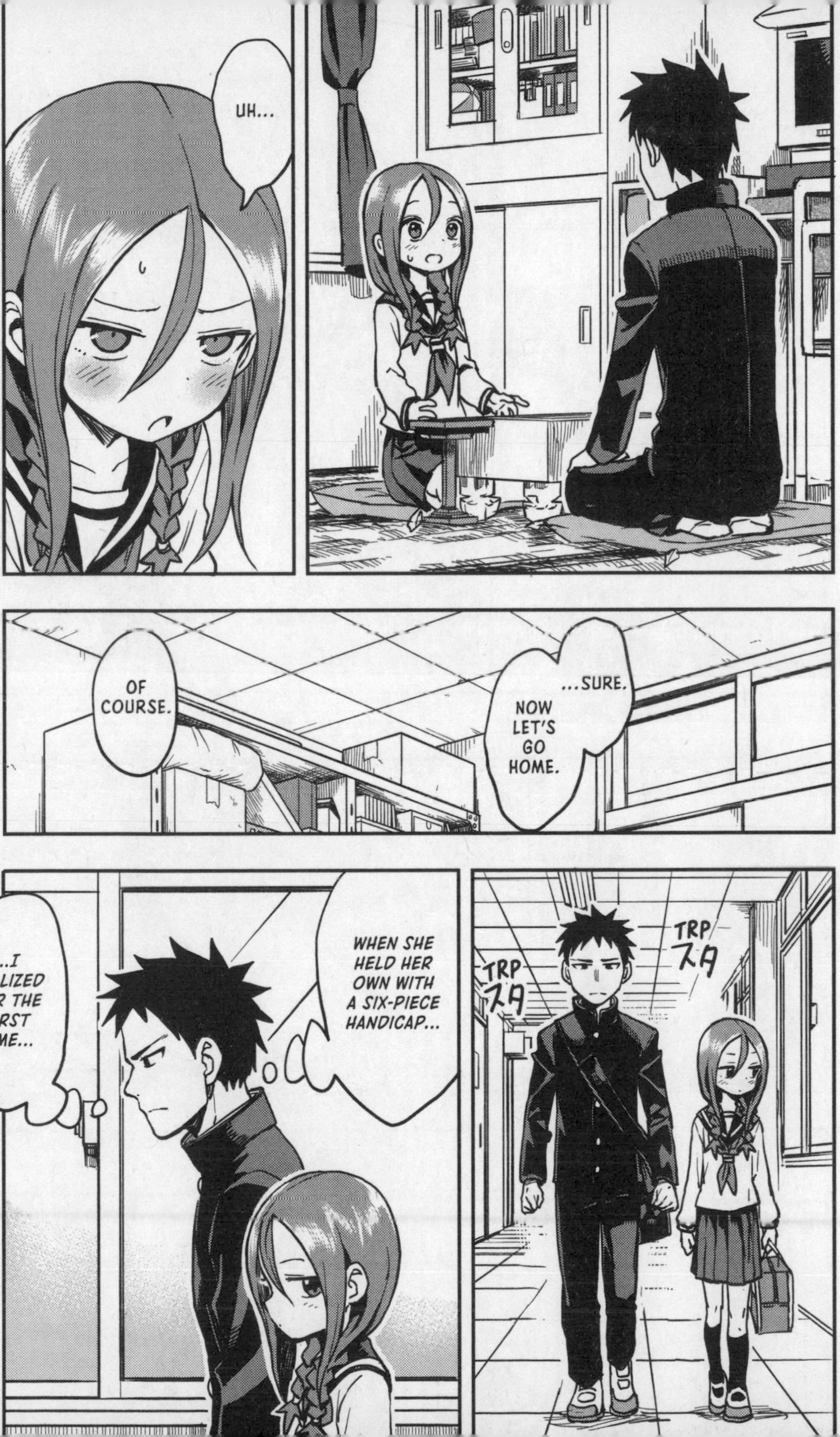
UH...
...SURE.
NOW LET'S GO HOME.
OF COURSE.
TRP スタ
TRP スタ
WHEN SHE HELD HER OWN WITH A SIX-PIECE HANDICAP...
...I REALIZED FOR THE FIRST TIME...

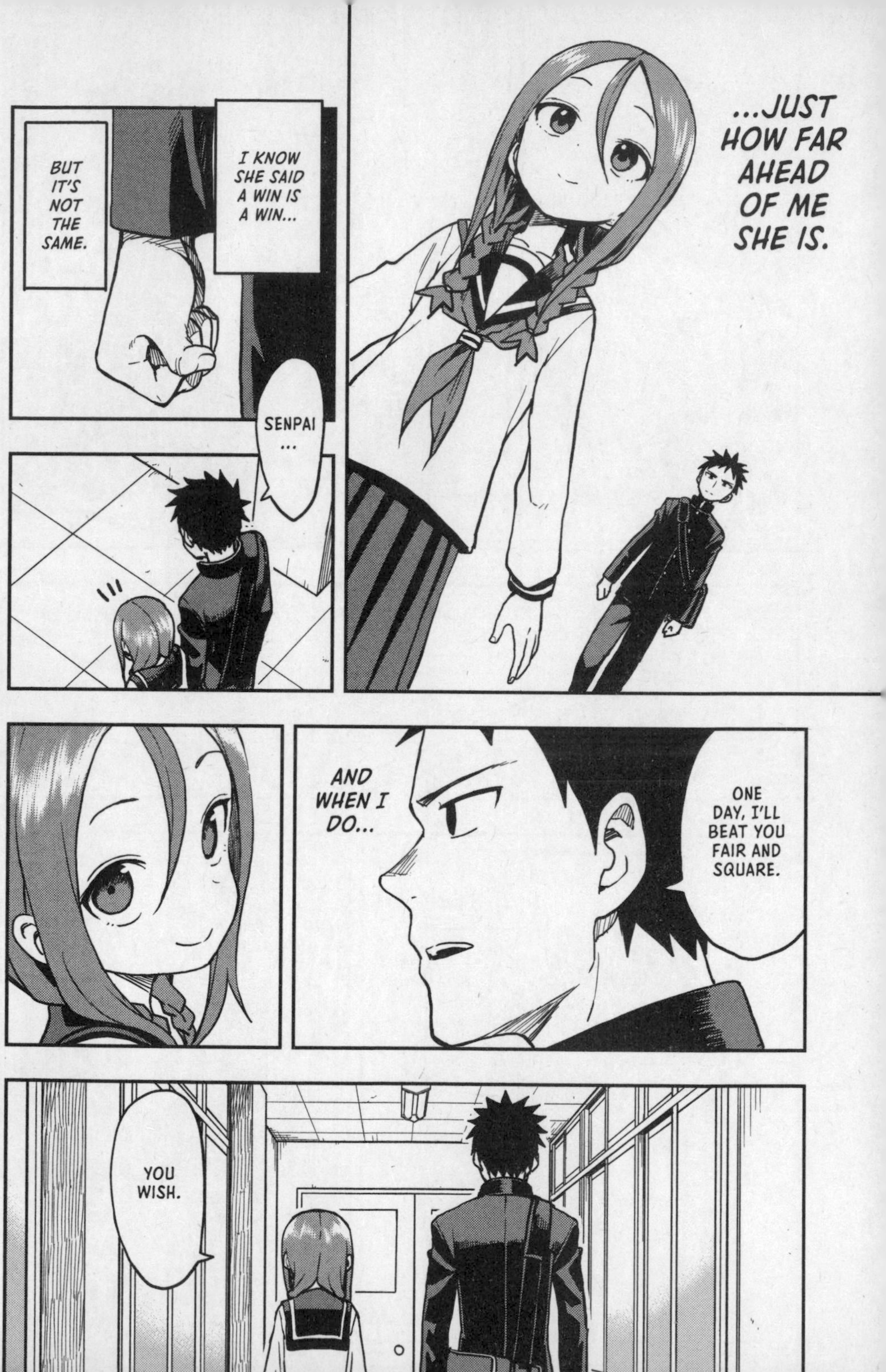
...JUST HOW FAR AHEAD OF ME SHE IS.
I KNOW SHE SAID A WIN IS A WIN...
BUT IT'S NOT THE SAME.
SENPAI ...
ONE DAY, I'LL BEAT YOU FAIR AND SQUARE.
AND WHEN I DO...
YOU WISH.

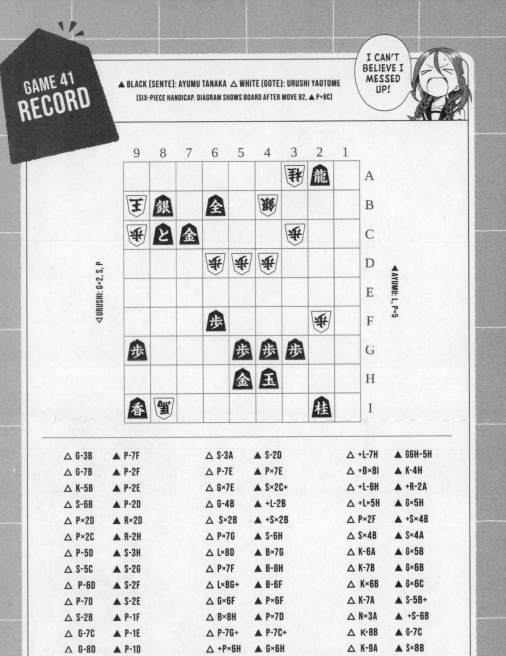

GAME 41 RECORD

▲ BLACK (SENTE): AYUMU TANAKA △ WHITE (GOTE): URUSHI YAOTOME
(SIX-PIECE HANDICAP. DIAGRAM SHOWS BOARD AFTER MOVE 92, ▲ P×8C)

I CAN'T BELIEVE I MESSED UP!

◁ URUSHI: G×2, S, P

▲ AYUMU: L, P×5

△ G-3B	▲ P-7F	△ S-3A	▲ S-2D	△ +L-7H	▲ G6H-5H
△ G-7B	▲ P-2F	△ P-7E	▲ P×7E	△ +B×8I	▲ K-4H
△ K-5B	▲ P-2E	△ G×7E	▲ S×2C+	△ +L-6H	▲ R-2A
△ S-6B	▲ P-2D	△ G-4B	▲ +L-2B	△ +L×5H	▲ G×5H
△ P×2D	▲ R×2D	△ S×2B	▲ +S×2B	△ P×2F	▲ +S×4B
△ P×2C	▲ R-2H	△ P×7G	▲ S-6H	△ S×4B	▲ S×4A
△ P-5D	▲ S-3H	△ L×8D	▲ B×7G	△ K-6A	▲ G×5B
△ S-5C	▲ S-2G	△ P×7F	▲ B-8H	△ K-7B	▲ G×6B
△ P-6D	▲ S-2F	△ L×8G+	▲ B-6F	△ K×6B	▲ G×6C
△ P-7D	▲ S-2E	△ G×6F	▲ P×6F	△ K-7A	▲ S-5B+
△ S-2B	▲ P-1F	△ B×8H	▲ P×7D	△ N×3A	▲ +S-6B
△ G-7C	▲ P-1E	△ P-7G+	▲ P-7C+	△ K-8B	▲ G-7C
△ G-8D	▲ P-1D	△ +P×6H	▲ G×6H	△ K-9A	▲ S×8B
△ P×1D	▲ P×1C	△ P-4D	▲ R-2C+	△ K-9B	▲ +P×8C
△ S×1C	▲ L×1D	△ S×6B	▲ +P-7D		[BLACK WINS AT MOVE 92]
△ S-2B	▲ L-1B+	△ B-7I+	▲ +S-3B		

WHEN WILL
AYUMU
MAKE HIS
MOVE?

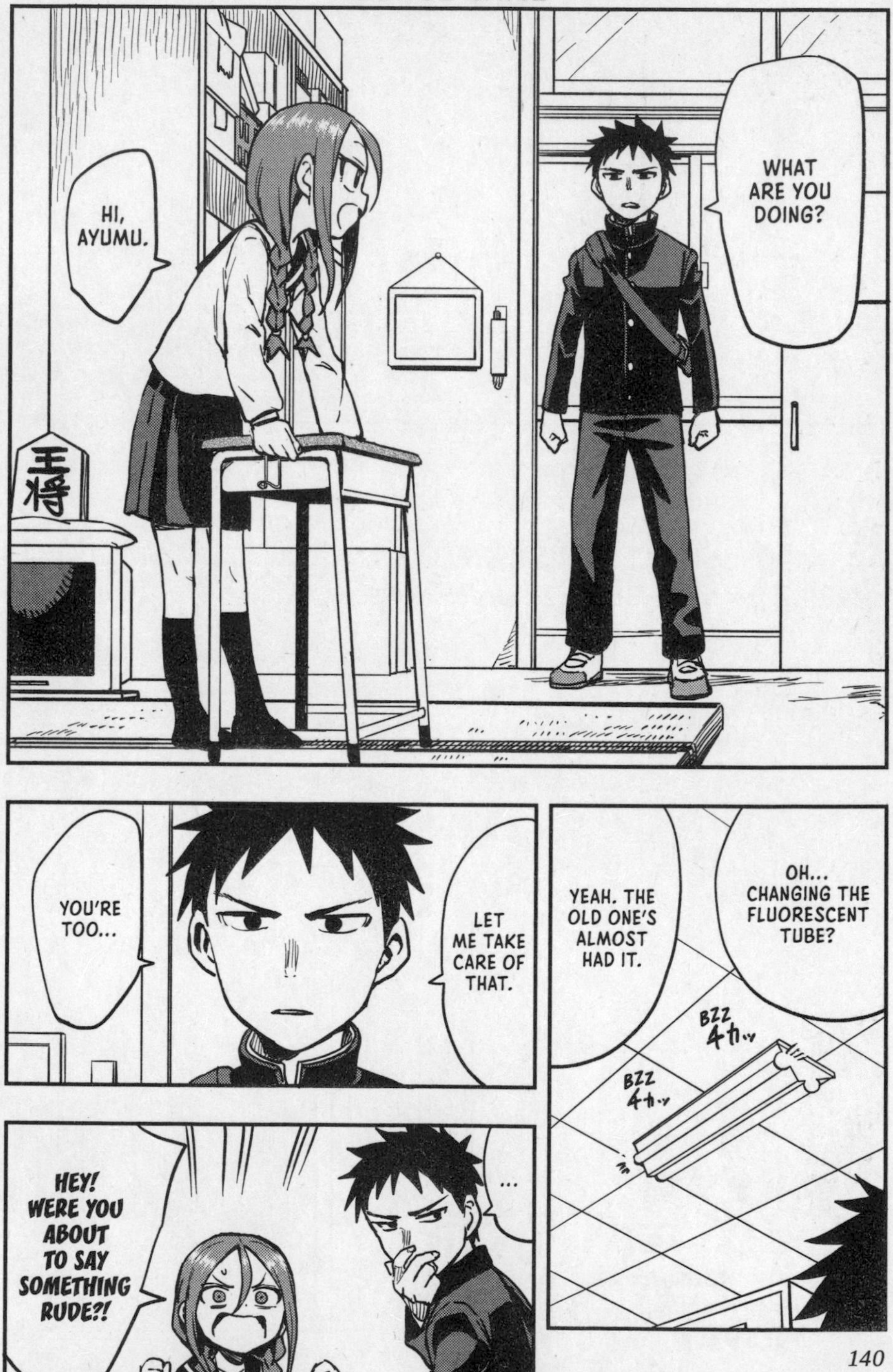
WHAT ARE YOU DOING?
HI, AYUMU.
OH... CHANGING THE FLUORESCENT TUBE?
YEAH. THE OLD ONE'S ALMOST HAD IT.
BZZ
BZZ
LET ME TAKE CARE OF THAT.
YOU'RE TOO...
...
HEY! WERE YOU ABOUT TO SAY SOMETHING RUDE?!

I CAN REACH JUST FINE!
SORRY.
BUT WOULD YOU LET ME CHANGE THE TUBE, ANYWAY?
IN CASE YOU FALL AND HURT YOURSELF.
ALL RIGHT, FINE.
IS THIS THE SHOGI CLUB?
I BROUGHT A NEW TUBE FOR YOU.
GREAT! THANK YOU!

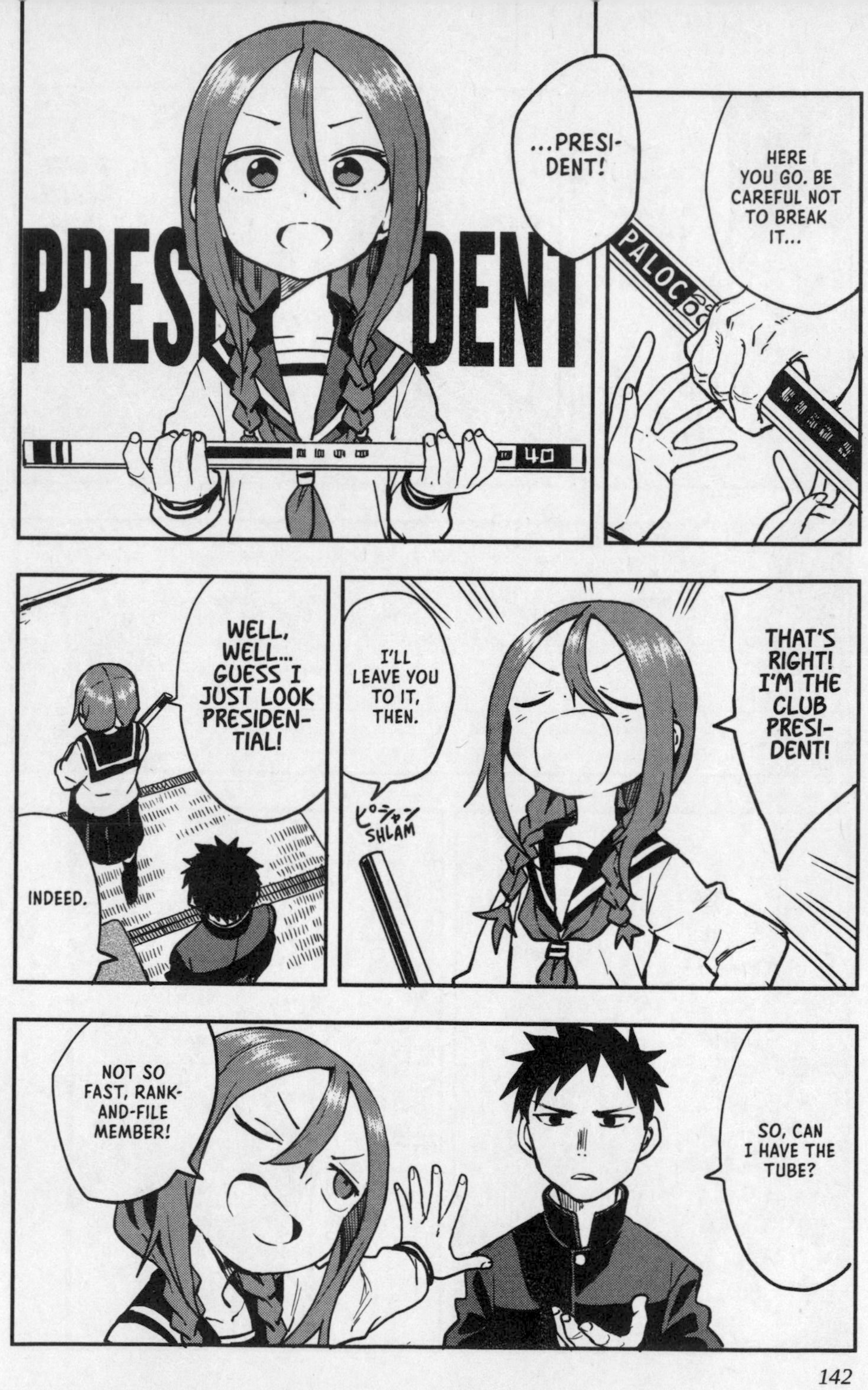
HERE YOU GO. BE CAREFUL NOT TO BREAK IT...
PALOC
...PRESIDENT!
PRESIDENT
THAT'S RIGHT! I'M THE CLUB PRESIDENT!
I'LL LEAVE YOU TO IT, THEN.
ピシャン
SHLAM
WELL, WELL... GUESS I JUST LOOK PRESIDENTIAL!
INDEED.
SO, CAN I HAVE THE TUBE?
NOT SO FAST, RANK-AND-FILE MEMBER!

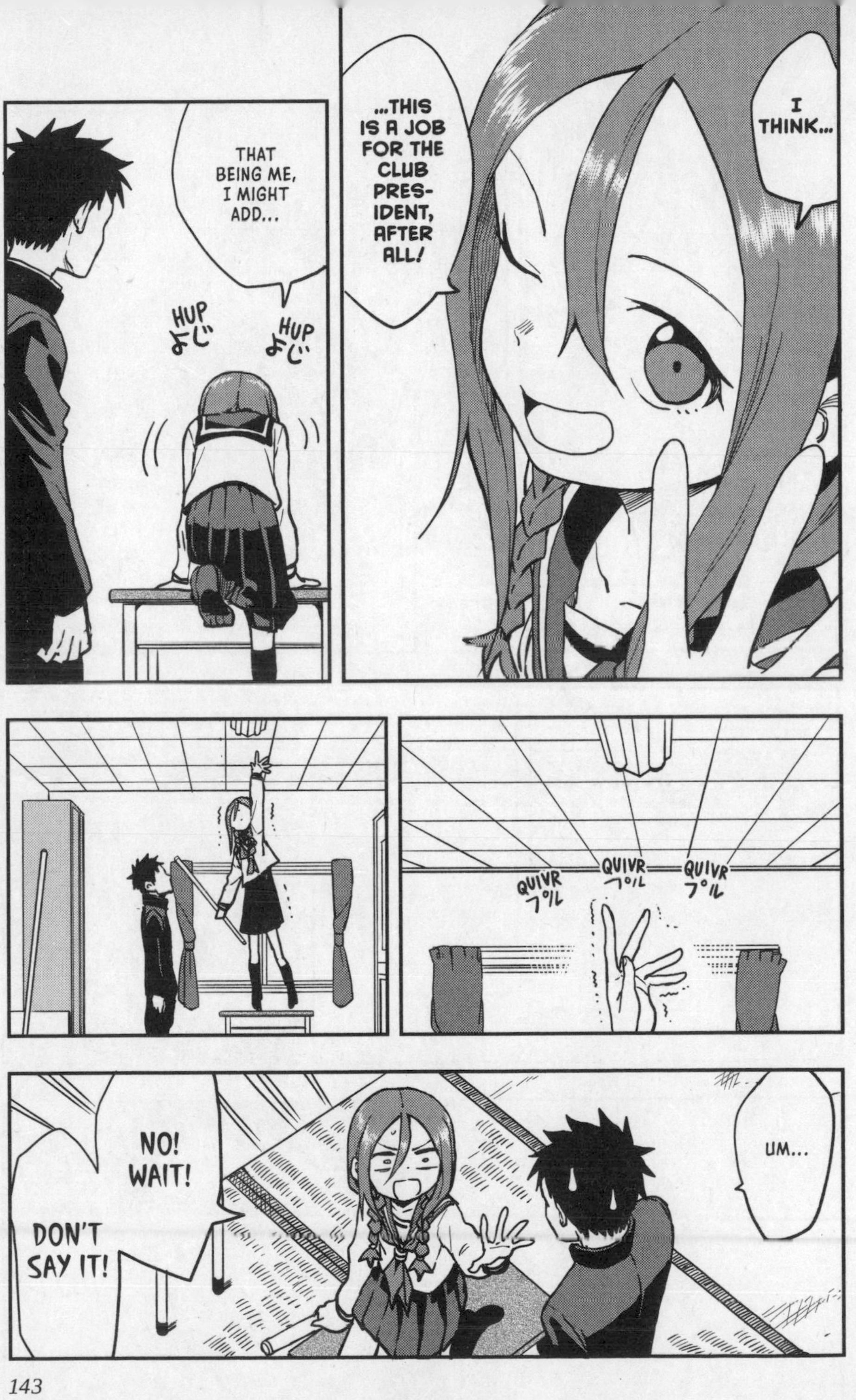
I THINK...
...THIS IS A JOB FOR THE CLUB PRESIDENT, AFTER ALL!
THAT BEING ME, I MIGHT ADD...
HUP よじ
HUP よじ
QUIVR フル
QUIVR フル
QUIVR フル
UM...
NO! WAIT!
DON'T SAY IT!

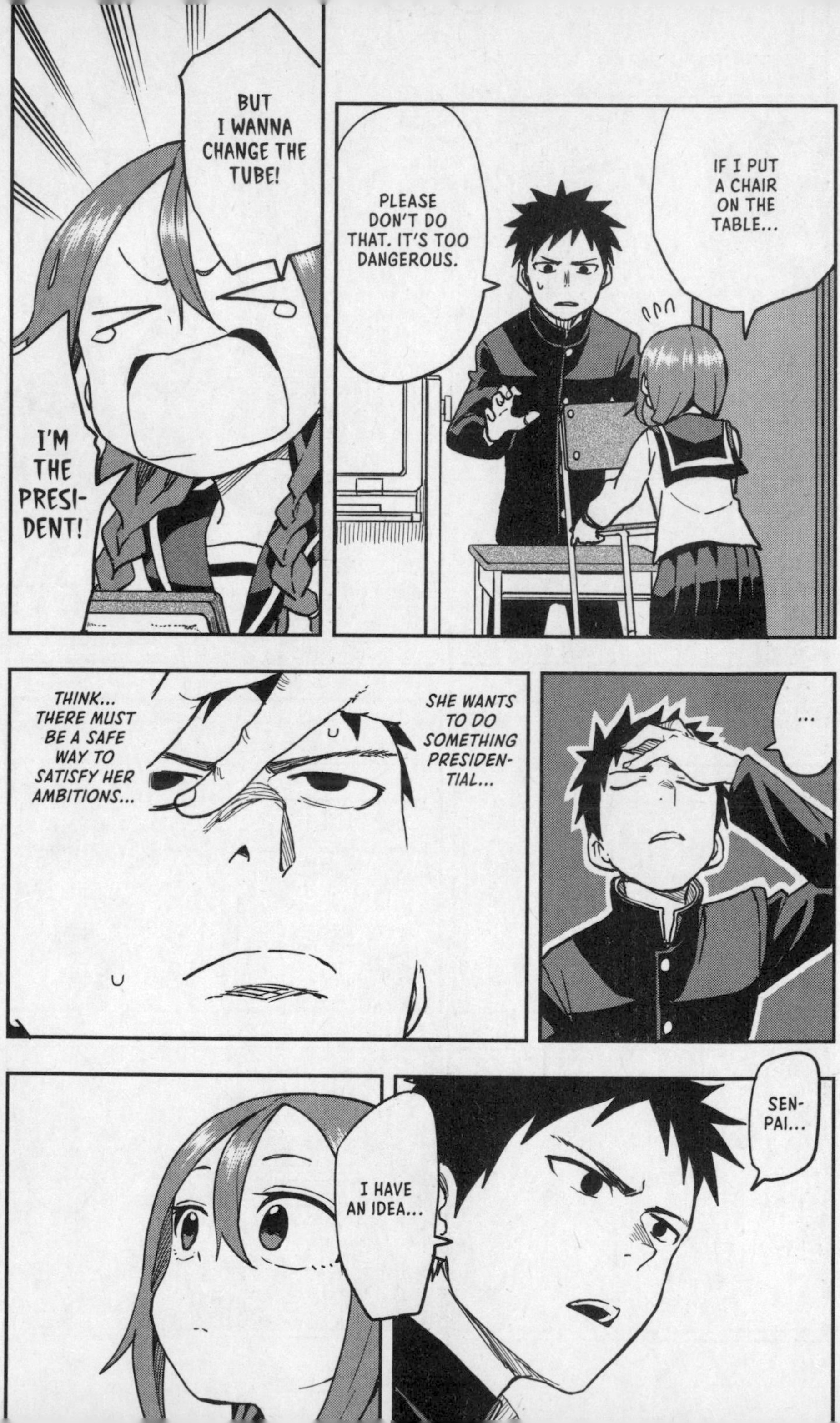
IF I PUT A CHAIR ON THE TABLE...
PLEASE DON'T DO THAT. IT'S TOO DANGEROUS.
BUT I WANNA CHANGE THE TUBE!
I'M THE PRESI-DENT!
...
SHE WANTS TO DO SOMETHING PRESIDEN-TIAL...
THINK... THERE MUST BE A SAFE WAY TO SATISFY HER AMBITIONS...
SEN-PAI...
I HAVE AN IDEA...

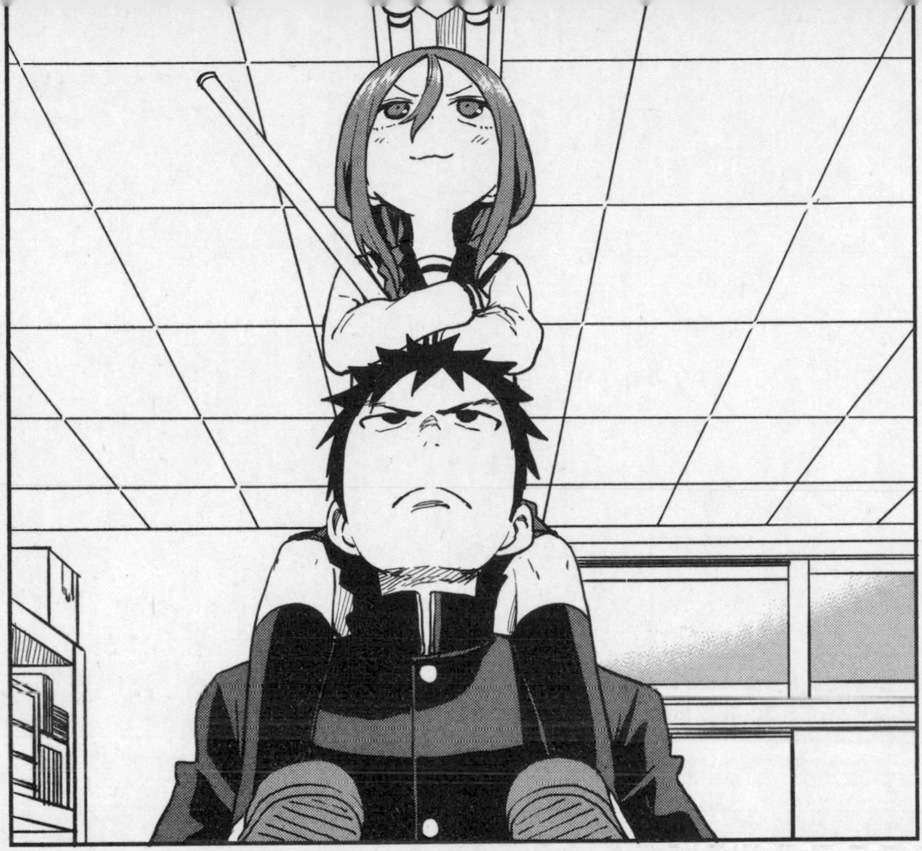

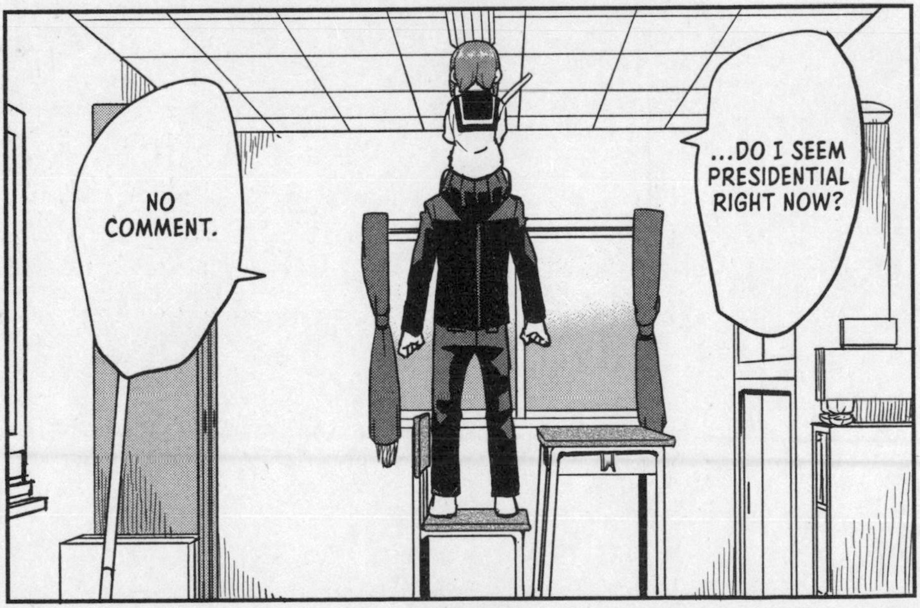
...DO I SEEM PRESIDENTIAL RIGHT NOW?
NO COMMENT.

THE END

TRANSLATION NOTES

CLIMBING SILVER, PAGE 123
A classic shogi strategy in which a silver general and a pawn, with a rook in the rear for support, push forward together to break into the enemy camp across the board. Climbing Silver is one type of Static Rook strategy (see below).

FOURTH-FILE ROOK, PAGE 123
The "fourth file" is the fourth column from the left from white's point of view (corresponding to the "sixth file" for the black side). Positioning the rook just left of center like this opens up a range of defensive possibilities.

STATIC ROOK RAPID ATTACK, PAGE 123
In a Static Rook strategy, the rook remains on the right side of the board—usually on its starting square—instead of crossing to the left as in Fourth-File Rook. This lets the rook support offensive strategies launched from that side. Climbing Silver is one type of Static Rook strategy.

SHITATE, UWATE, PAGE 137
Usually, the two players in a game of shogi are referred to as *sente* and *gote*, literally "player who goes first" and "player who goes next." However, in a handicapped game, the handicapped player is referred to as the *uwate* ("upper player"), and their opponent as the *shitate* ("lower player").

WHEN WILL AYUMU MAKE HIS MOVE?

Young characters and steampunk setting, like *Howl's Moving Castle* and *Battle Angel Alita*

Beyond the Clouds © 2018 Nicke / Ki-oon

A boy with a talent for machines and a mysterious girl whose wings he's fixed will take you beyond the clouds! In the tradition of the high-flying, resonant adventure stories of Studio Ghibli comes a gorgeous tale about the longing of young hearts for adventure and friendship!

Knight of the ICE

Knight of the ice ©Yayoi Ogawa/Kodansha Ltd.

Yayoi Ogawa

SKATING THRILLS AND ICY CHILLS WITH THIS NEW TINGLY ROMANCE SERIES!

A rom-com on ice, perfect for fans of *Princess Jellyfish* and *Wotakoi*. Kokoro is the talk of the figure-skating world, winning trophies and hearts. But little do they know... he's actually a huge nerd! From the beloved creator of *You're My Pet* (*Tramps Like Us*).

Chitose is a serious young woman, working for the health magazine *SASSO*. Or at least, she would be, if she wasn't constantly getting distracted by her childhood friend, international figure skating star Kokoro Kijinami! In the public eye and on the ice, Kokoro is a gallant, flawless knight, but behind his glittery costumes and breathtaking spins lies a secret: He's actually a hopelessly romantic otaku, who can only land his quad jumps when Chitose is on hand to recite a spell from his favorite magical girl anime!

PERFECT WORLD

Rie Aruga

A TOUCHING
NEW SERIES
ABOUT LOVE AND
COPING WITH
DISABILITY

An office party reunites Tsugumi with her high school crush Itsuki. He's realized his dream of becoming an architect, but along the way, he experienced a spinal injury that put him in a wheelchair. Now Tsugumi's rekindled feelings will butt up against prejudices she never considered — and Itsuki will have to decide if he's ready to let someone into his heart.

KC
KODANSHA
COMICS

The boys are back, in 400-page hardcovers that are as pretty and badass as they are!

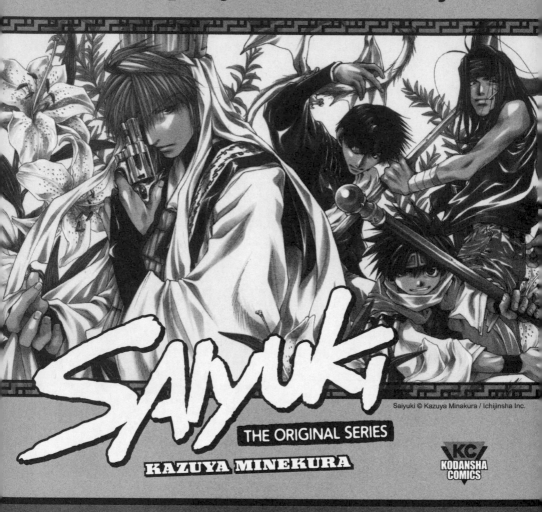

Saiyuki © Kazuya Minakura / Ichijinsha Inc.

SAIYUKI
THE ORIGINAL SERIES
KAZUYA MINEKURA

KC KODANSHA COMICS

"AN EDGY COMIC LOOK AT AN ANCIENT CHINESE TALE." —YALSA

Genjo Sanzo is a Buddhist priest in the city of Togenkyo, which is being ravaged by yokai spirits that have fallen out of balance with the natural order. His superiors send him on a journey far to the west to discover why this is happening and how to stop it. His companions are three yokai with human souls. But this is no day trip — the four will encounter many discoveries and horrors on the way.

FEATURES NEW TRANSLATION, COLOR PAGES, AND BEAUTIFUL WRAPAROUND COVER ART!

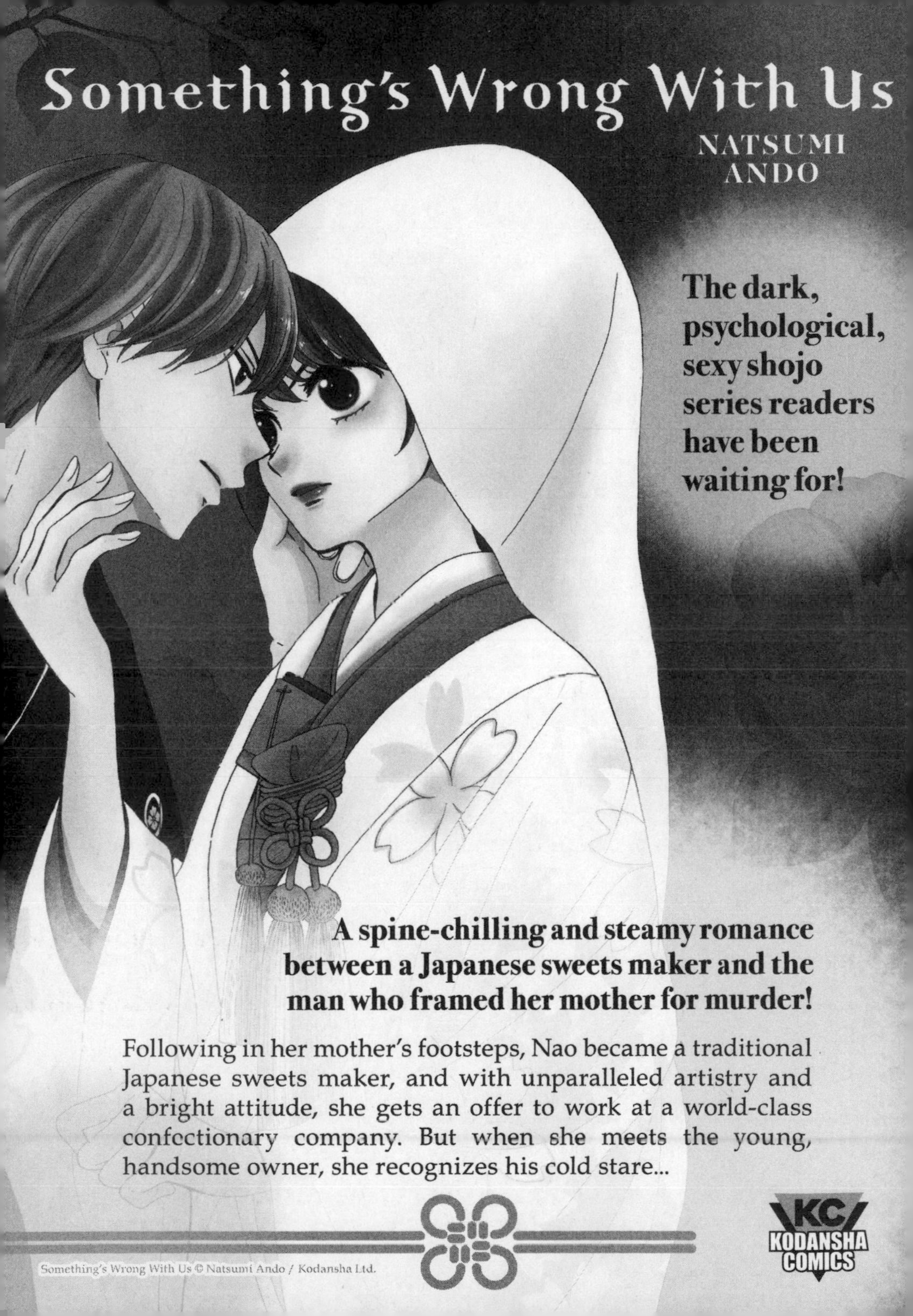
Something's Wrong With Us
NATSUMI ANDO
The dark, psychological, sexy shojo series readers have been waiting for!
A spine-chilling and steamy romance between a Japanese sweets maker and the man who framed her mother for murder!
Following in her mother's footsteps, Nao became a traditional Japanese sweets maker, and with unparalleled artistry and a bright attitude, she gets an offer to work at a world-class confectionary company. But when she meets the young, handsome owner, she recognizes his cold stare...
KC KODANSHA COMICS
Something's Wrong With Us © Natsumi Ando / Kodansha Ltd.

A Kodansha Trade Paperback Original

When Will Ayumu Make His Move? 3 copyright © 2020 Soichiro Yamamoto
English translation copyright © 2021 Soichiro Yamamoto

Published in the United States by
Kodansha USA Publishing, LLC, New York.

Publication rights for this English edition arranged through
Kodansha Ltd., Tokyo.

First published in Japan in 2020 by Kodansha Ltd., Tokyo
as *Sore demo Ayumu ha yosetekuru*, volume 3.

ISBN 978-1-64651-351-2

Printed in the United States of America.

1st Printing

Translation: Max Greenway
Lettering: Phil Christie
Editing: Nathaniel Gallant
Kodansha USA Publishing edition cover design by Phil Balsman

Publisher: Kiichiro Sugawara

Director of Publishing Services: Ben Applegate
Associate Director of Publishing Operations: Stephen Pakula
Publishing Services Managing Editors: Alanna Ruse, Madison Salters
Production Managers: Emi Lotto, Angela Zurlo

KODANSHA.US

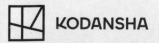